BEHAVIOR PATTERNS, STRESS, AND CORONARY DISEASE

COMPLEX HUMAN BEHAVIOR

A series of volumes edited by
Leon Festinger and **Stanley Schachter**

Behavior Patterns, Stress, and Coronary Disease

DAVID C. GLASS

THE GRADUATE SCHOOL AND
UNIVERSITY CENTER, CITY
UNIVERSITY OF NEW YORK

LAWRENCE ERLBAUM ASSOCIATES, PUBLISHERS
1977   Hillsdale, New Jersey

DISTRIBUTED BY THE HALSTED PRESS DIVISION OF

JOHN WILEY & SONS

New York   Toronto   London   Sydney

Lawrence Erlbaum Associates, Inc., Publishers
62 Maria Drive
Hillsdale, New Jersey 07642

Distributed solely by Halsted Press Division
John Wiley & Sons, Inc., New York

Library of Congress Cataloging in Publication Data

Glass, David C
    Behavior patterns, stress, and coronary disease.

    Includes bibliographical references and indexes.
    1. Coronary heart disease–Psychosomatic aspects.
2. Stress (Psychology).   I. Title. [DNLM: 1. Coronary diseases–Etiology.   2. Stress, Psychological.
3. Social behavior.   WG300 G549b]
RC685.C6G56   616.1'23'08   77-23788
ISBN 0-470-99294-8

Contents

Preface

The purpose of this book is to present experimental findings that support a conceptual approach to the interplay of uncontrollable stress and the Type A coronary-prone behavior pattern. Each of these variables has been implicated in the etiology of coronary heart disease. Uncontrollable stress involves the anticipation of psychic or physical harm which the individual believes he is relatively powerless to alter. The behavior pattern is believed to be a style of response to stressful stimulation that consists of excessive achievement striving, time urgency, and hostility. Indeed, this book is unique in providing behavioral validation for each of these components of Pattern A.

Our basic assumption is that Type A individuals exert greater efforts than their Type B counterparts to control stressful events that are perceived as threats to their sense of control. These active coping attempts eventually extinguish, for without reward, the relentless striving of the Type A individual leads to frustration and psychic exhaustion, which culminates in a reduction of efforts at control. An almost ironic reversal of behavior is then observed, with Type A individuals showing greater signs of helplessness than Type Bs. This sequence of reaction will often be referred to by the terms *hyperresponsiveness* and *hyporesponsiveness*. The focus of the book is a presentation of successive evaluations of the applicability of these ideas to an understanding of how Type A individuals respond to uncontrollable stress.

The major contribution of our research has been, perhaps, to formulate the role of behavioral factors in coronary disease in a new way. Our underlying notion is that the disease is a long-term risk involved in repeated cumulative efforts to adapt to uncontrollable stress. Although Type A individuals effectively adjust to, and even overcome, threats to their sense of environmental control, such adjustments have aftereffects that render them less resistant to subsequent stress and strain. These aftereffects are believed to entail autonomic and biochemical discharges which potentiate the pathogenesis of coronary disease. This is, admittedly, a oversimplified interpretation. We are fully aware of the fact that coronary disease has a multifaceted etiology, and that traditional risk factors (e.g., serum cholesterol) must eventually be incorporated in any complete analysis of its development.

This book is not devoted, however, to studies specifically linking the coronary disease process to behavioral and other risk variables. The research was designed to gain some understanding of two psychological factors that are known to be associated with cardiovascular disorders. While there is considerable value in examining demographic and psychosocial data from large samples of cases—the customary approach of epidemiology—nevertheless, the impact of behavior on coronary disease can, in our view, best be understood through systematic psychological research with small numbers of subjects in both laboratory and field settings. This is the type of approach taken in this volume. However, the topic of Pattern A and uncontrollable stress transcends narrow disciplinary lines and should, therefore, be of interest to a variety of specialists, including experimental social psychologists, cardiologists, and psychiatrists.

The plan of the book is outlined in the last section of the first chapter. Examination of the succeeding chapters reveals that, for the most part, support was generated for our initial theorizing about Pattern A as a style of coping with uncontrollable stressful events. However, we freely admit that our studies do not give rise to a complete theory of behavioral factors in coronary disease. This is not an admission of weakness or lack of completeness. The problem of how psychological factors influence the development and onset of disease is basic to the entire field of "behavioral medicine." In the case of our own research, a logical place has been reached to summarize and consolidate findings and theory, and to suggest directions for future experimentation. Indeed, a biobehavioral model outlined in the last chapter was specifically designed to indicate such directions.

The research reported in this book was a collaborative enterprise while I was at the University of Texas at Austin. While co-investigators have been cited at appropriate places throughout the text, the principal collaborators should be listed at this time. Most of these people were graduate students or postdoctoral fellows when the studies were being conducted. They are: David S. Krantz, James W. Pennebaker, Jack F. Hollis, Karen A. Matthews, Melvin L. Snyder, Charles S. Carver, M. Audrey Burnam, and David Harper. Jimme Davis provided outstanding electronic assistance required in many of the experiments.

My gratitude goes to Ray H. Rosenman and C. David Jenkins for their assistance in the classification of subjects as Pattern A and Pattern B, as well as their helpful support during the period of the project.

I extend my warmest thanks to Leon Festinger who read earlier versions of this manuscript. Dr. Festinger made important substantive contributions and suggestions that enabled me to improve the book substantially. I owe him a great debt of gratitude. My appreciation also goes to Ray H. Rosenman who assisted me in formulating certain sections of the manuscript pertaining to coronary artery disease.

Janet Peterson and Shirley Hodges performed most of the secretarial work connected with the project. I also wish to recognize Annette Howard who typed innumerable drafts of the manuscript and managed to meet often impossible deadlines. I thank her for her forbearance, loyalty, and competence.

The studies in this book were supported by grants from the National Science Foundation (GS-34329 and GS-37977X), the Hogg Foundation for Mental Health, and the University of Texas. The American Psychosomatic Society, the American Psychological Association, Academic Press, and Scripta Publishing Company granted permission to reproduce portions of articles that originally appeared in their journals. This book was written while I was a Visiting Scholar at Russell Sage Foundation in New York City. I wish to express my gratitude to the Trustees and Staff for making the book possible.

DAVID C. GLASS

To Palmer and Kate

BEHAVIOR PATTERNS, STRESS, AND CORONARY DISEASE

1
Introduction and Overview

Epidemiologists trace the beginnings of the widespread heart-disease problem in the United States to the early 1920s (Anderson, 1973). Since then, mortality rates due to cardiovascular disease have increased dramatically. Between 1940 and 1950, for example, the rate for white males, aged 35 to 64, increased by 23% (Borhani, 1966). Although a recent study reveals a significant decline in deaths due to coronary disease in American men during the 5 years from 1968 to 1972 (see *The New York Times*, January 23, 1975), the disease still remains the major source of death in the United States. The National Heart, Lung and Blood Institute estimated that 1.3 million Americans would experience coronary heart disease in 1975, of whom approximately 675,000 would die and 175,000 would be under the age of 65 (see, also, *The National Observer*, February 1, 1975). Indeed, a large percentage of the latter group would be classified as "premature" deaths, for they would occur during the middle years of 35 to 50.

CORONARY HEART DISEASE

Coronary heart disease (CHD) is a clinical disorder produced by lesions of the coronary arteries, the latter condition being called coronary artery disease (CAD), or atherosclerosis.[1] We will consider CAD at greater length in the next section. There are two major manifestations of clinical CHD: (1) angina pectoris, and (2) myocardial infarction.

[1] Arteriosclerosis is a generic term which includes a variety of pathological conditions that cause the arterial walls to thicken and lose their elasticity. A common term for this disorder is hardening of the arteries. Atherosclerosis is a form of arteriosclerosis in which the innermost layer of the coronary artery thickens due to fatty deposits. These deposits (atheromata) decrease the diameter of the central channel (the lumen) of the coronary artery and hence impede the flow of blood.

Angina Pectoris

The term angina pectoris designates a disorder involving a type of chest pain which arises when the heart muscle experiences anoxia because of an inadequate blood supply occasioned by occlusion of one or more of the coronary arteries (Friedberg, 1966). This state is called ischemia. In formal terms, ''angina pectoris is a clinical syndrome characterized by paroxysmal attacks of a distinctive pain or oppression,'' usually situated behind the sternum, radiating to the chest and left shoulder and down the left arm (Friedberg, 1966).

Angina is usually precipitated by physical exertion or psychological stress and is relieved relatively quickly by rest or drugs designed to produce dilation of the blood vessels and diminution of blood pressure. The pain of angina must be distinguished from the more prolonged chest pain resulting from acute myocardial infarction (discussed next). Moreover, anginal episodes rarely involve permanent and substantial damage to the heart tissue. By contrast, myocardial infarction signifies necrosis (death) of a portion of the heart muscle because of an interruption of its blood supply.

Acute Myocardial Infarction

Coronary occlusion, coronary thrombosis, and myocardial infarction (MI) are used synonymously, although the last term is the proper clinical designation for the disease being discussed here. It is the disorder commonly called a heart attack. An MI involves, as noted above, necrosis of heart tissue caused by insufficient oxygen supply over a relatively long period of time. In many, though not all cases, the infarction is a result of a clot or thrombus forming in a coronary artery. The thrombus obstructs the artery, thereby diminishing the blood supply to some portion of the left heart ventricle, which then dies.

An MI has a distinct clinical picture. There is usually pain in the chest, similar to that of angina pectoris but differing in its greater severity and duration and in its usual independence of exertion. The location and general size of a myocardial infarct can usually be determined by an electrocardiogram (EKG), as well as by various biochemical assays of the blood. The pathologic picture is complex and need not concern us here. Excellent discussions can be found in Friedberg (1966) and Brest and Moyer (1967).

An acute MI sometimes involves not only the heart muscle but, in addition, a portion of the heart's conduction system. In such cases arrhythmias like ventricular tachycardia may develop, or even ventricular fibrillation, which almost invariably results in sudden death.[2] Other complications and causes of

[2] Irregularities in the rhythm of the heart can occur in patients who have never suffered an infarct. Disorders such as tachycardia and bradycardia may result from a variety of factors, including those typically classified as psychological stressors (see Chapter 2).

sudden death following an MI include ventricular failures, pulmonary embolisms, heart rupture, and congestive heart failure, although the latter disease usually develops independently of an MI.

CORONARY ARTERY DISEASE

Coronary artery disease, or atherosclerosis, is a symptomless disorder characterized by thickening of the coronary arteries. The thickening may begin during the first few years of life and is attributable to tiny lesions produced by movements of the coronary artery as it carries blood to the heart. The artery engages in a self-healing procedure by which newly formed cells cover the lesion, thereby producing arterial thickenings. A succession of new lesions and repairs probably goes on continuously throughout childhood, adolescence, and adulthood.

The cells that compose the thickening consist, in large part, of lipids, hence the term "fatty streak" (Greer & McGill, 1967). Not all fatty streaks become atheromatous plaques, but many do, and it is the plaques which are considered the basis of CAD. The process of plaque formation begins when the fatty streak accumulates an excess amount of lipids and cholesterol. The overgrowth of cells expand and multiply, encroaching upon the lumen and narrowing its diameter. The excess lipids and cholesterol accumulating at the base of the plaque interfere with the blood supply needed by the living cells contained in the plaque. As a result, calcification often occurs which increases blockage of the arterial lumen.

The foregoing description of the evolution of a fatty streak into an arterial plaque is certainly over-simplified, though for our purposes it captures the essentials of the natural history of plaque formation. Most plaques are small and do not seriously obstruct the lumen. It is only when substantial occlusion occurs that the blood supply to portions of the heart is impaired and cardiac functioning affected. If the plaque grows at a rate exceeding the blood supply available for the nutrition of its cells, it is likely to decay and rupture. Thrombi may occur at this point and often close off the lumens of the coronary arteries already severely narrowed by the plaques (cf. Friedman & Byers, 1967). When this occlusion occurs, myocardial necrosis may develop and CAD has evolved into CHD. Myocardial infarctions can, of course, also occur without the specific production of thrombi (see Friedberg, 1966 for a discussion of this issue).

A number of investigators have been searching for possible abnormalities in the blood of coronary patients that might explain the genesis of a coronary thrombus (cf. Mustard & Packham, 1969). The adhesiveness of the blood platelets—one of the clotting elements in the blood—has received particular attention. One hypothesis is that an excess of catecholamines leads to increased adhesiveness and hence to deposition of blood platelets on the internal surface of a coronary artery plaque. This deposition is believed to lead to enlargement of the atheromatic plaque as the clotted platelets gradually change into tissue indistinguishable from that making up the initial plaque (see Duguid, 1946). Some investigators suggest that the aggregation of platelets with resulting increase in plaque size hastens the rate of development of coronary disease, including the occurrence of myocardial lesions (see Raab, Stark, MacMillan, and Gigee, 1961; Raab, Chaplin, and Bajusz, 1964; Theorell, 1974).

TRADITIONAL RISK FACTORS FOR CORONARY DISEASE

Data collected in various epidemiologic studies, such as the Heart Disease Epidemiology Study of the National Heart and Lung Institute at Framingham, Massachusetts (Dawber & Kannel, 1961), suggest that the individual prone to CAD and CHD can be identified by certain specific features, although there is little experimental evidence directly implicating these factors in the etiology of coronary disease. Among the principal factors often regarded as associated with high risk from CHD are the following: (1) aging; (2) sex (being a male); (3) elevated serum cholesterol, that is, 250–275 mg per 100 ml or greater of blood serum; (4) elevated serum lipoproteins, including triglycerides; (5) hypertension, that is, systolic and diastolic blood pressure above 160/95 mm Hg; (6) dietary intake of animal fats (for instance, fats in milk) and cholesterol; (7) heavy cigarette smoking, that is, 20 cigarettes or more per day; (8) diabetes mellitus; (9) genetic factors; (10) specific diseases such as hypothyroidism; (11) obesity[3]; (12) physical inactivity; and (13) electrocardiographic evidence of left ventricular hypertrophy (LVH).

In general, the more risk factors present, or the greater severity of the abnormality of any factor, the greater the risk (Insull, 1973). Note, however, that actuarial tables of coronary risk published by the American Heart Association include only 7 variables: age, sex, cigarette smoking, elevated systolic blood pressure, serum cholesterol, LVH, and diabetes measured by biochemical procedures (Insull, 1973).

It is unnecessary for purposes of this monograph to present evidence for and against each of the traditional risk factors. Such discussion can be found in Friedberg (1966) and Rosenman (1975). Suffice it to say here that CAD and CHD have a multifaceted etiology that probably involves all of the factors identified by the American Heart Association, as well as some of the others listed above (like dietary intake of animal fat). Nevertheless, a careful survey of the literature on risk of coronary disease leads to the inescapable conclusion

---

[3]It should be noted here that some researchers believe there is no predictive value of obesity per se for clinical CHD by any of several commonly used indices of obesity (e.g., Mann, 1974; Insull, 1973).

that the best combination of traditional risk factors would still fail to identify most new cases of CHD (Jenkins, 1971). The majority of heart patients do not have a serum cholesterol exceeding 250 mg per 100 ml; only a small number are hypertensive (for example, 160–170/95 mm Hg); and even fewer are diabetic. Admittedly, the simultaneous presence of two or more factors is associated with extremely high risk of CHD, but such conditions still predict only about half the incidence from an epidemiologic point of view (cf. Gordon & Verter, 1969; Keys, Aravanis, Blackburn, van Buchem, Buzina, Djordjevic, Fidanza, Kavonen, Menotti, Pudov, & Taylor, 1972).

Even more important, perhaps, is the uncertainty which exists regarding the predictive status of the most widely accepted risk factors themselves. With a few exceptions (like smoking—Friedman, 1969), there is considerable lack of knowledge regarding the mechanisms mediating the effects of the risk factors on the pathogenesis of coronary disease. The role of dietary fat in atherosclerosis is a commonly cited case in point (cf. Friedman, 1969). Physical inactivity is still another poorly understood variable in the development of coronary disease (cf. Fuller & Eliot, 1974). In general, although a great deal is known about the factors that increase the risk of coronary disease, unanswered questions remain about how these factors exert their influence and, in some cases, whether they actually increase the risk of disease.

PSYCHOLOGICAL AND SOCIAL RISK FACTORS FOR CORONARY DISEASE

The limitations in current knowledge of the etiology of coronary disease argue for "broadening the search for contributing causes . . . of pathogenesis" (Jenkins, 1971). There is, in fact, a sizeable body of empirical research, primarily epidemiologic and clinical, designed to elucidate social and psychological variables that place individuals at higher risk of clinical CHD. Several reviews of this literature (e.g., Keith, 1966; Mordkoff & Parsons, 1968) have concluded that there is little clear-cut evidence implicating psychological factors in coronary disease. Other papers (e.g., Syme, 1968) suggest that the evidence for behavioral variables (both psychological *and* social) is stronger than the support for the role of diet in coronary risk. A monograph published by the Milbank Memorial Fund contains an article (Smith, 1967) which provided the definitive summary of the status of social and psychological risk factors, until the recent appearance of two comprehensive review papers published in the *New England Journal of Medicine* (Jenkins, 1971; 1976). The first paper covers 162 research articles, published between 1965 and 1969, concerned with psychosocial variables associated with risk of coronary disease. The second paper presents more recent evidence and covers the time period since 1970.

We are indeed fortunate in having available such thorough collations of empirical research. Therefore, little effort will be made here to review all of the material on psychosocial risk factors. Suffice it to note that sociological indices such as marital status, religion, ethnicity, occupation, and income level have not shown consistent associations with CHD morbidity and mortality. Race has been somewhat more predictive of CHD, with black males showing lower CHD death rates than white males (Borhani, 1966). Level of education has generally shown an inverse relationship with CHD rates (e.g., Hinkle, Whitney, Lehman, Dunn, Benjamin, King, Piakun, & Flehinger, 1968; Rosenman, Brand, Jenkins, Friedman, Straus, & Wurm, 1975), although some studies suggest that the direction of the relationship depends upon the nature of CHD; that is, angina occurs in higher educational groups and infarction in groups with less education (e.g., Shekelle, 1969). Social mobility, at least where it results in "status incongruity,"[4] appears to raise the risk of coronary disease. This variable may actually reflect personal dissatisfaction, in which case it might be more parsimonious to conceptualize status incongruity in terms of the more general rubric of stress, as discussed in Chapter 2.

As for personality factors, Jenkins' (1971; 1976) summaries suggest that prior to illness, CHD patients differ from healthy controls on Minnesota Multiphasic Personality Inventory (MMPI) indices of neuroticism and somatic preoccupation (that is, Hysteria, Depression, and Hypochondriasis). The difference appears to be largely the result of high scores obtained by persons in whom angina is about to develop rather than in those who subsequently have myocardial infarctions. Studies measuring manifest anxiety in coronary and noncoronary patients indicate that the former group have higher anxiety scores than their noncoronary controls. A word of caution is needed here, however. Most of the research is retrospective, and the observed anxiety may well be a reaction to the coronary event rather than a precursor of the disease. Excessive use of denial and repression by myocardial infarct patients has also been reported in the literature (e.g., Olin & Hackett, 1964). There are even data indicating that the use of these defense mechanisms is a major factor contributing to a patient's delay in seeking medical attention after experiencing symptoms of myocardial infarction (e.g., Greene, Moss, & Goldstein, 1974).

Despite the results just cited, the fact remains that it is extremely difficult to establish a relationship between coronary disease and personality. Part of the difficulty stems from limitations inherent in the techniques of personality measurement used in this area of research, but there is also the more basic problem of employing personality constructs which may be inappropriate to the issues under investigation. A serious attempt to explore the relationship between personality predispositions and coronary disease should involve an

---

[4]Status incongruity refers to a condition in which different characteristics of an individual simultaneously place him at different levels of a social hierarchy. An extreme example would be the urban derelict who comes from a well-to-do upper-class family.

explicit search for psychological variables that are theoretically coordinate with the conditions which increase proneness for CAD and CHD.

Two promising variables have been identified in recent years, namely, psychological stress and the so-called Type A coronary-prone behavior pattern. Both factors have been implicated in the pathogenesis of atherosclerosis and the onset of clinical coronary heart disease. Psychological stress involves the anticipation of harm or injury, whether psychic or physical (see Chapter 2). The behavior pattern is a style of overt response to certain forms of stressful stimulation. It consists of such traits as excessive achievement striving, time urgency, and hostility (see Chapter 3).

Documentation for the association between coronary disease and each of these variables (stress and Pattern A) comes from several sources, including epidemiological research and more focused studies relating specific types of stressors and stress responses to cardiovascular pathology. These data are reviewed in Chapters 2 and 3, since the empirical relationships between coronary disease, Pattern A, and psychological stress provided the original rationale for our program of research. This book is not, however, devoted to a presentation of studies linking coronary disease to behavioral variables. Its major purpose is, rather, to present experimental findings which support a specific conceptual approach to the motivational dynamics underlying the interplay of Pattern A and stress. The crux of this approach is outlined in the next section.

FOCUS OF THIS BOOK

In this monograph I take the position that Type A individuals exert greater efforts than Type B individuals to master stressful events which they perceive as a threat to their sense of control. These active coping attempts eventually extinguish in the face of uncontrollable stimuli, for without reward the relentless striving and time urgency of the Type A individual leads to frustration and psychic exhaustion, which culminate in giving up efforts at control. An almost ironic reversal of behavior is then observed, with Type A individuals showing greater signs of helplessness than their Type B counterparts. We will often refer to this sequence of reaction to uncontrollable stress by the terms *hyperresponsiveness* and *hyporesponsiveness*. Indeed, the major focus of the book is the presentation of successive evaluations of the applicability of these ideas to an understanding of how Type A individuals respond to uncontrollable stressors.

While my earlier concerns with uncontrollable stress (Glass & Singer, 1972) affected my approach to the conceptualization of Pattern A, nevertheless the notion of the behavior pattern as a strategy for coping with uncontrollable aversive events took final shape only after considerable experimentation. The method was inductive, empirical, and phenomenon-oriented. It reflected a style of research that has gained some modicum of acceptance in experimental social psychology over the past few years. However, my concerns and methods also reflected those of the field in general, and to this extent I did not assume a patently atheoretical approach. On the contrary, the program of research was designed to provide systematic documentation for a general model of the interaction of uncontrollable stress and the coronary-prone behavior pattern.

For the most part, the results provide support for the notion of Pattern A as a style of coping with uncontrollable stress. However, I freely admit to a number of unresolved issues and inconsistencies in the data. These are discussed in connection with each study, as well as in a more general summary of the research presented in the final chapter of this book. Moreover, the studies reported here do not give rise to a complete theory relating Pattern A and uncontrollability to coronary disease. While preliminary evidence is presented for biochemical (specifically, catecholaminic) processes that might mediate the effects of behavioral factors on cardiovascular function and pathology (see Chapter 12, the experimentation has not yet been conducted designed to test this line of thought. However, this is hardly a confession of weakness or incompleteness. I am, after all, working on a fundamental problem in what has recently been called the field of "behavioral medicine" (see Miller, 1975). I have now arrived at a logical place to take stock, summarize, and consolidate my work, and to suggest directions for future research. This book is less than a final accounting, but more than a progress report.

PLAN OF THIS BOOK

I have arranged the almost two dozen experiments and studies reported in this monograph into chapters that permit an organized development of successive tests of my major propositions. As I indicated earlier, however, Chapters 2 and 3 are preliminary insofar as they are designed to document the involvement of psychological stress and Pattern A in the pathogenesis of coronary disease. Having established these empirical relationships, the remaining chapters present my own research on the interplay of Pattern A and uncontrollable stressful events. Chapters 4–6 present data concerning the construct validity of the behavior pattern. These findings provide systematic confirmation of previous descriptions of Pattern A. However, close examination of the results also helped lead to the notion of Pattern A as a response style for coping with uncontrollable stressors in the physical and social environment.

Chapter 7 reports studies that support the hypothesis that Type A individuals, in contrast to Type Bs, respond to uncontrollable stress with an initial increment in efforts at control. While most of the studies were conducted with college-student populations, research is also presented using middle-aged subjects. These results add to the external validity of my work, for coronary disease is considered an affliction of the middle years. Chapter 8 indicates that while Type As try harder to assert control than do Type Bs after brief exposure to uncontrollable stimulation, prolonged exposure under certain conditions actually leads to hyporesponsiveness in Type A subjects. Subsequent experimentation suggested that this learned-helplessness effect (see Seligman, 1975) may be dependent upon the salience of uncontrollability cues. Chapter 9 develops this theme further and presents relevant experimental results. Chapter 10 describes additional data concerning the relationship between Pattern A and uncontrollable stress. A study is discussed showing that, compared with healthy controls, coronary patients score higher on the Type A–Type B dimension and experience greater losses in their lives during a 1-year period prior to hospitalization. Chapter 11 is concerned with the origins of the Type A pattern; it presents several studies bearing on genetic and environmental antecedents of the behavior pattern. A final chapter summarizes and interprets the results of all the research, and then attempts to integrate the findings with data presented in Chapters 2 and 3 on biochemical processes implicated in cardiovascular function and pathology. The last section of Chapter 12 is devoted to some general observations concerning the feasibility of modifying the Type A behavior pattern.

2
Psychological Stress and Coronary Disease

An examination of stress research over the past several decades reveals a variety of specific definitions of stress (see, for example, Appley & Trumbull, 1967; Cofer & Appley, 1964; Lazarus, 1966; McGrath, 1970; Rahe, 1975a; Selye, 1956). We do not propose to give extensive treatment to elusive definitional problems, but in the interests of clarity, a brief discussion of the meaning of stress seems appropriate. Such considerations are particularly important in view of continuing confusion regarding the mechanisms of stress reactions. The crux of the difficulty stems from the fact that the term *stress* has been used sometimes to designate arousal conditions (both behavorial and physiological), sometimes to identify instrumental responses, sometimes to describe stimulus conditions, and sometimes for state and trait variables. There is obviously a need to spell out the relationships among these concepts, and we shall now offer an approach which attempts to do just this.

PSYCHOLOGICAL STRESS DEFINED

Psychological stress refers to affective, behavioral, and physiological responses to aversive stimuli in the environment (Appley & Trumbull, 1967). A great variety of environmental events (namely, stressors) are capable of producing stress responses, exemplars ranging from a student failing an examination to a supine patient undergoing cardiac catheterization and fluoroscopy. However, it is also recognized that the induction of stress responses depends upon the mediation of various cognitive factors (Glass & Singer, 1972). As we go up the phylogenetic scale, stress reactions become less dependent on the magnitude of the impinging stimuli and more on associated cues that signify or symbolize the implictions and consequences of these stimuli. Therefore, we prefer to follow

10

Lazarus (1966; 1975) in speaking of psychological stress as the threat or anticipation of future harm, whether that harm is physical (say, electric shock) or psychological (say, an event which lowers self-esteem).

When confronted by any of a range of environmental events, the individual first engages in perceptual–cognitive activity designed to appraise the event as threatening or benign. Stress responses occur if the stimulus is appraised as threatening, at which point the individual begins to mobilize his resources in an effort to eliminate or at least reduce the effects of the stressor stimulus. These coping processes may involve direct actions against the stressor and/or realistic or defensive reevaluation of the stimulus as benign. In either case, the subsequent occurrence of the stimulus will elicit a diminished stress response, and the individual is said to have achieved adaptation (see Glass & Singer, 1972).

The overall process of primary appraisal (that is, threat evaluation) and secondary appraisal (coping[1]) is more complex than we have presented here, since it involves a number of servomechanisms in which stress responses act upon the cognitive appraisal processes and thus affect their outcomes. For our purposes, we need not enter into such complexity; it is enough to emphasize that the central concept in our definition of stress is perceived threat and its attendant coping processes. It should be noted, however, that primary threat appraisal depends upon two general classes of factors: (1) factors in the stimulus and its context, including the imminence of harmful confrontation and, especially, perception of the stimulus as potentially controllable or uncontrollable; (2) factors within the individual, including his intellectual resources, coping strategies, and related personality predispositions. These same factors, along with degree of threat, determine the coping processes used by the individual to reduce or eliminate the anticipated harm.

Psychological stress is defined, then, not solely in terms of stimulus conditions, nor solely in terms of response variables. It is defined with respect to both sets of factors and, more importantly, with respect to mediating cognitive activity. While it is recognized that certain life events are almost universally appraised as stressful, for example, the death of a loved one, an assessment of the individual's primary and secondary appraisal processes is nevertheless essential to a firm designation of an event as stressful or benign.

Consider the case of two 65-year-old men who retire from their respective occupations. One, who had few sources of gratification other than his job, appraises retirement as a threat to his self-esteem and way of life, whereas the

---

[1] We recognize that some investigators prefer to distinguish between coping and defense (e.g., Haan, 1963; Rahe, 1975a), but the distinction strikes us as less than necessary in the stress schema being presented here. The individual may use ego-defensive mechanisms (such as denial or isolation) to reduce the stressor's impact, or he may engage in behaviors designed to alter the effect of the stimulus more directly (such as covering his ears against aversive sound). In each instance, the individual may be characterized as coping with the stressor confronting him.

other, who derived personal gratification from varied sources such as family, friends, and sports, views his retirement as an opportunity to indulge his nonwork interests. The first man may be said to experience retirement as stressful; the second has appraised it as benign, indeed as a pleasurable event. Consider another instance of two men competing for promotion in a large commercial organization. Both appraise each other as threatening, yet one will respond with calculated efforts to further his own cause with his boss, whereas the other takes a more fatalistic view and exerts little effort in his own behalf. He may even deceive himself into believing that there is nothing to be concerned about and, in any event, he is not that interested in promotion. Each man has reduced the stressful impact of the experience—one by direct action and the other by defensive processes.

EFFECTS OF PSYCHOLOGICAL STRESS
ON CORONARY DISEASE

With these definitional considerations as a background, we turn to a discussion of the influence of psychological stress on coronary disease. Indeed, our approach to the stress concept encourages us to think of the breakdown of secondary appraisal processes as a disturbance of organismic adaptation to the environment that may eventually lead to the production of cardiovascular dysfunction. Three general classes of psychological stressors have been studied in connection with coronary disease: (1) general dissatisfaction with various aspects of life; (2) chronic or relatively long-term life events experienced by the individual as stressful; (3) acute life events, defined by the individual (as well as by the culture) as stressful. In addition, there is a group of experimental studies concerned with psychophysiological reactions to all three categories of environmental stressors. The separation of these types of research is, of course, artificial, and much of what will be said in one section applies to the others. It is, however, convenient to draw distinctions for clarity of exposition.

Life Dissatisfactions

Jenkins (1971; 1976) notes that studies from several countries agree that coronary patients report dissatisfaction in many areas of their lives. In Oklahoma, Bruhn, McGrady, and duPlessis (1968) found more frequent job difficulties among 64 workers with coronary disease than among matched controls. Wolf (1969) has also implicated job dissatisfaction and inability to derive satisfaction from leisure activities in myocardial infarction and sudden death in the United States. Dutch investigators report that an infarction is often preceded by a setback in work involving loss of prestige (Kits van Heijningen

& Treurniet, 1966), and in a postmortem study in Israel, Groen and Drory (1967) found that individuals with atherosclerosis were likely to be described by their next of kin as having had severe work problems. A recent investigation of Swedish coronary patients indicates that they experienced less satisfaction with their jobs than healthy controls (Theorell & Rahe, 1972). The study also showed that post-MI patients reported working more hours overtime than did comparison subjects. Sales and House (1971) provide further support for the job-dissatisfaction hypothesis by secondary analyses of data from several American social surveys. They found that occupational groups with higher job dissatisfaction had consistently higher mortality rates due to coronary disease, independent of social class. No relationships were found between average levels of job dissatisfaction and mortality from a variety of other diseases, including cancer, accidents, and pneumonia.

Dissatisfaction with aspects of life other than in the occupational sphere has also been reported to be more frequent among coronary patients than controls. Jenkins (1971; 1976) reviews a number of relevant studies and concludes that coronary cases experience more unhappiness over their level of education, adult interpersonal relations, and marital relations. Explicit cross-cultural comparisons suggest that life dissatisfactions may be greater in some societies than in others. Thus, Romo, Siltanen, Theorell, and Rahe (1974) found that there was nearly twice the dissatisfaction with level of education and achievement of life goals among Finnish coronary patients than among their Swedish and American counterparts.

Despite the consistent pattern of results obtained in the dissatisfaction research, a word of caution must be introduced here. The findings are almost entirely retrospective and could, therefore, result from a tendency among individuals with coronary disease to be more critical and irritated with their life circumstances. This problem of design severely restricts causal inferences.

Chronic Stress

Sales (1969) and House (1975) suggest that excessive work and responsibility, when it approaches the limits of the individual's capacity to control the work, precipitate the development of coronary disease. Evidence to support this hypothesis comes from epidemiologic research, most of which is reviewed in T. Smith (1967), Jenkins (1971; 1976), and House (1975). Additional documentation for the association between occupational stress and coronary disease can be found in more focused studies of job stressors and coronary disease. For example, French and his colleagues (French & Caplan, 1972; French, Rodgers, & Cobb, 1974; French, Tupper, & Mueller, 1965) have found that feelings of work overload are related to elevated serum cholesterol.

Work overload refers to feelings that the demands of the job are beyond the individual's control.

House (1975) reviews a number of other studies that, by and large, produce results not unlike those reported in the research of French and associates. The review also cites studies that document a correlation between occupational stress (for example, excess of overtime work) and actual CHD (e.g., Russek, 1965; Theorell & Rahe, 1971). Thus, there is increasing evidence that chronic work overload—or at least its implications for lack of felt control—plays a significant role in increasing the risk of coronary disease.

Acute Stress

Death of a close relative appears to increase the likelihood of death in next of kin, particularly due to coronary disease (e.g., Parkes, Benjamin, & Fitzgerald, 1969). Rejection by a loved one or a sudden loss in self-esteem sometimes precede an acute MI (e.g., Engel, 1970). Recent studies also indicate that abrupt economic downturns are associated with increased mortality from heart disease and that, conversely, heart disease mortality declines with economic upturns (Brenner, 1971). Holmes and Rahe (e.g., 1967; also Holmes & Masuda, 1970; Rahe *et al.*, 1974) have developed an objective instrument for measuring a variety of such stressful life events in an individual's immediate and past environment. The instrument is called the Social Readjustment Rating Scale. It is based on values assigned by groups of judges to 45 different kinds of life events (death of a spouse, retirement, son or daughter leaving home, marriage, etc.). The judges were asked to weight these items in terms of the intensity and length of time necessary to accommodate to them, irrespective of whether positive or negative feelings are likely to be associated with the events. They were given an anchor point of "marriage" with which to compare the other events. The resulting estimates of scale values are called *life change units*; for example, the item "death of a spouse" has the highest value at 100, "marriage" ranks seventh with 50, and "vacation" is forty-first with a value of 13.

The actual procedure used by Holmes and his associates has a subject complete a form called the SRE, that is, the Schedule of Recent Experience (Hawkins, Davies, & Holmes, 1957). The subject indicates which of 45 events on the SRE happened to him during various time intervals in the recent past; for example, 6 months ago, 6 months to 1 year ago, 1 to 2 years ago, and 2 to 3 years ago. The scale value of each event is multiplied by the number of times the event occurred in a given time period, and the resulting values for the 45 events are added up for a total score in life change units for the time interval under consideration.

Several variants of the Holmes procedure have been reported in the literature, including variations of the events included in the SRE, different time intervals, and the construction of indices based on subsets of items from the SRE. Paykel, Myers, Dienelt, Klerman, Lindenthal, and Pepper (1969), for example, have shown that "social exits" (events like death of a close family member, divorce, or a family member leaving home) were more frequent among depressed patients than among controls during a 6-month period immediately prior to the onset of depression. The total of "entrance" items (for instance, marriage, or birth of a child), on the other hand, was about equal in the two groups during the same time period.

Of particular relevance to the present discussion is the application of the life change scale to studies of the antecedents of coronary disease (e.g., Rahe & Lind, 1971; Rahe & Paasikivi, 1971; Theorell & Rahe, 1971). A very recent study in this series (Rahe, Romo, Bennett, & Siltanen, 1974) gathered life-change data from 275 survivors of myocardial infarctions and from 22 cases of abrupt coronary death in Helsinki. Spouses provided life change information for all of the victims. The results indicated marked elevations in the magnitude of total life changes during the 6 months prior to infarction compared to the same time interval 1 year earlier. These data generally agree with earlier studies conducted in Sweden showing an increase in total life change during the 6-month period prior to infarction (e.g., Rahe & Lind, 1971).

Despite the seeming impressiveness of the preceding results, it should be emphasized that most of the research is retrospective and could easily be contaminated by the subject's knowledge of his own illness. A systematic attempt to overcome this limitation is currently underway in Stockholm (Theorell, 1974) using the life change approach and a 2-year follow-up of mortality and morbidity due to coronary disease.

Prospective studies of life change and coronary disease provide only one direction for future research. Of equal importance to an understanding of the role of acute stress in the occurrence of CHD is a more fine-grained analysis of the nature of life events preceding infarction. The work of Paykel (e.g., Paykel *et al.*, 1969) with indices of life change illustrate this approach. Theorell, Lind, and Floderus (1975) have also used specific items and subsets of items (for example, responsibility in work, perception of financial status) from the SRE in a moderately successful effort to predict near-future myocardial infarctions.

It may also be that the simple total of stressful events during a given time period is less critical in predicting CHD than the significance of these events for the individual. Following our earlier definition of psychological stress, we suggest that the way in which an event is appraised and how the individual copes with it must be considered in any serious effort to understand psychophysiological (and specifically cardiovascular) effects of acute life stressors. While the use of indices of life change items, as described here, does not guarantee an accurate reflection of the individual's threat appraisal, such indices do move us somewhat closer to this goal than a simple sum of weighted life changes.

Loss, helplessness, and illness. A program of studies not unrelated to the life change approach is currently underway at the University of Rochester (e.g., Engel, 1968, 1970; Greene, Goldstein & Moss, 1972; Schmale, 1972). According to these investigators, there is a psychological state called helplessness that commonly precedes the onset of illness and death. The passing of a loved one upon whom the individual has depended, a sudden loss of prestige or self-esteem, a decline of physical abilities in old age—all may precede illness from a sense of helplessness. An individual experiencing helplessness perceives a noncontingency between his responses and outcomes. He attributes his feelings to failures emanating from his environment, and it is to the environment that he looks for a solution to his problems. From a behavioral point of view, the helpless person shows a decrement in response initiation and simply gives up efforts to interact with his physical and social surroundings.

There is, in fact, some documentation for the hypothesized helplessness–illness association. We cited one relevant study in the introduction to this section (i.e., Parkes *et al.*, 1969), and Engel (1970) has documented the role of helplessness in disease and death by analyzing press accounts of some 160 instances of sudden death over a 6-year period. Despite the anecdotal and uncontrolled nature of his primary data, there is an impressive consistency to the circumstances surrounding the deaths, for they all involved some form of helplessness for the victim. For example, the largest group in the sample were people who died soon after receiving news of the death of a loved one. Another group died suddenly during situations of danger beyond their control, such as riots and personal assault. The immediate cause of death was usually some form of CHD.

Additional support for the helplessness–death relationship comes from the research of Greene *et al.* (1972). Twenty-six male patients who died suddenly from CHD in an industrial population of 44,000 were the focus of study. Data were obtained from plant medical records and from direct interviews with the surviving next of kin. The results indicate that at least 80% of the 26 patients were reported to have had clinical symptoms of depression for a week up to several months prior to death. A study by Kavanagh and Shephard (1973) of 122 coronary victims in Toronto obtained similar results. In the year prior to their attack, these patients were beset with problems in business and elsewhere, and increased fatigue was noted in the week prior to attack.

While the prodromal depression noted in these two studies could have been a direct result of an impending heart attack, the Rochester group has initiated a promising line of research which is certainly relevant to this book's approach to the role of psychological factors in coronary disease (see Chapters 7–10). It is, moreover, a good illustration of the importance of considering the individual's perception of life events and their implications. Cardiovascular effects of psychological stressors are not simply a function of their intensity or frequency; they also depend upon the cognitive context in which the stressors occur, that is, their perceived uncontrollability which may lead to feelings of helplessness.

Psychophysiology of Stress

The credibility of the stress hypothesis in cardiovascular disease does not depend exclusively on the preceding data and theory. Research has been conducted showing that stressful events provoke changes in physiological and biochemical functioning that are present in coronary compared to noncoronary subjects. Consider those studies which demonstrate a relationship between stressor stimuli and changes in cardiovascular function that could lead to vascular injury and coronary disease.

Stress and cardiovascular activity. There is an extensive literature on the relationship between environmental stressors and cardiovascular function in man and animals. Williams (1975) cites a number of experiments indicating that stress increases cardiac output, decreases total peripheral resistance, and shunts blood away from skin and viscera to the skeletal muscles. It turns out, however, that the picture is more complicated. Heart rate slows down in the face of certain types of stressor stimuli, as when an individual is trying to detect and control potentially stressful events in the environment (e.g., Lacey, Kagan, Lacey, & Moss, 1963). Moreover, vasoconstriction in the skeletal muscles is associated with heart-rate decrements, whereas vasodilation appears with stressors (for instance, mental arithmetic) that do not involve scanning the environment. Plasma catecholamines increase only in the presence of vaso-constriction and, as noted in later chapters, norepinephrine and epinephrine may be implicated in the risk of coronary disease.

Several studies have shown relationships between the actual occurrence of coronary disease and the cardiovascular response patterns described here. A prospective study in Minnesota, for example, indicates that the degree of rise of diastolic blood pressure in a cold pressor test (immersing the subject's limb in ice water) has major predictive powers with regard to the coronary incidence observed during 20 years of the study (Keys, Taylor, Blackburn, Brozek, Anderson, & Simonson, 1971). The cold pressor test is known to induce sympathetic nervous system discharge, including increased peripheral vas-oconstriction, elevated blood pressure, and increased heart rate (Sternbach, 1966). Williams (1975) has summarized other research in the area and con-cludes that both in attempting to control and in failing to control stressful events, individuals subject their cardiovascular systems to response patterns that are potentially injurious.

Further support for this view comes from research on stress and predisposition to ventricular fibrillation (VF), the mechanism of sudden coronary death. Lown, Verrier, and Corbalan (1973) have recently shown that the amount of electrical current needed to trigger a repetitive ventricular response in a dog (a precursor of VF) was considerably reduced if testing was done in what they called a nonstressful as compared to a stressful environment. The data were obtained on the fourth and fifth day of experimentation. The nonstress condition consisted of a cage which permitted freedom of movement during testing. The stressful condition consisted of placing the dog in a Pavlovian sling which did not permit free movement. The results were interpreted in terms of psychologic stress lowering the threshold for VF by triggering increased sympathetic activity and resultant rapid heart rate.

The results of Lown and colleagues might also be explained in terms of the notions of uncontrollability and helplessness (cf. Seligman, Maier, & Solomon, 1971). Dogs in both conditions were exposed to the stress of cardiac catheterization for several days, but those in harness had the added experience of being immobilized. The unharnessed animals were able to move about during stressful stimulation, and these movements may well have reduced the affective and physiological responses associated with the shocks. Indeed, Lown *et al.* (1973) note that the harnessed dogs showed more restlessness and somatic tremor than the unharnessed animals. It might be concluded, therefore, that *uncontrollable* stressors affect the conduction system of the heart to a greater extent than do controllable stressors.

Stress and serum cholesterol.   As noted earlier, serum cholesterol level is widely accepted as one of the more important risk factors for coronary disease (see Friedman, 1969). There is a sizable literature concerning the relationship between environmental stressors and serum cholesterol response. A few illustrative findings should clarify the nature of this association. Friedman, Byers, and Brown (1967) exposed rats to an intermittent 114-dB, 200-Hz square-wave sound superimposed upon continuous 102-dB noise stimulation. The animals showed substantial elevations of postprandial plasma triglycerides for a period of about 21 days. Cholesterol-fed rabbits exposed to similar auditory stimulation for 10 weeks exhibited higher blood cholesterol and more extensive atherosclerosis than similarly fed control animals. The unpredictable nature of the noise schedule may have been critical here, for other research (e.g., Glass & Singer, 1972; Weiss, 1970) indicates that unpredictable and uncontrollable stressors are necessary conditions for producing stress responses in animals and humans. Indeed, Paré, Rothfeld, Isom, and Varady (1973) demonstrated that rats fed a high lipid diet and also exposed to uncontrollable (that is, unavoidable) and unpredictable grid shock for 2 to 8 days showed higher levels of accumulated serum cholesterol than control rats fed only the high lipid diet.

Rahe and his colleagues (e.g., Rahe, Rubin, & Arthur, 1974; Rahe, Rubin, Arthur, & Clark, 1968; Rahe, Rubin, Gunderson, & Arthur, 1971; Rubin, Rahe, Clark, & Arthur, 1970) have conducted an extensive series of studies of the association of human subjects' psychological states with their serum concentrations of cholesterol. Most of the research used navy personnel exposed to a variety of stressful training situations; the group included underwater demolition trainees, submariners, or naval aviators. Elevated serum cholesterol levels were observed when subjects felt overburdened by demands of the training (for example, during exams and periods of learning new skills); when subjects reported feeling depressed, angry, fearful, and lethargic; and when there was a threat of imminent failure.

Such results are obviously subject to a number of theoretical interpretations, but it can at least be argued that cholesterol elevations occurred when subjects believed that the stressful events were beyond their control, that is, during imminent failure and when environmental demands were overburdening them. The correlations with mood are less easily explained, although a negative association between cholesterol level and reported motivation to perform well suggests someone who believes he is in potential control of the situation. This finding adds a further dimension to the observations of several investigators that "active" psychological states such as motivation to master events accompany low levels of serum cholesterol and high levels of serum uric acid (e.g., Brooks & Mueller, 1966; Rahe et al., 1968; Wolf, McCabe, Yamamoto, Adsett, & Schottstaedt, 1962).

Further support for the association between serum cholesterol level and psychological stress comes from a study by Friedman, Rosenman, and Carroll (1958). These investigators studied a group of accountants who agreed to be bled twice monthly for approximately 6 months beginning in the first month of the year. For at least 1 week prior to April 15, the final date for tax returns in the United States, the accountants were subjected to the stressful experience of finishing all the tax forms they had contracted to complete. Many of the accountants were also subjected to the same type of stressful experience in January, when tax inventories had to be prepared for various corporate clients. Along with serum cholesterol determinations taken twice monthly during the 6-month period (January through June), the accountants each kept a dietary history for the week of April 2 to 9 and again on May 14 to 21.

The results showed that during the first two weeks of April, serum cholesterol levels were significantly higher than during February and March. The average cholesterol level in April for the accountants who were also engaged in estimating January tax inventories was higher than the level for those who did not have to work on the inventories. No change was noted in the diets of any of the accountants during the periods in which cholesterol rose. The average cholesterol level of all accountants fell sharply after April 15.

A number of studies have confirmed the foregoing results (Dreyfuss &

Czaczkes, 1959; Grundy & Griffin, 1959; Peterson, Keith, & Wilcox, 1962; Thomas & Murphy, 1958; Wertlake, Wilcox, Haley, & Peterson, 1958). There were also several experiments antedating the 1958 publication showing that cholesterol levels are appreciably higher during periods of stress than at other times (e.g., Mann & White, 1953). Most of this research used university or medical-school examinations as the stressor stimulus and the period of regular academic work as baseline.

Stress and adrenal cortex secretions.   The adrenal cortex is known to be involved in the regulation of cholesterol metabolism and may thus play a role in the pathogenesis of coronary disease (Friedberg, 1966). An extensive body of research documents a positive association between psychological stress and certain adrenocortical hormones such as 17-hydroxycorticosteroids (e.g., Hamburg, 1962; Mason, 1972; Mason & Brady, 1964). Elevation of these hormones is not, however, related to specific stressor stimuli; rather it appears to reflect a relatively undifferentiated state of affective arousal.

Of greater significance for a stress–coronary disease relationship is secretion of the corticosteroid, cortisol, since it increases FFA release and generally leads to a rise in serum lipids and cholesterol (Netter, 1969). It is now well established that secretion of cortisol in humans and animals increases in response to psychological stressors (Mason, 1972). The kinds of situations used in this research include venous catheterization (Rose & Hurst, 1975), underwater demolition team training (Rubin, Rahe, Arthur, & Clark, 1969), and, in animals, capture and chair restraint (Brown, Schalch, & Reichlin, 1971).

Stress and adrenal medulla secretions.   The best known hormones secreted by the adrenal medulla are epinephrine and norepinephrine. These catecholamines are related to sympathetic nervous system activity (indeed, norepinephrine is secreted from sympathetic nerve endings), which in turn is responsive to the impact of psychological stressors (Greenfield & Sternbach, 1972). What has probably made the catecholamines important in stress research is evidence suggesting that epinephrine is associated with fear or passive responding and norepinephrine with anger or aggressiveness (Ax, 1953; Funkenstein, King, & Drollette, 1957; Silverman & Cohen, 1960). This set of associations is, however, by no means firmly established (e.g., Levi, 1965). Indeed, the work of Schachter and Singer (1962) indicates that behavioral and subjective effects of catecholamines are dependent upon cognitive activity, that is, the psychological significance of the situation for the individual and not merely on the release of the hormones per se. Whatever the final resolution of these issues, the fact remains that alterations in catecholamine levels coincide with the application of external stressors. Excellent summaries of relevant research can be found in Mason (1972) and Frankenhaeuser (1971).

Stress, catecholamines, and coronary disease. It is entirely appropriate, however, to examine some of the evidence bearing on the correlation among environmental stressors, catecholamines, and cardiovascular function and pathology. Epinephrine and norepinephrine induce acute hemodynamic effects related to CAD, including elevations of cardiac rate, blood pressure, and release of lipids into the blood (e.g., Friedman, 1969; Steinberg, 1966). A recent review paper, summarizing physiological research on the role of catecholamines in coronary disease, concludes that these hormones may be causally implicated in the pathogenesis of myocardial infarction (Januszewicz & Sznajderman, 1972; see also Frankel, 1969). The catecholamines can contribute to an infarction by facilitating the aggregation of thrombocytes (blood platelets), which may then lead to thrombosis (Mustard & Packham, 1969; Theorell, 1974). Since the catecholamines elevate blood pressure, they can potentiate bleeding in arterial atheromata induced by enhanced mechanical strain in the vessel wall. Moreover, epinephrine and norepinephrine may lead to a narrowing of the capillaries nourishing the blood vessels and associated coronary plaques. Such narrowing eventually interferes with nourishment of the plaques which leads to further arterial damage, and even an infarction.

It would thus appear that the catecholamines may have a special significance in the development of coronary disease. It follows that any psychological agent which increases circulating catecholamines may be potential pathogen for cardiovascular function. Several studies document the relationship between psychological stressors and catecholamines (see Mason, 1972). Consider, for example, a study by Nestel, Verghese, and Lovell (1967), which shows that subjects with angina pectoris responded to a test of intellectual ability with a greater average increase in secretion of vanilmandelic acid (VMA), a metabolite of norepinephrine, compared to patients with CHD but no anginal pain. The authors suggest that the effect may have been due to the way in which their subjects responded to the test rather than to the disease.

Friedman, Byers, Diamant, and Rosenman (1975) report that under competitive conditions the plasma norepinephrine concentration of coronary-prone subjects rose an average of 30%, while that of noncoronary-prone subjects remained unchanged. There were no differences between the two groups under resting conditions, and epinephrine concentrations were virtually the same in both groups under resting as well as competitive conditions. This result suggests that norepinephrine, in particular, may be influenced by efforts to cope with psychological stressors.

Earlier research (e.g., Elmadjian, 1963; Elmadjian, Hope, & Larson, 1958), indicates that active coping with a stressor leads to the increased specific discharge of norepinephrine, and we have already cited studies showing a linkage between norepinephrine and aggressiveness (e.g., Funkenstein *et al.*, 1957). More recent work suggests that norepinephrine levels in blood and urine remain elevated in subjects engaged in active efforts to escape or avoid stressors (Frankenhaeuser, 1971; Frankenhaeuser & Rissler, 1970; Weiss, Stone, & Harrell, 1970), whereas substantial depletions in brain norepinephrine occur when subjects react to uncontrollable stressors with helplessness or giving-up responses (e.g., Weiss, Glazer, & Pohorecky, 1977). It is not surprising that concomitant increases in epinephrine levels have also been observed following a reduction in coping activity (cf. Anisman, 1975).

The foregoing set of data will be referred to again later in the book, when an attempt is made to relate our behavioral results to coronary disease. Suffice it to note here that (1) catecholamines seem to play a role in producing arterial injury and are thus implicated in plaque formation and coronary artery disease; (2) catecholamines have other effects that may contribute to myocardial infarction; (3) environmental stressors produce elevations in catecholamine levels; and (4) norepinephrine levels are increased during active efforts to control psychosocial stressors, whereas they are depleted when the individual gives up these coping efforts.

SUMMARY

This chapter was designed to summarize the evidence for an empirical linkage between psychological stress and coronary disease. The stress factor is, as noted in Chapter 1, one of the two principal variables involved in the program of behavioral experimentation presented in this book. For this reason, a brief summary is appropriate here.

Psychological stress was defined in terms of a conceptual model that emphasizes cognitive processes mediating the relationship between external stressors and measurable stress responses. Three classes of stressors were identified as involved in the onset of coronary disease. Thus, there is a consistent pattern of results indicating that excessive work and responsibility is associated with the development of CAD and CHD. Research on acute stressors indicates that the onset of CHD (and sudden death) is characteristically related to an increase of life events during the previous 6-month period. Unfortunately, most of the studies were retrospective; moreover, no effort was made to determine whether subjects appraised life changes as in fact stressful.

Psychophysiological research has demonstrated an association between cardiovascular function and both acute and chronic environmental stressors. Similar relationships seem well established between stress and (1) serum cholesterol and (2) catecholamines. However, the nature of the stressor is not irrelevant in these associations, for analysis of some of the literature suggests that the physiological effects of chronic and acute stressors may depend upon whether they are experienced as controllable or uncontrollable.

3

The Coronary-Prone Behavior Pattern and Coronary Disease

The idea of a "coronary-prone behavior pattern" has been discussed by cardiologists and researchers for a good many years. It is present in the writings of the Menningers, Flanders Dunbar, and even a nineteenth century cardiologist, Sir William Osler. In more recent times, deep involvement in job or profession—one of the presumed components of the behavior pattern—has been linked to the occurrence of coronary disease. Some of the relevant research in this area was cited in the last chapter. House (e.g., 1975) has also implicated "work overload" as a risk factor for CHD, and aggressive striving for achievement, difficulty in relaxing, and the need to maintain a rapid pacing of activities have all been noted as characteristics of coronary patients compared to their controls (e.g., Dreyfuss, Shanan, & Sharon, 1966; Liljefors & Rahe, 1970; Theorell & Rahe, 1972). These traits are considered to be major aspects of the coronary-prone behavior pattern.

Wolf and his colleagues (e.g., see Wolf, 1969) suggest the term "Sisyphus pattern" to characterize the coronary-prone individual. The Sisyphean type is described as someone who "strives without joy" and frequently without success. He is a relentless striver who tends to experience little sense of accomplishment or satisfaction. Wolf's description of the Sisyphus reaction stresses the individual's lack of fulfillment and satisfaction, whereas with the Type A behavior pattern somewhat less emphasis is placed on these features of the coronary-prone subject. On the other hand, recent evidence indicates a relationship between extreme Pattern A responses and the joyless striving behavior of the Sisyphus complex (Bruhn, Paredes, Adsett, & Wolf, 1974).

It should be emphasized that the notion of a coronary-prone behavior pattern is not quite the same as the idea of a "coronary personality," which quite correctly fell into disfavor for lack of empirical support (see, for example, Mordkoff & Parsons, 1968). The behavior pattern is a set of overt behaviors resulting from the interaction of a specific set of predispositions with appropriately eliciting situations. This may sound like a needless distinction and really not all that different from certain approaches to personality (e.g., Bowers, 1973; Mischel, 1968). However, we wish to emphasize that personality traits do not lead to behavioral and physiological responses by some invariant process. One must take into account a variety of situational factors and how they interact with individual predispositions. In these terms, we must construct models of specific person–situation interactions in order to give etiologic significance to psychological factors in coronary disease. Such an approach is, of course, the major thrust of our research and, we should add, an underlying assumption of the coronary-prone behavior pattern.

TYPE A CORONARY-PRONE BEHAVIOR PATTERN: DEFINITION

Progress toward an integrated description of the coronary-prone behavior pattern comes from the laboratories of Friedman and Rosenman (e.g., Friedman, 1969; Rosenman, 1975; Rosenman & Friedman, 1974). The pattern is described by these investigators as "a characteristic action–emotion complex which is exhibited by those individuals who are engaged in a relatively *chronic struggle* to obtain an *unlimited* number of *poorly defined* things from their environment in *the shortest period of time* and, if necessary, against the opposing effects of other things or persons in this same environment" (Friedman, 1969, p. 84). Individuals who manifest this behavior pattern to a greater degree are called Type As, whereas those who tend to show the opposite pattern of relaxation, serenity, and lack of time urgency are designated Type Bs.

We can probably define Pattern A[1] in terms of a limited set of descriptive characteristics: (1) competitive achievement striving; (2) exaggerated sense of time urgency; (3) aggressiveness and hostility. At least two of these components correspond to factors extracted in various analyses of data on which the diagnosis of Pattern A is based (e.g., Zyzanski & Jenkins, 1970). In other words, our selection of the principal components of the behavior pattern has some empirical foundation. However, it should be emphasized that the components correlate substantially with the total A–B pattern and, indeed, they have been shown to load a single factor orthogonal to other factors loading subscale scores from standard personality tests (Caffrey, 1968).

---

[1] Throughout this book, we shall use the terms Type A–Type B or Pattern A–Pattern B interchangeably. They are simply a shorthand for the Type A coronary-prone behavior pattern and the Type B noncoronary-prone behavior pattern. Similarly, Type As will mean Type A individuals; Type Bs will mean Type B individuals.

There are several additional points that need to be made with regard to the definition of Pattern A. First, no one Type A individual manifests all of the characteristics constituting the pattern, and even a Type B individual will show some A-like features. In clinical practice, the designation of a person as Type A or Type B depends upon a summation of the number of Pattern A characteristics and their intensity (Jenkins, 1975). We will return to this issue when we consider measurement procedures. Another point to be emphasized is that the behavior pattern is not a typology. Descriptions of Type A and Type B individuals represent extremes of a bipolar continuum that is, in all likelihood, normally distributed in the United States (see Rosenman, Friedman, Straus, Wurm, Kosichek, Hahn, & Werthessen, 1964).

It might be argued that Pattern A is simply a reflection of socioeconomic status; after all, its descriptive characteristics are similar to the "work ethic" of the middle classes of Western society. While there is no evidence linking Pattern A to level of education per se (see, for example, Caffrey, 1968), one recent study has shown consistent though weak correlations (around .20) between an objective measure of the behavior pattern and a social class index based on educational and occupational rank (Shekelle, Schoenberger, and Stamler, 1976). Other research indicates an association between occupational rank and Pattern A (e.g., Rosenman et al., 1964; Rosenman, Friedman, Straus, Jenkins, Zyzanski, & Wurm, 1970). Individuals in professional and managerial occupations tend to have a higher frequency of Pattern A behavior than individuals at lower levels of the occupational hierarchy. On the other hand, the linkage of Pattern A to social class level is far from an invariant relationship. There are many Type Bs in top management positions and one can easily find relatively uneducated As in the laboring occupations (see, for example, Friedman, 1969).

MEASUREMENT OF PATTERN A

There are three principal techniques for the measurement of the coronary-prone behavior pattern, and each of these is discussed in this section.

Standardized Stress Interview

The classification of individuals as Pattern A or Pattern B is often based on a standardized stress interview developed by Friedman and Rosenman (e.g., see Rosenman et al., 1964). This interview relies on both the content and overt behavioral style of the subject's responses to rate his behavior pattern on a 4-point scale: fully developed As (A_1); incompletely developed As (A_2); incompletely developed Bs (B_3); and fully developed Bs (B_4). In addition, there is an intermediate pattern called Type X, which is found in persons who exhibit some of the characteristics of both the incompletely developed A_2 and B_3 types. Estimates indicate that about 10% of the population fall in the X category (Friedman & Rosenman, 1974).

The stress interview is a standardized clinical technique. The subject is asked approximately 25 questions dealing with the intensity of his ambitions, competitiveness, sense of time urgency, and the nature and magnitude of his hostile feelings. The interviewer deliberately phrases his questions so as to create a stressful atmosphere for the subject. It is assumed that these conditions are optimal for eliciting signs of impatience, aggressiveness, competitiveness, and the like, if these traits are, in fact, characteristic of the subject. The manner and tone in which the subject responds to the questions (for example, his general appearance, bodily movements, explosive speech accentuations and inflections) are somewhat more important than the content of his answers, though the latter is certainly a determinant of an individual's behavior pattern classification. The interviews are typically tape recorded for later assessment.

The coronary-prone behavior pattern is judged on the basis of overt behavior. Such behavior is best observed when an individual is responding to questions about areas in his life that are important to him or in some way threaten him. It is for this reason that it is extremely difficult to assess the behavior pattern of a person who has disengaged himself from his surroundings or is, in some other way, bored and disinterested. But with appropriate stimulus conditions, such as the stress interview just described, behavior pattern classifications can be made by a trained interviewer and assessor.

Pattern A characteristics may be grouped into several indicator categories, ranging from values and styles of thought to overt behaviors such as gestures, facial expressions, and breathing. For example, the fully developed Pattern A subject usually reacts and speaks rapidly, enunciates words with emphasis, and anticipates what is going to be said next. He hurries the person with whom he is talking by anticipatory nods and "ahems." Along with these motor signs, other indicators of Pattern A include: a craving for power and recognition; compulsive attraction to competition; few sources of gratification other than the job; compulsiveness about getting things done; a tendency to be easily aroused to anger by other people and things; and the belief that one can overcome any obstacle with sufficient effort.

The Pattern B subject will often exhibit many of these Pattern A characteristics, but rarely in such exaggerated form. Individuals classified as Pattern B display little evidence of chronic time urgency, although they may occasionally feel some pressure due to deadlines. They tend to show a relatively relaxed pattern of gestures and unhurried movements. They are not easily aroused to anger, though there are situations in which they can behave in a hostile manner. Pattern B subjects recognize their own limitations and do not show an intense inclination to compete.

Discussion of the replicability and test–retest reliability of the interview method of assessing Pattern A is presented in Appendix A.

Self-Administered Questionnaire

Another commonly used technique for assessing Pattern A is an objective self-administered questionnaire developed by C. David Jenkins of Boston University Medical School. The test is called the JAS, that is, the Jenkins Activity Survey for Health Prediction, and it provides continuous scores on the A–B dimension (Jenkins, Rosenman, & Friedman, 1967; Jenkins, Zyzanski, & Rosenman, 1971; Zyzanski & Jenkins, 1970).[2] Form B (and more recently, Form E) of the JAS (Jenkins, Rosenman, & Zyzanski, 1972) was designed for adult working males, much as the interview procedure was developed for this type of population. It consists of 54 items which yield several scores, including a Pattern A or A–B scale score based on 21 of the items.

Typical questions are the following:

1. "Has your spouse or some friend ever told you that you eat too fast?"; a Pattern A response is "Yes, often," and Pattern B responses are "Yes, once or twice" or "No, no one has told me this."
2. "How would your wife (or closest friend) rate you?"; Pattern A responses are "Definitely hard-driving and competitive" and "Probably hard-driving and competitive," and B responses are "Probably relaxed and easy going" and "Definitely relaxed and easy going."
3. "How would your spouse (or best friend) rate your general level of activity?"; an A response is "Too active, needs to slow down," and B responses are "Too slow, should be more active" and "About average, is busy much of the time."
4. "Do you ever set deadlines or quotas for yourself at work or at home?"; an A response is "Yes, once per week or more often," and B responses are "No" and "Yes, but only occasionally."

Scoring of the JAS items is based on a series of optimal weights derived from discriminant function equations generated from scores of adult subjects used in a prospective study designed to establish the predictive validity of the structured interview (discussed later in this chapter). The JAS scores of this sample were normally distributed. A linear transformation applied to all scores was incorporated into the computer program which scores the test. Thus, the mean of A–B scale scores for this sample was 0.0 with a standard deviation of

---

[2] Permission to use the JAS must be obtained from Dr. C. David Jenkins, Department of Behavioral Epidemiology, Boston University Medical School, Boston, Massachusetts. The student version of the JAS, described in the next section and in Appendix A, can be obtained by writing directly to the author of this monograph.

10.0. Positive scores denote the Pattern A direction, and negative scores denote the Pattern B direction.

In addition to the A–B scale, the JAS can be scored for three factors which are correlated with the overall A–B score but which are independent of each other. These dimensions were derived from a series of factor analyses of JAS responses. A complete description of the samples used, as well as of all JAS items and their factor loadings, is given by Zyzanski and Jenkins (1970). The three factor scales have been named Speed and Impatience (S), Hard Driving (H), and Job Involvement (J). In view of their disappointing ability to predict CHD (e.g., Jenkins, Rosenman, & Zyzanski, 1974), the factor scores were used only once in our own research.

Appendix A contains data on the test–retest reliability of the JAS, as well as on its degree of agreement with the interview method of assessing Pattern A.

Student version of the JAS.   Most of the experiments reported in this monograph used college students as subjects. Administration of the intact JAS to such a population is not entirely appropriate. The test was, after all, designed for working male adults. Accordingly, a modified, student version of the JAS was designed for young men and women attending college. A discussion of the modification, its scoring, and reliability is contained in Appendix A. Suffice it to note here that the A–B scale of the student JAS contains 21 items, just as in the original JAS. Note, also, that with one exception each item was virtually identical to the corresponding item in the adult version.

A description of how subjects were classified as Pattern A or Pattern B in terms of the student JAS is also contained in Appendix A. For the most part, we relied on a division at the median of the A–B scale score distribution, although several studies selected subjects who scored at the extremes. These exceptions are noted in appropriate places in subsequent chapters.

Performance Battery

A third technique for measuring Pattern A consists of 11 cognitive and psychomotor tests developed by Rayman W. Bortner of Pennsylvania State University. Twenty-one different scores were derived from this battery of tests. Using stepwise multiple regression procedures, only 9 of the scores made significant contributions to the prediction of Pattern A as assessed by the stress interview (Bortner & Rosenman, 1967).

Descriptions of the tests included in Bortner's battery are deliberately omitted here. This technique was employed only once in our research, and the tests are better described at the time the relevant experiment is presented (Chapter 11). Suffice it to note that Bortner's battery includes a flicker-fusion task, a writing speed test, the Thurstone (1944) Embedded Figures test, and a general measure of the motor activity of the subject as he or she works on the different tests.

EFFECTS OF PATTERN A ON CORONARY DISEASE

The preceding two sections defined Pattern A and outlined the principal methods of assessing the behavior pattern. We now turn to a review of data bearing on the influence of Pattern A on coronary disease. This section is organized according to research findings germane to different types of criterion-related validity, rather than in terms of the methods of measuring Pattern A. We are specifically concerned with the Pattern A construct and only secondarily with the instruments *currently* being used to measure the behavior pattern. Psychometric properties of measuring instruments are certainly important, but a theoretical understanding of the constructs being measured is more likely to lead to a dynamic rather than static interpretation of experimental results produced by the instruments.

Predictive Validity

Several studies have documented an association between Pattern A and the occurrence of CHD. For example, Caffrey (1968; 1969) studied some 1500 Trappist and Benedictine monks in 26 different monasteries. The highest prevalence rates of CHD occurred among those group of monks having a higher proportion of Pattern A individuals (as measured by a modified stress interview), living in what was characterized as a Type A monastery, and taking a high-fat diet. When any one of these three factors was missing, the groups had low and comparable rates.

Jenkins *et al.* (1971) found that 83 coronary patients, selected from the Western Collaborative Group Study (WCGS) to be described shortly, scored significantly higher on the A–B scale of the JAS than a sample of 524 men without coronary disease. In another study in Connecticut (Kenigsberg, Zyzanski, Jenkins, Wardwell, & Licciardello, 1974), the JAS was administered to 48 hospitalized coronary patients and 42 patients hospitalized for other diseases. The results showed that CHD patients, regardless of age and sex, scored more in the Pattern A direction than those with other diseases.

It would appear, then, that research findings with different population groups show some consensus regarding the relationship between Pattern A and CHD. However, all of the studies cited above are retrospective, that is, the JAS or interview was administered after subjects had clinical CHD. It is entirely possible that the disease itself affected the subject's perceptions and behavior, hence his classification as A or B. In order to determine if Pattern A bears a prognostic relationship to CHD, Friedman and Rosenman initiated the WCGS in 1960–1961 (see Rosenman *et al.*, 1964). Let us examine this study more closely.

The WCGS study.   The WCGS was conducted as a double-blind prospective investigation in which the researchers rating the behavior pattern had no knowledge of other risk factors and did not participate in subsequent diagnosis of the presence or absence of coronary disease. The responsibility for diagnostic judgments was vested in two cardiologists, both of whom worked independently of the study and had no knowledge of the behavior-pattern classifications and of the presence or absence of other risk factors. Of 3524 men, aged 39 to 59 years at intake, 3154 completed participation in the longitudinal study.[3] All were employed in 10 California companies. The following kinds of data were obtained: medical and socioeconomic histories; dietary and smoking habits; blood pressure; serum cholesterol; triglycerides and lipoproteins; blood clotting times; and anthropometric measurements. These data were obtained at intake and annually until the study was terminated, providing 8 to 9 years of follow-up.

Reports of the incidence of clinical CHD after 2½ and 4½ years (Rosenman, Friedman, Straus, Wurm, Jenkins, & Messinger, 1966; Rosenman *et al.*, 1970) revealed that healthy men judged to possess Pattern A at intake had between 1.7 and 6 times the rate of disease of men judged to be Pattern B, the higher ratios occurring among men in the 39- to 49-year-old age group. Furthermore, the association of Pattern A with CHD was maintained even after partialing out the effects of traditional risk factors on which Type As and Type Bs differed (for example, levels of serum cholesterol[4]).

On August 25, 1975, a final follow-up report of the WCGS was published in the *Journal of the American Medical Association* (Rosenman, Brand, Jenkins, Friedman, Straus, & Wurm, 1975; see also Rosenman & Friedman, 1971). Of the 3154 initially healthy subjects in 1960–1961, clinical CHD occurred in 257 subjects during the 8½ year follow-up, an average annual incidence of 9.6/1000 subjects at risk. This incidence was found to be significantly associated with (1) the presence of CHD in the subjects' parents; (2) reported diabetes; (3) current cigarette smoking; (4) reported daily amount smoked at intake; (5) elevated systolic and diastolic blood pressure at intake; (6) elevated serum levels of cholesterol, triglycerides, and the β/α lipoprotein ratios at

---

[3] Excluded from the study were 370 cases for the following reasons: 78 men under or over the specified intake age; 141 cases with CHD at intake; 106 employees of one firm that refused to participate in follow-up; and 45 cases who relocated, or suffered non-CHD death.

[4] There was no difference at intake between As and Bs in the qualitative or quantitative aspects of their food ingestion.

intake. With only one exception (parental CHD), the preceding associations were statistically significant in both age decades of 39–49 and 50–59. There was also a significant relationship between amount of schooling and CHD incidence, with higher rates occurring in those with a high school education or less.

Of greater interest to our current discussion is the result indicating that men judged at intake to be Pattern A had more than twice the rate of new CHD during 8½ years as men originally judged to possess Pattern B behavior. Of approximately 1500 men classified as Pattern A, 178 developed clinical CHD 8½ years later. Only 79 of the some 1500 men diagnosed as Pattern B developed CHD during the period of the prospective study. The results also showed that Pattern A subjects with CHD were 5 times more likely to have a second myocardial infarct than were Pattern B subjects with CHD.

Analysis indicated that a higher CHD incidence in Type As still prevailed when subjects were stratified by each of the risk variables listed earlier, that is, cholesterol, smoking, blood pressure, etc. Moreover, when simulataneous adjustment was made for combinations of traditional risk variables, the CHD-behavior pattern relationship still obtained. The relative risk ratio for As and Bs was 1.87 in the younger age group and 1.98 in the older group. Thus, the predictive relationship of Pattern A to CHD incidence cannot be "explained away" by other risk factors; Pattern A exerts an independent pathogenic influence (see, also, Brand, Rosenman, Sholtz and Friedman, 1976).

The WCGS results were based on a classification of cases in terms of the stress interview. It is of some interest, therefore, to examine a study by Jenkins et al. (1974), who administered the adult JAS to 2750 of the subjects in the WCGS. All cases were free of CHD at the time of testing in 1965. The follow-up period lasted 4 years through the end of 1969. The major results showed that higher scorers on the JAS (the top third) had 1.7 times the incidence of new CHD of low scorers (the bottom third of the JAS distribution). Moreover, there was a continuous and significant relationship between JAS scores and the incidence of CHD, with high, middle, and low Pattern A scores being associated with high, middle, and low CHD incidence rates. As noted previously, the factor-analytically derived scales (H, S, and J) failed to predict coronary disease. A more recent study using the A–B scale score of the JAS found that it was the strongest single predictor of recurrent CHD among a set of available variables, including serum cholesterol and number of cigarettes smoked daily (Jenkins, Zyzanski, and Rosenman, 1976).

Concurrent Validity

The research on Pattern A described thus far has been concerned with how well the behavior pattern predicts (or at least is associated with) clinical manifestations of coronary disease. Other studies indicate that Pattern A is related to some of the traditional risk factors for CHD, as well as to the atherosclerotic process which culminates in myocardial infarction or angina pectoris. Such data provide, in effect, concurrent and construct validation of the behavior pattern.[5]

Pattern A and degree of atherosclerosis.   The increasing clinical use of coronary angiography (cf. Friedberg, 1966) has resulted in at least two independent studies of the association between Pattern A and the extent of atheromatic deposition in the coronary arteries of living patients. Blumenthal, Williams, Kong, Thompson, Jenkins, and Rosenman (1975) conducted a double-blind study of 156 patients referred for diagnostic angiography at Duke University Medical Center. Each patient was classified as Pattern A or Pattern B on the basis of the interview technique. Fifty-nine (82%) of the 72 patients with at least a 75% narrowing of one coronary artery turned out to have been classified as Pattern A, whereas 44 (63%) of the 70 patients without significant disease were classified as Pattern B. Moreover, the average degree of atherosclerosis was significantly greater in As than Bs, even when age and sex were covaried in the analysis. These findings were replicated in a study at Boston University School of Medicine that used the JAS to classify 94 patients as A or B (Zyzanski, Jenkins, Ryan, Flessas, and Everist, 1976). Fifty-five men with more than 50% arterial obstruction in two or more vessels scored significantly higher on the A–B scale than the 36 men whose arteries were less diseased.

The preceding studies point to the possibility that Pattern A increases the risk of CHD at least in part through an association with the atherosclerotic process. Further evidence on this issue comes from research on the relation of the behavior pattern to some of the traditional factors increasing the risk of clinical CHD. A detailed discussion of these studies is probably not needed here, but we mention some of the major findings in the next section.

Pattern A and risk factors for CHD.   Friedman and Rosenman (1959) and Rosenman and Friedman (1961) showed that the average serum cholesterol levels of both men and women with fully developed Pattern A behavior (225 mg per 100 ml and 272 mg per 100 ml, respectively) were significantly higher than those of their fully developed Pattern B counterparts (218 mg per 100 ml and 214 mg per 100 ml). While E. H. Friedman, Hellerstein, Eastwood, and Jones (1968) were unable to replicate these findings, a more recent study by Blumenthal *et al.* (1975) found reliable total serum cholesterol differences between men classified simply as A and B on the basis of the interview. Rosenman *et al.* (1966) report a similar difference for the 39- to 49-year-old

---

[5] Another form of concurrent validity consists of the pattern of relationships existing between Pattern A and various standardized personality inventories and related psychological tests. Appendix B presents such data for the adult JAS and the stress interview method of assessing the behavior pattern. A similar discussion for the student JAS is contained in Appendix C.

age group at intake in the WCGS, and Jenkins, Zyzanski, and Rosenman (1973) present indirect evidence linking Pattern A, as measured by the JAS, with increased levels of serum cholesterol.

Additional results relating Pattern A characteristics to serum lipid levels can be found in Rosenman *et al.* (1966), Friedman, Rosenman, and Byers (1968), Jenkins, Hames, Zyzanski, Rosenman, and Friedman (1969), and Sloane, Davidson, Holland, and Payne (1962). It is not surprising, therefore, that fully developed Pattern A subjects also show a fasting level of serum triglycerides greater than that of subjects with the fully developed form of Pattern B (e.g., Friedman, Rosenman, & Byers, 1964). Elevated triglycerides in healthy Pattern A subjects indicate that long before they experience CHD, Type As already exhibit serum lipid abnormalities which are frequently found in patients with the disease.

There are no published studies, to our knowledge, directly associating hypertension (another risk factor) with Pattern A. Indeed, there is evidence from at least one study (Shekelle, Schoenberger, and Stamler, 1976) which indictes that prevalence of hypertension is unrelated to Pattern A in men. On the other hand, the WCGS suggest that Type A men at intake had higher diastolic blood pressure than Type B men (Rosenman *et al.*, 1966). Of greater significance, perhaps, is the finding in the 2½-year follow-up that elevated diastolic blood pressure (that is, exceeding 94 mm Hg) significantly enhanced the risk of CHD only when this factor occurred in Pattern A subjects (Rosenman *et al.*, 1966). There are, of course, a host of experiments showing that psychological stimuli indicative of Pattern A (say, hostility) produce episodic rises in blood pressure (Hokanson, Burgess, & Cohen, 1963; McGinn, Harburg, Julius, & McLeod, 1964), but it is not at all certain that such elevations are closely related to coronary disease (cf. Graham, 1972; Gutmann & Benson, 1971). At best, these data indicate that Type As may react to induced frustration with greater blood-pressure elevations than Type Bs.

There appear to be about as many cigarette smokers in a group of Pattern B subjects as in a group of Pattern A subjects (Rosenman *et al.*, 1966). On the other hand, of those who smoke, fully developed As consume more cigarettes per day than comparable Pattern B individuals (Friedman & Rosenman, 1959; Rosenman & Friedman, 1961). An intensive study of the smoking habits of the WCGS sample (Jenkins, Rosenman, & Zyzanski, 1968) revealed that men who were judged to exhibit Pattern A behavior were significantly more likely to smoke 26 or more cigarettes per day and were less likely to be in the "never smoked" category. Considering the simultaneous influence of smoking and Pattern A on CHD incidence rates in the 4½ year follow-up of the WCGS, Jenkins *et al.* (1968) report that coronary rates in the smoking categories of 16–25 cigarettes per day and 26 or more per day ranged from 2.7 to 5.1 times greater in Pattern A subjects than in their Pattern B counterparts.

Pattern A, catecholamines, and platelet adhesiveness.   In Chapter 1, emphasis was given to the possible importance of the adhesiveness of blood platelets in the genesis of coronary disease. Friedman *et al.* (1958) showed a significant degree of hastening of blood coagulation in their accountant subjects on the April 15 tax deadline. Such data suggest the possibility of rapid platelet aggregation under stress. It is not surprising, therefore, to find that the average clotting time of As is significantly faster than that of Bs (e.g., Friedman & Rosenman, 1959).

The discharge of catecholamines is believed to potentiate platelet aggregation (e.g., Mustard & Packham, 1969). It was already suggested that individuals engaged in an active struggle to master uncontrollable stimuli show increased specific discharge of norepinephrine, whereas passive responding to such stimuli coincides with a decrement in norepinephrine. Given the characteristics of Pattern A, we might expect such subjects to excrete more norepinephrine than Pattern B subjects—at least in response to stressful stimulation. This was found to be the case in an experiment cited earlier; Type As exhibited enhanced plasma norepinephrine levels in response to competitive situations, whereas Type Bs did not show this type of responsiveness (Friedman *et al.*, 1975). Simpson, Olewine, Jenkins, Ramsey, Zyzanski, Thomas, and Hames (1974) have confirmed this result by showing that physically fit Pattern A men have the largest increase in plasma norepinephrine immediately after a stressful treadmill test; the less fit among the Bs exhibited the lowest increase in norepinephrine. Other data indicate that extreme Type As excrete more norepinephrine in their urine during active working hours than do Type Bs (Friedman, St. George, Byers, and Rosenman, 1960).

SUMMARY

The major descriptive components of Pattern A are competitive striving for achievement, an exaggerated sense of time urgency, and aggressiveness and hostility. Several techniques for measuring behavior pattern A have been developed and standardized, including the stress interview, the adult JAS, and the student JAS. There seems to be a fair amount of consensus among studies now available that lend support to the hypothesis that Pattern A is significantly related to the risk of clinical CHD. There is, in addition, evidence linking Pattern A to the pathogenesis and extent of atherosclerosis. Most of the research indicates that associations between the behavior pattern and cardiovascular pathology are neither spurious nor secondary to other risk factors and related peculiarities of any single population.

Since Pattern A can be defined and measured reliably, and since there is a body of data in support of its validity, what was the rationale for initiating the program of studies reported in this book? Two answers may be given to this question. First, research on Pattern A has been largely concerned with measurement reliability and criterion-related validities, that is, efforts to infer from a behavior-pattern score an individual's most probable standing on some cardiovascular variable. But science is not simply a matter of prediction; its goal is the understanding of phenomena which can rarely be gained from a single validity coefficient, or even from a set of such coefficients. To what extent is Pattern A a reflection of a more fundamental psychological dimension? How does it relate to other psychological variables and to classes of stimulus conditions in the physical and social environment? Systematic demonstration of behavioral differences between As and Bs is clearly needed as a first step toward answering these questions. This was the rationale for the specific studies reported in the next three chapters.

A more general rationale for our research was the conceptualization of a psychological dimension underlying behavior pattern A—one that would, at once, encompass the descriptive components of the pattern, and elucidate its motivational dynamics. Such a dimension was suggested by earlier work on uncontrollable stress (cf. Glass & Singer, 1972), as well as by the experiments reported in Chapters 4–6. Accordingly, we generated the model outlined in the first chapter. It treats Pattern A as a style of response to uncontrollable stressors in the physical and social environment. The model is based on an interactionist view, in which uncontrollable stimuli elicit Pattern A behavior in susceptible individuals. The bulk of this book reports experimentation designed to test some of the implications of this line of thought. The goal of the research is to explicate the interplay of the behavior pattern and uncontrollable stressful events, for both factors appear to be implicated in the development of coronary disease. An understanding of the nature of the relationship between the two variables should help to clarify the processes by which behavior becomes involved in cardiovascular pathology.

4
Pattern A and Achievement Striving

There are virtually no systematic data demonstrating that individuals classified as Pattern A do, in fact, exhibit excessive achievement striving, time urgency, and hostility. Since these aspects of the behavior pattern are its defining characteristics, their empirical documentation was taken as the first order of business in developing the program of research described in this book. Systematic demonstration of Pattern A characteristics was also important because most of the studies reported in subsequent chapters used college-student populations classified as A or B on the basis of the student JAS. Basic to the validity of the behavior pattern in college students is experimental evidence relating the student JAS to Pattern A versus Pattern B behavior.[1] This chapter and Chapters 5 and 6 present such evidence.

THE DEADLINE EXPERIMENT

The Type A individual is described as having an intense drive to succeed in achievement-related activities. We should thus expect Type A subjects to work at near maximum capacity even in the absence of a specific deadline for task completion. By contrast, Pattern B subjects might be expected to work as hard as their Pattern A counterparts only when confronted by a concrete deadline. The hypothesis received explicit test in the following experiment (see Burnam, Pennebaker, & Glass, 1973, Experiment II).

---

[1] Correlations of the student JAS with various objective psychological tests can be found in Appendix C. These data constitute additional information relevant to the validity of the test.

Subjects and Procedure

A total of 62 male and female subjects participated in the study. Subjects were randomly assigned to the two experimental treatments, regardless of their location on the A–B dimension. Subjects were designated as Pattern A if they scored above the median for the sample of 62 cases and as Pattern B if they scored below the median (see Appendix A). There were 33 As and 29 Bs.

Subjects were tested individually. In most of our studies, including this one, the experimenter was unaware of the subject's A–B classification. After introductory comments, instructions were given for a time-estimation task. Description of this task and the resulting data are deferred until Chapter 5, where we discuss the time-urgency component of Pattern A. Immediately after time estimation, subjects listened to instructions for the next task, which consisted of 240 simple arithmetic problems (for instance, 6 + 9 − 2). Subjects were told to begin with the first problem and solve each problem before going on to the next. They were cautioned against making written computations. Only the final answer was to be given on the test sheets.

The basic experimental design involved telling half of the subjects, "I will be timing you on these problems, but there is no time limit" (No Deadline condition), whereas the other half of the subjects were informed, "You have exactly 5 minutes to do as many of these problems as you can" (Deadline condition). All subjects were in fact allowed 5 min in which to solve the problems.

Results

There were no differences between experimental conditions and subject groups in percentage of errors on the arithmetic task ($ps > .20$). However, the picture is very different when we examine the number of problems attempted during the testing session.

Analysis of variance of these data revealed a significant main effect for the Deadline versus No Deadline treatment, $F(1, 58) = 4.57$, $p < .05$, and a reliable interaction between this variable and the A–B classification, $F(1, 58) = 3.84$, $p < .05$. Subsequent contrasts using the error-mean-square from the variance analysis showed that As attempted more problems than Bs in the No Deadline condition ($Ms = 86.0$ and 71.6, $p < .06$), whereas the difference between As and Bs in the Deadline condition was not statistically significant ($Ms = 87.0$ and 94.5, $p > .20$). Comparisons between the two experimental treatments indicated that As performed at a similar level under Deadline and No Deadline conditions ($p > .20$), but Bs attempted more problems under Deadline than No Deadline ($p < .01$).

Discussion

While the significance levels in this study were sometimes less than over-whelming (perhaps because of misclassification of subjects inherent in a crude median split on the A–B scale), nevertheless the data are generally in accord with initial expectations. The results suggest that the achievement drive of Pattern A individuals produces high levels of effort, even when task demands are not made explicit. Pattern B subjects, in contrast, appear to respond to the perceived requirements of the situation. These conclusions are based on the fact that As performed at the same level under Deadline and No Deadline conditions, whereas Bs attempted more arithmetic problems only when given instructions about a 5-min deadline.

A specific feature of the results worth noting here is the comparatively large number of problems completed by Bs in the Deadline condition. We might have expected As to exceed Bs in this treatment as well. The null effect underscores the importance of describing the A–B dimension in terms of an interaction between predispositions and eliciting situations. Type Bs will, under some circumstances, behave like As insofar as the Bs accelerate the pace of their activities in order to master a prescribed task. The notion of Bs behaving like As in certain situations may have profound implications for understanding life in contemporary Western societies: It is precisely these cultures that may encourage the prevalence of Pattern A by rewarding those who can think, perform, and communicate more rapidly than their peers.

THE IMMEDIATE RECALL EXPERIMENT

Further support for the notion that As are more hard driving and achievement oriented than Bs comes from an experiment conducted by David S. Krantz (1975) as part of his doctoral dissertation. A practice slide and three experimen-tal slides were flashed on a screen for a brief period of time. The slides contained either lists of words (like *rat, pin*) or pictures of objects (like a house, a boat). They were taken from research recently reported in Schachter and Rodin (1974). Subjects were instructed to repeat out loud as many of the items as they could recall after each slide went off the screen. The major dependent measure was mean number of items recalled correctly per slide. For reasons that need not concern us here (see Krantz, 1975), two durations of slide presentation were used, namely, 5 sec (5-sec condition) or 8 sec (8-sec condition). Sixty Type A and 65 Type B male undergraduates participated in the study. It might be expected that the success drive of Type As would lead them to recall more items correctly than their Type B counterparts.

Procedure

The subject was seated in a darkened room 10 ft (about 3.1 m) from a white screen. He was told that the purpose of the study was to "measure reactions to various sensory stimuli" and that the task involved recall of visually presented objects. "When each of several slides come on, try to remember as many things [on the slide] as you can. As soon as each slide goes off, recite aloud as many items as you can remember." The four slides were presented in the same order to all subjects. The practice slide was always given first, followed by the three experimental slides.

Results and Discussion

Table 4.1 presents the group means for number of items recalled correctly per experimental slide. Analysis of these data revealed a main effect for slide duration, such that subjects viewing the slide for 8 sec remembered more items per slide than those viewing it for 5 sec ($p < .001$). Of greater interest was a significant A–B main effect ($p < .02$), such that As recalled more items than Bs.

TABLE 4.1
Mean Number of Slide Items Correctly Recalled

Subject	8-sec condition		5-sec condition	
classification	Mean	N	Mean	N
Pattern A	5.22	34	5.32	26
Pattern B	5.12	31	4.29	35

Analysis of variance was also computed on total number of errors made on the three experimental slides. There were no significant effects or intereactions in these data ($ps > .20$).

The superior performance of Type As can be interpreted in terms of their greater achievement motivation. Put very simply, Type As showed better recall because of their enhanced tendency to perform at near maximum capacity, which in this experiment was defined by the instruction to attend to the slides and correctly recall as many items as possible.

THE INTERVIEW STUDY

The presence of excessive drive in As should be evident not only in structured laboratory situations of the kind reported above. Achievement striving should also appear in the everyday activities of Type As as well. Indeed, the interview assessment of Pattern A relies, in part, on questions concerning the individual's past and present achievements and accomplishments. Involvement in multiple activities, numerous community and social commitments, and participation in competitive athletics are often characteristic signs of the working adult with behavior pattern A. It seemed reasonable, therefore, to determine whether college-student subjects classified by the student JAS also had more of these signs than their Pattern B peers. A recent study by James W. Pennebaker and the writer was undertaken for this purpose.

University of Texas undergraduates scoring in the upper and lower fifths of a distribution of JAS scores were selected as the potential sample. From this group of approximately 100 cases, 46 white males aged 18 to 20 agreed to participate in a study on "the relationship of psychological test data to health behavior." Subjects received $5.00 for their participation, and they understood that the study involved not only an interview but also a physical examination, including a blood sample. The physical data are reported in Appendix D. They were collected in an effort to relate Pattern A behavior in college students to such traditional risk factors as serum cholesterol, blood pressure, and smoking.

The interview was given immediately after the medical examination. It consisted of questions pertaining to the subject's past and present involvement in athletic, social, and related extracurricular activities, as well as his past and current scholastic and athletic achievements. There were 14 such questions. Information was also obtained on the educational and occupational levels of the subject's parents. There were no differences between As and Bs on these indices of social class (Hollingshead, 1957).

Table 4.2 presents the subjects' responses to 12 of the interview questions. Five items show significant or near-significant differences between Pattern A and Pattern B subjects. On the average, As report having participated in more sports during high school than do Bs ($p < .05$). Although not specifically tabulated in Table 4.2, 18 of the 22 As and only 10 of the 24 Bs were on a high school athletic team. Type As tended to win more athletic awards in high school than Type Bs.

The results also indicate that, on the average, As participated in more college extracurricular activities (other than sports) than did Bs ($p < .01$). These activities included community and church work as well as campus politics. The difference between As and Bs in average number of high school academic honors does not attain statistical significance ($p > .20$), but Type As reported having earned reliably more honors in college than did Type Bs ($p < .05$).[2] Table 4.2 shows an interesting reversal for involvement in high

[2] It should be noted here that Pattern A is unrelated to performance on standardized tests of ability and intelligence (see, for example, Appendix C, Tables C.1 and C.2). Type A college students may be more hard driving and thus gain greater academic recognition than their Type B counterparts, but they are not necessarily more able and intelligent as measured by objective tests.

TABLE 4.2
Mean Responses to Achievement-Related Interview
Questions

Item	Pattern A ($N = 22$)	Pattern B ($N = 24$)
Number of sports (high school)	2.2**	1.4
Number of athletic awards (high school)	1.5*	0.9
Number of sports (college)	1.4	1.3
Number of athletic awards (college)	0.1	0.0
Extracurricular activities in high school (other than sports)	2.5	2.2
Positions of leadership in high school extracurricular activities	1.2	0.9
Extracurricular activities in college (other than sports)	0.9***	0.3
Positions of leadership in college extracurricular activities	0.2	0.0
Academic honors (high school)	1.6	1.2
Academic honors (college)	0.7**	0.3
High school social activities	1.4	2.3***
College social activities	2.1	2.0

*$p < .10$.   **$p < .05$.   ***$p < .01$.

school social activities, where a score of 1 means "very active" and 4 means "not active at all." Type Bs report somewhat greater social life in high school than do As.

A final note on the interview. When asked about their "plans after college," approximately 60% of the As said they would "go on to graduate or professional school," whereas 70% of the Bs said they intended to "go to work, get a job."

The interview results are not surprising, for they indicate that in contrast to Bs, As exhibit more drive, ambition, and involvement in multiple activities in their everyday life. Even where mean differences did not reach statistical significance (as with number of athletic awards in high school), As had a higher mean score than Bs. Pattern A students, like their older counterparts, are simply more active and involved in a variety of enterprises than Pattern B students. The fact that As reported fewer high school social activities is actually consistent with other data. One would not expect Type A students to drive satisfaction from purely social encounters when they could be spending their time in community, campus, and athletic activities that might bring them recognition and power. The Type A is a hard-driving man of action who has his sights set on achievement and success, not on pleasures to be derived from interpersonal pursuits.

The preceding findings call to mind descriptions of the Pattern A individual as confidently believing that with sufficient effort he can master any task, overcome any obstacle (e.g., Friedman, 1969). This thought led to the speculation that As might suppress or deny feelings of fatigue to a greater extent than their Pattern B counterparts in order to persist at a task and thus achieve success in its mastery. The next experiment was designed to test this idea (see Carver, Coleman, & Glass, 1976).

THE FATIGUE SUPPRESSION EXPERIMENT

A task was chosen for this experiment that was likely to produce veridical feelings of fatigue; that is, subjects were required to walk continuously on a motorized treadmill at increasingly sharp angles of incline. This procedure provided a test of the hypothesis that Pattern A individuals will suppress feelings of fatigue to a greater extent than Pattern B individuals. It was also expected that As would exert greater efforts in walking on the treadmill, thereby causing them to work closer to the limits of their endurance as measured by a physiological index of aerobic capacity.

Subjects

A total of 21 Texas undergraduates participated in the study, 10 of whom were designated Pattern A and 11 Pattern B. Subjects were selected as Pattern A if their scores were in the upper 20% of a pretest distribution of approximately 800 cases, and as Pattern B if their scores were in the lower 20% of the distribution. Members of university athletic teams and individuals whose body weight was more than 20% above the average for their height and age were excluded from the study.

Procedure

Two experimenters were present at each testing session. The primary experimenter informed the subject that the session would consist of two parts and then explained the treadmill procedures of Balke (1954) and Costill and Fox (1969). These procedures are described in the following subsections. Each subject was told that the primary experimenter would terminate the Balke procedure after a predetermined length of time. The subject was also told that he could terminate the test prior to the predetermined time by giving an appropriate signal to the experimenter. In reality, there was *no* predetermined length of time. Instead, all subjects ended the session by indicating their desire to stop. As the experimenter gave these instructions, he attached EKG leads to the subject's chest.

After determining the subject's height and weight, three skinfold thickness measures were made at each of three sites (chest, abdomen, and thigh). Body fat was estimated from skinfold data using the equations of Jackson and Pollack (1975).

The subject was then given instructions and practice in walking on a motor-driven treadmill. Each subject warmed up on the treadmill for 5 min by walking at 3.3 miles per hour (90 m per minute) on a level grade. At this point, the subject was allowed a 5-min rest while a second experimenter explained that he (the subject) would be required to rate himself for freshness or fatigue periodically during the Balke procedure. Fatigue ratings were made from a scale printed on a board located in direct view of the subject. The scale had 11 linear points, with the end points labeled "As fresh as I have ever been" (11) and "As tired as I have ever been" (1). Additional verbal labels at four other points were "Quite fresh" (9), "Somewhat fresh" (7), "Somewhat tired" (5), and "Quite tired" (3). The subject was to rate himself by choosing one of the 11 numbers from the scale and signaling the number with his fingers. Verbalization was impossible because the subject was to be wearing a mouthpiece for collection of expired air. It was emphasized that the subject's response should indicate how he felt at the exact time he was asked for his rating. Following these instructions, the subject rated his degree of freshness (premeasure). Next, the subject was told to do his best—but not to overdo it—and the treadmill procedure began.

Throughout the procedure, the second experimenter recorded the subject's ratings of fatigue after every 2 min of elapsed time until termination of the session.

Balke test.   The treadmill test used to assess performance and fatigue has been employed extensively in research on exercise physiology (e.g., Balke, 1954; Balke, Grillo, Konecci, & Luft, 1954). Treadmill speed was set at 90 m per minute (that is, 3.3 miles per hour, equivalent to a brisk walk) and the subject walked at 0% grade for 1 minute. The grade was then raised to 1% and increased 1% per minute thereafter until the subject terminated the session. During the test, the subject was given no feedback concerning the amount of time he had walked or his current rate. No attempt was made to encourage or discourage his efforts during treadmill activity.

The subject's heart rate was monitored periodically, using a CMS lead system and a Physiograph.[3] Expired air was collected continuously through a

---

[3] Heart rate was recorded in order to monitor the subject's progress on the treadmill test. Systematic readings were taken only at the termination of the Balke procedure. No significant difference between groups in mean heart rate was observed, $t < 1$.

two-way Daniels valve inserted in the subject's mouth. All metabolic measures were determined by standard techniques of open spirometry. Expired air was analyzed by means of a Beckman E2 Oxygen Analyzer and a Beckman Medical Gas Analyzer. Gas volume was assessed by a Parkinson–Cowan CD-4 gas meter. All volumes were corrected to standard temperature and pressure dry.

Max VO$_2$ test.   A second procedure was included in the study for the purpose of assessing as precisely as possible each subject's physical capabilities (Costill & Fox, 1969). Exercise physiologists have long associated the limits of a person's endurance with his maximum rate of oxygen consumption, also referred to as "aerobic capacity," or "Max VO$_2$" (cf. Hill & Lupton, 1923; Karlsson, Astrand, & Ekblom, 1967).

Upon completion of the Balke test, the subject rested for 15 min and was then administered a Max VO$_2$ test. Administration of the Max test after a short rest is reported to produce Max values comparable to those obtained by techniques utilizing longer rest periods (Saltin, 1964). The subject ran for 3 min at 201 m per minute (or 7.5 miles per hour, the pace of an 8-min mile) at a 0% grade. The treadmill elevation was then increased by 2.5%, and further increased by 2.5% for each successive 3 min run, until the subject could no longer continue. The end point of the Max test was subjectively determined by the subject himself, although this time all subjects were encouraged to achieve their highest level on the test. If a subject completed 3 min at any given incline during the test, he was required to attempt the next higher incline. It was assumed that maximum oxygen consumption was reached when O$_2$ uptake values for successive inclines ceased to increase linearly and differed by ±5% or less (cf. Larson, 1974). The highest level of oxygen consumption achieved during the test was chosen as the subject's Max value. Fatigue ratings were not made during this procedure.

Analysis of expired air.   Samples of expired air from the last minute of the Max VO$_2$ test were analyzed to determine each subject's maximal level of oxygen uptake (milliliters of O$_2$ per kilograms of body weight per minute). Samples of expired air from the final minute of the subject's Balke test were also analyzed to determine the level of oxygen uptake at the point at which he terminated the procedure. Each subject's aerobic performance on the Balke was then compared to his own aerobic limit, that is, his Max VO$_2$ performance. The resulting value expresses the subject's efforts on the Balke test as a proportion of his maximum aerobic capacity.

There were two reasons why this index was chosen as our measure of effort. First, as stated earlier, a person's aerobic capacity—his maximal rate of oxygen absorption—is accepted by exercise physiologists as representing the limit of his endurance (Karlsson et al., 1967). Indeed, it has been suggested that "factors such as . . . oxygen consumption may more accurately reflect physiological strain and, therefore, perceived exertion'' than other factors such as heart rate (Noble, Metz, Pandolf, Bell, Cafarelli, & Simes, 1973, p. 119). It thus seems reasonable that a person working near the limit of his aerobic capacity is exerting greater effort than is one who is working at a level further removed from that limit. Sensitivity of measurement was a second reason for using the percentage measure; that is, each subject's performance on the Balke was compared with his own ability to perform.

Results

Physical characteristics of the subjects. Pattern A and Pattern B subjects who participated in the study did not differ significantly in weight ($p > .6$), height ($p > .2$), age ($p > .2$), or percentage of body fat ($p > .6$); nor did the groups differ reliably in aerobic capacities ($p > .3$). Group means on all of these measures are presented in Table 4.3. Of the 20 cases in the study, only two As and two Bs used tobacco. Each one smoked about 20 cigarettes per day.

Balke performance. Each subject's efforts on the Balke test were determined by the percentage-of-aerobic-capacity method outlined earlier. Analysis of these percentage values revealed a significant difference between As and Bs, $F(1, 18) = 8.74$, $p < .01$. On the Balke test, As reached an oxygen absorption rate equal to 91.4% of their capacities, whereas Bs reached a rate equal to only 82.8% of their capacities. The groups did not differ in the total amount of time they walked on the treadmill ($p = .68$).

TABLE 4.3
Average Physical Characteristics of the Subjects

Characteristic	Pattern A ($N = 10$)	Pattern B ($N = 10$)
Weight (pounds)	159.2 (71.6 kg)	155.0 (69.8 kg)
Height (inches)	72.5 (184.2 cm)	71.4 (181.4 cm)
Age (years)	19.7	20.7
Body fat (%)	4.29	4.46
Maximum rate of O_2 consumption (ml O_2/kg/min)	48.25	51.74

Fatigue ratings.   Pattern A and Pattern B subjects did not differ significantly in their initial self-ratings of fatigue (Ms = 9.9 and 9.7, p > .6). The most obvious analysis of the subsequent fatigue ratings would seem to be a groups-by-trials analysis. However, the amount of time spent on the Balke procedure varied considerably between subjects; elapsed times ranged from 17 min, 13 sec to 16 min, 3 sec. The resulting differences in number of actual ratings made a trials analysis impractical. However, two other analyses were performed on the fatigue ratings. The first involved computing a mean rating for each subject, which provided a rough index of self-rated fatigue over the entire walking session. Analysis of these mean ratings showed that As expressed less overall fatigue than did Bs, $F(1, 18)$ = 4.90, p < .04. The respective means were 6.19 and 5.21.

The argument that As would suppress or deny fatigue to a greater extent than Bs is obviously applicable only after fatigue has been produced. Therefore, as a more sensitive test of the hypothesis, we examined the last four ratings of fatigue made by each subject prior to termination of his Balke session. Table 4.4 presents the relevant data.

TABLE 4.4
Final Four Fatigue Ratings[a]

Subject classification	Fourth-to-last rating	Third-to-last rating	Second-to-last rating	Last rating
Pattern A	5.30	4.10	3.10	2.20
	(SD = 1.72)	(SD = 0.94)	(SD = 0.70)	(SD = 0.60)
Pattern B	3.40	2.80	2.20	1.50
	(SD = 0.92)	(SD = 0.60)	(SD = 0.60)	(SD = 0.67)

[a] A small number indicates greater fatigue on an 11-point scale; for example, 1 represents "As tired as I have ever been."

A separate analysis of variance was conducted for each of the four sets of ratings. These results revealed that in each case As rated their fatigue as significantly lower than Bs. The difference was strongest on the third-to-last rating, $F(1, 18)$ = 12.17, p < .003, but was also statistically reliable on the final rating, $F(1, 18)$ = 5.44, p < .03. A repeated-measures analysis confirmed that the overall mean of the last four ratings was significantly greater for Bs than As, $F(1, 18)$ = 12.27, p < .003.

Discussion

Both of our hypotheses received support in the results. Pattern A subjects worked at a level closer to the limits of their endurance than did Pattern B subjects. Moreover, even as they did so, As suppressed feelings of fatigue to a greater extent than did their Type B counterparts. This was true whether the fatigue ratings were taken as an average over the entire session or examined only toward the end of the session. It should be pointed out that at least one factor militated against the hypothesized result being produced in the end-of-session analyses. Compared with Bs, Pattern A subjects were reaching a performance level closer to their upper limits by the end of the session. Thus, As should have been experiencing more rather than less fatigue relative to Type B subjects. It is therefore noteworthy that As continued to deny fatigue even on the final rating.

It is somewhat surprising that the two groups did not differ in the amount of time spent on the Balke treadmill test. It is possible, however, to isolate at least two factors which may have contributed to the absence of a time difference. One stems from the fact that subjects received only minimal training for walking on the treadmill (which is not as easy a task as it appears to be). Thus there was probably a great deal of variability in walking efficiency. Inefficient walking increases a subject's workload and thus decreases the time required to approach maximal capacity. Since As closely approximated their aerobic limits but took comparatively less time to do so than Bs, it could be argued that the sample of As that happened to be recruited tended to be less efficient walkers than the Bs. There is some evidence to support this statement. Comparisons of As and Bs who walked the same amount of time revealed a trend toward higher rates of oxygen consumption among the As. This tendency suggests that the As were somewhat less efficient walkers than the Bs.

A second possible reason for the absence of a time difference is the fact that Bs who participated in this study tended to have greater aerobic capacities, that is, higher scores on the Max VO_2 test, than did Type As [although the difference was not statistically significant ($p > .3$)]. Since the Bs' aerobic limits were somewhat higher than those of the As, the Bs should have taken longer to approximate their own maximal capacities, thereby increasing their elapsed times on the treadmill and minimizing any time difference between groups.

If one accepts this line of thought, an alternative interpretation of the percentage-of-capacity results is immediately suggested. It could be argued that As more closely approximated their capacities only because their capacities were lower. However, there appears to be little basis for this argument either in logic or in fact. There is no reason to believe, a priori, that a high aerobic capacity should lead to reduced efforts relative to capacity. The subjects were tested individually and no standard of persistence was provided against which they might judge their own behavior. Moreover, this interpretation would require that there be an inverse relationship between the Balke percentage-of-capacity performance and total aerobic capacity. The correlation between those two variables was in fact quite low ($r = -.14, p > .55$).

The subjective fatigue results clearly showed that Pattern A subjects suppressed feelings of fatigue to a greater extent than did Pattern B subjects, even though they exerted greater efforts than the Bs. Indeed, Type As reported reliably less fatigue even on the final rating, which, it will be recalled, occurred immediately prior to termination of the treadmill session. It would appear that despite their stated unwillingness to continue walking, As continued to have difficulty in explicitly admitting their fatigue. This exaggerated tendency toward fatigue suppression—or at least public denial of fatigue—may be understood in terms of the hard-driving character of Type As. Thus, denial of fatigue has instrumental value for As because it aids in their struggle for attainment of achievement-related goals. The acknowledgement of fatigue, on the other hand, might interfere with successful task mastery—a situation which As could not tolerate easily.

THE RESPONSE THRESHOLD EXPERIMENT

Closely related to the tendency of As to deny fatigue in the interests of task mastery are their efforts to conceal other signs of inability to cope with environmental stimulation (Friedman, 1969). Compared to Type Bs, Type As are alleged to express overt bravado, or, at minimum, a reluctance to reveal themselves as being bothered by stressful stimuli. Given this clinical description, we might expect As to show a higher threshold for responding to aversive events than their Type B counterparts, providing the As believed that their responsiveness could be interpreted as an indication of weakness. Some support for this notion can be gleaned from a study by M. Audrey Burnam, Karen Matthews, and the writer. Subjects were exposed to a high-frequency (3100 Hz) tone which was systematically increased over the course of an experimental session. The intensity level at which the subject tried to terminate the tone was the major dependent variable.

Subjects

Twenty-two Type A and 20 Type B female undergraduates participated in the study. Behavior pattern classification was determined by whether subjects scored above or below the median of a pretested sample of approximately 800 cases.

Procedure

Subjects were greeted by a male experimenter who said that the regular experimenter was about 15 min late; hence, he would begin the first part of the experiment. The subject then was told that she was participating in a study of the relationship between mood and reaction time to various visual and auditory stimuli. It was explained that since red goggles would be worn during the reaction time test, the first step consisted of a 10-min period of visual adaptation. The red goggles were placed on the subject, and she was asked to examine five art prints to assist in the adaptation process. At this point, a 55-dB(A) tone was delivered via a wall speaker. The experimenter shook his head, pushed several buttons on a small metal box located across the room, and the tone eventually stopped. The experimenter explained:

> This noise generator has been switching on by itself every once in a while. It's not working right. If it does that while you're in here and it gets annoying, you might be able to turn it off by pushing a couple of those buttons. Otherwise, just ignore it.

The experimenter then left. Two minutes later, as the subject sat looking at the prints, the tone came on suddenly at an intensity of 46 dB(A), for a period of 30 sec. The tone increased about 4 dB(A) every 30 sec until it reached 81 dB(A), or until the subject pushed a button. If the tone continued at 81 dB(A) for 30 sec without action by the subject, the tone was discontinued.

Results

Subjects could terminate the tone at any one of ten decibel levels, ranging from 46 to 81 dB(A). Index numbers were assigned to each of these levels, where 1 represented 46 dB(A) and 10 represented 81 dB(A). The mean of the index numbers was 4.8 for As and 2.7 for Bs, $F(1, 40) = 8.12, p < .01$.

Discussion

The results of this study indicate that compared to Bs, Type As wait longer before trying to terminate unwanted sound. Since Type As and Type Bs did not differ in postexperimental ratings of the intensity of the 46-dB(A) and 81-dB(A) tones ($ps > .20$), we are inclined to dismiss the possibility that the noise was experienced as differentially intense by two types of subjects. The elevated threshold of response among As might then be interpreted as reflecting their reluctance to admit that the noise was bothersome. This finding supplements the fatigue-suppression effect observed in the previous experiment. Not only do As deny subjective states that might directly degrade task performance, but given the option, they will also behave in ways that suggest they can withstand unwanted stimulation.

CONCLUSIONS

The range of results reported in this chapter indicate that Pattern A individuals are indeed more hard driving and achievement oriented than their Pattern B counterparts. These conclusions were reached on the basis of both systematic experimental manipulations and self-reports of everyday activities. They thus provide some behavioral validation for the achievement-striving component of Pattern A. It would appear that As believe that with sufficient effort they can overcome a variety of obstacles or frustrations; at least their behavior in the studies reported here is consistent with such an inferred cognitive and motivational pattern.

5
Pattern A and Time Urgency

A second feature of Pattern A is an exaggerated sense of time urgency. The experiments reported in this chapter were designed to document some of the behavioral consequences of this Type A characteristic. The first experiment examined time consciousness in As and Bs; the second and third experiments attempted to arouse impatience directly and thus impair the performance of As on timing tasks; the final study was concerned with the enhanced irritation of As when they are slowed down in their efforts to complete an assigned task.

TIME CONSCIOUSNESS

It will be recalled that the Deadline Experiment in the last chapter included a time-estimation task prior to the performance phase of the study. The rationale behind the estimation task was as follows. It was assumed that the impatience of As would lead to an experience of time passing slowly. Research in time perception indicates that increasing the number of stimuli or stimulus changes during an interval heightens its apparent duration (e.g., Frankenhaeuser, 1959). Moreover, Fraisse (1963) has suggested that impatience leads to increased attentiveness to stimulus changes, which in turn results in the experience of time passing more slowly. It might be expected, therefore, that the impatience of As would lead them to report the passage of a fixed time interval (say, 1 min) sooner than their Pattern B counterparts. This prediction was tested in the time estimation part of the Deadline Experiment.

Procedure

Instructions for the time-estimation task were as follows:

> The first task you will be working on today involves time estimation. After I say "Start," I want you to guess when 1 minute has elapsed. During this time you will be reading a passage aloud. When you think a minute has passed say "Stop." Please do not use any objective cues such as heart rate, breathing, or counting . . .

Subjects who had wristwatches were asked to hand them to the experimenter, after which they were given a technical paper in cognitive psychology to read aloud. The time between starting to read and saying "Stop" was recorded.

Results

Analysis of time estimates revealed that As signaled the passage of 1 min sooner than did Bs. The mean number of seconds that actually elapsed before the signal was 52.6 for As and 75.0 for Bs; $F(1, 58) = 12.48$, $p < .001$. The average estimates for both types of subjects were significantly different from 60 sec ($ps < .05$), and the average deviation from 1 min was not significantly greater for Bs than for As ($p > .20$). These data indicate that As and Bs depart equally (though in opposite directions) from an accurate estimate of the passage of 1 min.

Discussion

This study demonstrates a relationship between the alleged time-urgent features of Pattern A and a tendency to perceive time as passing slowly. The finding that a specific time interval elapsed sooner for As than for Bs is in accord with other research on Pattern A and perceptions of time (Bortner & Rosenman, 1967). The fact that Bs overestimated the passage of a minute is not inconsistent with psychophysical studies of time estimation, which show that subjects often give much longer estimates when they pass the time performing a monotonous task than when they are engaged in interesting work (cf. Woodrow, 1951).

The struggle of As to overcome the constraints of time may stem from their excessive drive to master a large number of aspects of their environment. It should be noted in this connection that achievement-related experiences foster characteristic attitudes toward the lapse of time; for example, highly motivated individuals become angry if the clock is not exact and feel vaguely guilty if time is wasted (Heckhausen, 1967). These reactions are precisely what we would expect from a Pattern A individual. Moreover, they suggest that the arousal of time urgency may have behavioral as well as perceptual consequences. More systematic documentation of behavioral effects can be found in the experiment reported next (see Glass, Snyder, & Hollis, 1974 Experiment I).

THE DRL EXPERIMENT

The performance of As and Bs was compared on a task involving differential reinforcement of low rates of response (DRL). To obtain reinforcement on a DRL schedule, the subject must wait during a fixed time interval before responding; any premature response resets the time contingency (cf. Singh, 1973). For example, DRL 20 sec means that the subject should not respond for at least 20 sec following the preceding response. If he responds within 20 sec, he must wait 20 sec after premature response to obtain reinforcement on the next trial. The DRL task is difficult and can be mastered only with considerable patience. It was expected, therefore, that As would experience difficulty in correctly delaying their responses on a DRL task. The less time-urgent Bs, by contrast, should have less trouble in responding slowly, hence their DRL performance was expected to exceed that of the As.

It seemed intuitively reasonable that As would show greater tension and hyperactivity than Bs while working on the DRL task. This hunch was tested by recording behavioral signs of hyperactivity during the session.

Subjects

A total of 36 male undergraduates (18 As and 18 Bs) were randomly selected from the upper and lower thirds of a distribution of several hundred JAS scores. Three As and two Bs were subsequently eliminated from the study because of equipment failure, prior knowledge of how to solve the DRL task, or other procedural problems. The final experimental sample consisted of 15 As and 16 Bs.

Apparatus

The DRL apparatus was a modification of a device developed by Singh (1971; 1973). It consisted of a small metal box in which an illuminating push button and two signal lights were embedded. A 20-sec DRL with a 5-sec limited hold was programmed with integrated circuits and a Foringer punched-tape reader. Each trial was initiated by illumination of the push button, which was automatically turned off by the subject's response. If the subject pressed the button within the 20–25-sec interval, a green signal light containing a plus sign came on for 3 sec; if he pressed the button earlier than 20 sec or did not press within the interval, a red light containing a minus sign was illuminated for 3 sec.

Procedure

The following taped instructions were played to each subject:

> This is a test of time judgment. We would like to know how accurately you can judge time without the aid of a watch. We are not going to tell you what this time interval is; you must figure it out by trial and error. You have complete freedom to use any strategy to figure out this interval. The interval will always remain constant. Every time you press the button in front of you, either the plus sign or the minus sign will light up on the box. If you guess the correct time interval, and press the button during this interval, the plus sign will light up. If you have pressed at the wrong time, a minus sign will light up. Also, if you do not press the button for some time, a minus sign will automatically appear. We are going to give you a 50-cent bank. Every time you get a plus sign, we will add 2 cents to your bank. Every time you get a minus sign, we will subtract 2 cents from your bank. If you are correct enough times, it is possible to make 3 to 4 dollars during the experiment. Try to get as many plus signs as possible.

All subjects were tested for 45 min on the DRL schedule. The number of responses during the 45-min period were recorded on an Anadex digital printer for each subject.

During the testing session, an observer recorded a variety of behaviors indicative of tension and general hyperactivity. These included pounding on the response box; walking around the room; looking through books or newspapers the subject may have brought with him; sighing; clenching his fist and jaw muscles. It was expected that more As than Bs would show these behavioral signs during the session.

Results

The percentage of reinforcement [(number of reinforced responses/total number of responses) × 100] for the entire 45-min DRL session was calculated for each subject. Pattern A subjects received a significantly lower percentage of total reinforcements than Pattern B subjects. The respective median percentages were 66.5 and 77.6 (p = .05, by a two-tailed Mann–Whitney U Test).[1]

The total number of responses made by As and Bs was approximately the same for the entire 45-min session—slightly more than 104.

Error distributions. Type As may have performed more poorly than Type Bs did because As (1) responded immediately after receiving reinforcement; (2) did not wait long enough after receiving reinforcement; or (3) responded after the 20- to 25-sec interval. Accordingly, we determined whether As and Bs had different error distributions by analyzing the number of responses within each of four time segments (0–10, 10–20, 20–25, and 25+ or overshot). There were no appreciable differences within the 0–10 and overshot categories (ps > .20).

Pattern A subjects certainly performed more poorly than did Pattern B subjects, but not because As responded immediately after reinforcement or too long after reinforcement. They were simply unable to wait long enough after prior reinforcement, as can be seen in the greater proportion of responses for As than Bs within the 10–20-sec time period. The median percentage of responses in this period across trial blocks was about 15 for As and 10 for Bs (p = .10, by the two-tailed U-test). Note, in this connection, that both As and Bs were able to estimate the correct time interval for reinforcement. Mean postexperimental estimates were 23 and 25 sec for As and Bs, respectively. It would appear that As could not act upon this estimate, whereas Bs had little difficulty in correctly delaying their responses.

Behavioral signs and other data. Subjects were categorized as to whether or not they showed behaviors indicative of tension and hyperactivity during the DRL session. Approximately 47% of the As and only 12% of the Bs showed tense and hyperactive behavioral signs (p = .086, by Fisher's Exact Test). The time-urgent tendencies of As appeared to conflict with the slow-response demands of the DRL task, thereby causing increased tension along with impaired performance. Still further support for this conclusion comes from a postexperimental questionnaire item asking subjects to rate their experienced difficulty with the task on a scale ranging from 1 = "Not at all difficult" to 7 = "Very difficult." The mean rating was 2.9 for the As and 1.9 for the Bs; $t(29)$ = 2.25, p = .03.

[1] Nonparametric statistics were used here because assumptions of homogeneity of variance could not be satisfied by the DRL data (cf. Singh, 1973). However, analysis of the *mean* percentages for As (63.6) and Bs (73.4) revealed a near-significant difference between the two groups, $F(1, 29)$ = 3.41, p = .07.

Discussion

The behavioral effects reported here are probably not limited to a DRL reinforcement schedule. If As are indeed more impatient than Bs, As should do more poorly on a variety of tasks involving a period of delay before response. The literature of experimental psychology contains a number of time-related tasks which are characterized by this parameter; or at least they can be modified to include a foreperiod of varying length. To test the general notion that As would do more poorly than Bs on tasks involving delayed response, David Krantz, David Harper, and the writer conducted the following choice reaction time (RT) experiment.

THE CHOICE REACTION TIME EXPERIMENT

It was predicted that Type As would show longer response latencies than Type Bs on a choice RT task involving relatively long preparatory intervals (PIs) and intertrial intervals (ITIs). The rationale for this prediction was that lengthy foreperiods arouse impatience in As, with resultant restless behavior and distraction. Such activity might be expected to divert the attention away from the task at hand, thereby causing the Type A subject to respond more slowly than his Type B counterpart when the stimulus light finally comes on.

This interpretation of the superiority of Bs over As on a choice RT task implies that short PIs and ITIs would reduce performance differences between the two types of subjects. Indeed, As might show shorter response latencies under certain parametric conditions, for example, where the foreperiod was set for a few milliseconds. Pattern A individuals tend, after all, to exhibit more rapid pacing of their motor activities than do Pattern B individuals, in which case As might actually exhibit lower RT latencies.

Design

The foregoing line of thought was tested by comparing RT latencies of As and Bs in two conditions: one with short PIs and ITIs (from 1.5 to 2.0 sec), and one with longer intervals (from 4 to 9 sec). For logistical reasons, it was necessary to test all cases in the so-called Long condition first and then all cases in the Short condition. However, the basic analysis of RT data was conducted as a 2×2 analysis of variance.

Subjects

Subjects were 71 college-age males. Those scoring in approximately the upper third of a larger JAS distribution were designated Pattern A; those scoring in the lower third were classified Pattern B.

Apparatus

The choice RT apparatus consisted of an upright wooden panel, which displayed two small white bulbs spaced 18 in. (46 cm) apart at eye level. Directly beneath each bulb was a telegraph key. A red signal light was located in the center of the panel between the white bulbs forming the apex of a triangle made up of the three bulbs. Stimuli were presented and reaction times recorded by a PDP-8 computer and teletype in an adjoining room. Reaction times were recorded to the nearest thousandth of a second.

Procedure

When a subject arrived at the laboratory, he was seated in front of the RT apparatus and told that the purpose of the study was to measure "reactions to various sensory stimuli." The tests he would be taking, he was instructed, "provide information on how people encode and respond to their sensory environment." Instructions for the RT task were then given as follows. When the signal light comes on, "keep your hands on the table with your forefingers pressed down on both keys." Upon seeing the right light, "you are to release the left key as quickly as you can." Upon seeing the left light, "you are to release the right key as quickly as possible." In other words, the correct response was to release the key opposite to the light which appeared on the RT board.

There were 52 stimulus presentations—4 practice trials followed by 48 experimental trials. Twenty-four of the experimental trials were with each bulb on a random basis. In the Long condition, intervals between ready signal and light onset (that is, the PI) were randomized, ranging from 4 to 9 sec. The signal light went off contiguous with onset of the stimulus light. Intertrial intervals were randomized and also ranged from 4 to 9 sec.

The procedure was identical in the Short condition, except that the PIs ranged from 1.5 to 2.0 sec in random steps of .01 sec and the ITIs were constant at 1.5 sec.

Results

Each subject received two RT latency scores: the first was based on his mean response latency for the first 10 experimental trials; the second was based on his mean latency for the entire series of 48 trials.[2] The mean group scores are presented in Tables 5.1 and 5.2. Analysis of variance of the data in Table 5.1 revealed a marginally significant A–B main effect, $F(1, 67) = 2.89, p < .09$; a significant Long-Short effect, $F(1, 67) = 10.22, p < .003$; and a significant interaction between the two variables, $F(1, 67) = 5.23, p < .03$. The variance analysis for Table 5.2 confirmed the interaction, $F(1, 67) = 3.26, p < .07$, and the Long–Short effect, $F(1, 67) = 29.81, p < .001$. The A–B main effect, however, failed to reach statistical significance: $F(1, 67) < 1$.

The results indicate that subjects generally have faster response latencies under conditions of short versus long PIs and ITIs—a not very surprising finding. Of greater interest is the interaction term which reflects the fact that Bs are faster than As in the Long treatment, whereas As are faster than Bs in the Short treatment. Individual contrasts between cell means, using the error-mean-square from the appropriate analysis of variance, revealed that the difference between As and Bs in the Long condition was marginally significant for the 48 RT trials ($p = .08$) and clearly significant for the first 10 trials ($p = .01$). Comparisons between As and Bs in the Short condition indicated that the differences for both 48 trials and 10 trials were not statistically significant ($ps > .20$).

The nonsignificant reversal of means in the Short condition suggests that even where impatience is presumably not at issue, As fail to exhibit substantially faster reaction times than Bs. It may be that achievement-motivated As do not exceed Bs in the Short condition because of their concern with avoiding errors. Table 5.3 presents the average number of errors made during the 48 RT trials. (The error results are virtually identical for the first 10 trials.) Analysis of these data revealed a significant interaction, $F(1, 67) = 6.52, p = .01$, which corresponds to the interaction obtained with the response-latency means. There were no significant main effects in the analysis ($ps > .20$). Individual contrasts indicate that in the Long condition, Pattern B subjects made more errors than did their Pattern A counterparts ($p = .08$), whereas the reverse difference in the Short condition failed to attain statistical significance ($p > .10$). It would appear that Bs are not only faster than As in the Long condition, but they also make more errors. Similarly, As are somewhat faster in the Short condition, and they also tend to commit more mistakes than Bs.

---

[2] Latencies for incorrect responses were not included in the calculation of average reaction times for a given subject. Errors included the release of an incorrect key, as well as failure to make a response on a particular trial.

TABLE 5.1
Mean Reaction Time Latencies (in Milliseconds)
for the First 10 Choice RT Trials

| Subject | Experimental condition | |
classification	Long	Short
Pattern A	494.88 ($N = 17$)	397.75 ($N = 20$)
Pattern B	424.24 ($N = 17$)	408.12 ($N = 17$)

TABLE 5.2
Mean Reaction Time Latencies (in Milliseconds)
for the 48 Choice RT Trials

| Subject | Experimental condition | |
classification	Long	Short
Pattern A	484.82 ($N = 17$)	382.95 ($N = 20$)
Pattern B	445.71 ($N = 17$)	394.88 ($N = 17$)

TABLE 5.3
Mean Number of Errors for the 48 Trials of the Choice RT
Task

| Subject | Experimental condition | |
classification	Long	Short
Pattern A	4.2	5.1
Pattern B	5.9	3.7

Discussion

The results of this experiment indicate that lengthening the PI and ITI on a complex RT task results in increased response latencies among As as compared to Bs. This effect was strongest for the first 10 RT trials and marginally significant for all 48 trials. This latter result is somewhat surprising. However, comparison of the 10-trial and 48-trial means for As and Bs in the Long condition (Tables 5.1 and 5.2) reveals that Bs showed a greater decrement in speed than As over the course of the RT session. Indeed, As actually became slightly faster. The marginal A–B difference for 48 trials may, then, be attributable to increased fatigue and/or depressed motivation among Bs relative to As as the experiment progressed.

In any event, the overall pattern of results for both 10 trials and 48 trials in the Long condition accords rather nicely with data reported by Abrahams and Birren (1973). These investigators showed that with 4-sec PIs and 5-sec ITIs, Pattern A adults (25 to 59 years of age) had reliably longer response latencies on choice RT than Pattern B adults. This result was interpreted as suggesting that As are slow discriminators because their tension level rises when patience is required to absorb information (Birren, 1974). Such an explanation is consistent with our own view of the importance of impatience in interfering with choice RT responses in Type A subjects.

It was precisely this notion that led to the prediction that shortening PIs and ITIs would result in greater improvement of timing behavior in As than in Bs. While the mean response latency of As was lower than that of Bs in the Short condition, the difference failed to achieve an acceptable level of statistical significance. An attempt to explain this nonsignificant reversal in terms of the Type A subject's concern with accuracy was not supported by the data.

Despite this puzzling feature of our results, the present study supports the view that the time-urgency component of Pattern A affects timing behavior in predictable ways. Type As react more slowly under conditions which place a premium on patience compared to conditions which do not require a delayed response. Such documentation lends credence to the idea that Pattern A individuals are time urgent and impatient, which, after all, was the principal purpose for conducting the study.

THE INTERRUPTION EXPERIMENT

It has been alleged that, compared to Bs, As exhibit irritation and anger when forced to slow down the rapid pacing of their activities (e.g., Friedman, 1969). While there is clinical support for this hypothesis, little systematic data exist showing greater irritation in As than in Bs after interruption of task-relevant activities. An experiment was designed to provide such data (see Glass *et al.*, 1974, Experiment II). Subjects engaged in a discussion with a confederate of the experimenter in order to reach consensus on a series of decision problems. The confederate deliberately slowed down the discussion for half of the subjects, whereas he allowed it to proceed at normal pace with the remaining subjects. Behavioral signs of impatience and irritability were recorded for all subjects.

Subjects

Fifty-three college males, with A–B scores in the upper and lower thirds of a larger JAS distribution, participated in the study. Seven were eliminated from analysis because of their suspicions that the confederate was not really another subject. Another six cases were deleted because the confederate was unable to shift their positions on certain discussion items described later. The final sample consisted of 40 cases.

Procedure

Upon arriving at the laboratory, each subject was asked to wait a few minutes for the arrival of a "second subject"—actually a confederate of the experimenter. When he arrived, both subject and confederate were taken into the laboratory chamber and given introductory instructions. The study was presented as an investigation of cooperative decision making. Ten life-dilemma items from studies of the "risky-shift phenomenon" (e.g., Wallach, Kogan, & Bem, 1962) were presented separately to the subject and confederate. The questionnaires contained descriptions of hypothetical situations requiring decisions. The central figure in each situation must choose between two courses of action, one of which is more risky than the other but also more rewarding if successful. For each situation, the subject was told to indicate the lowest probability of success he would accept before recommending that the riskier alternative be chosen. Possible responses were listed as 1, 3, 5, 7, and 9 chances of success in 10, plus a final category in which the subject could simply refuse to recommend the risky alternative. The situations covered a wide range of choices such as the following: (1) a secure job versus an uncertain but more profitable one; (2) an easy versus a rigorous doctoral program in chemistry; (3) remain a prisoner of war or attempt to escape; (4) go for a tie or a win against an arch football rival. The questionnaire was administered using standard instructions from Wallach et al. (1962).[3]

After completing the 10 life-dilemma items, the experimenter returned to the laboratory chamber and told the subject and the confederate to discuss their individual answers for the purpose of reaching consensus as quickly and carefully as possible. They were asked to indicate their joint answers on new questionnaires. The experimenter then returned to the observation room to record the subject's behavior through a one-way mirror. During the ensuing discussion, the confederate slowed down the decision process for half of the As and half of the Bs by belaboring points and reiterating arguments (Slowdown condition). The remaining half of the subjects were in the Control condition, where discussion proceeded at a normal pace without systematic interference from the confederate.

Discussion of each item began with the confederate soliciting the subject's personal response to the item. In this way, he was able to take a position systematically different from the one chosen by the subject. On the first item, the confederate announced his position as one response category removed from that of the subject and then proceeded to accept the view taken by the subject. For example, the confederate might move from a response of "5 in 10" to "7 in 10." On the second item, the confederate again took a position one category

---

[3] There were no A–B differences in the average risk-conservatism scores of the subjects ($p >$ .25).

removed from that of the subject, but this time he convinced the subject to shift his response.

On six of the eight remaining life-dilemma items, the confederate established an initial discrepancy of two response categories between himself and the subject, for example, "7 in 10" versus "3 in 10." The confederate shifted to the subject's initial position on the third and eighth items in the discussion sequence. He persuaded the subject to shift his position on items 4 and 7 in the sequence, and there was a compromise on items 5 and 10. Initial agreement with the subject was established on the remaining two items (6 and 9). Discussion was systematically slowed down on each of the items except for 1 and 2, which constituted a baseline measure of the subject's general impatience and irritability.

After the discussion was completed, the experimenter returned to the laboratory and administered postexperimental questionnaires, including a 20-item attraction scale adapted from Davis and Jones (1960). The subject rated the confederate on such dimensions as likeability, intelligence, and maturity.

Behavioral observations. The subject was rated on three behavioral dimensions: (1) nervous touching of his hands to his body; (2) impatient tapping on the table; (3) displaying facial annoyance toward the confederate. These dimensions were selected as indicators of impatience and irritation on the basis of earlier pilot work with college students. Ratings on the three dimensions were made during discussion of each of the life-dilemma items. The rating scale consisted of four categories: none (1); a little (2); somewhat (3); a lot (4). Each subject was given five behavioral rating scores as follows: Values assigned to the four rating categories were summed across the three behavioral dimensions and then across the two discussion items making up each of five decision-item classifications. Thus, each subject received a score for the two items on which he and the confederate agreed (*agree* items); another score for two items on which he shifted to the confederate's position (*subject shift* items); still another score for items on which the confederate moved to the subject's position (*confederate shift* items); and a score for the two items on which a compromise was reached (*compromise* items). As indicated above, the score for the first two items discussed in the session constituted a *baseline* measure of impatience and irritability. The other four scores were treated as deviations from this baseline.

Results and Discussion

Effectiveness of the Slowdown manipulation. The five behavioral observation scores were subjected to a repeated-measures analysis of variance, with the A–B and Slowdown versus Control variables as between factors, and decision-item categories as the within factor. The results indicated greater irritation and impatience among Slowdown subjects than among Control subjects; $F(1, 36) = 11.76, p < .002$. There was also a significant repeated-measures effect, $F(4, 144) = 13.28, p < .001$, and an interaction between this variable and the Slowdown manipulation, $F(4, 144) = 5.76, p < .004$. The latter result occurred principally because the confederate did not begin his manipulations until after the two baseline decision items.

It would appear, then, that the manipulations of impatience and irritation were generally successful. Slowdown subjects certainly showed reliably greater signs of such affect than Control subjects. It is interesting to note that the former group rated themselves as having felt slowed down to a greater extent than the Controls. These postexperimental ratings were made on a 7-point scale, where a high score indicated that the subject "felt very slowed down" by the confederate. The mean rating was 2.4 for the Slowdown condition and 1.5 for the Controls, $F(1, 36) = 3.19, p = .08$. In actual fact, it took an average of about 21 min to complete the discussion in the Slowdown condition and slightly over 15 min in the Control condition, $F(1, 36) = 7.50, p < .01$.

Relative impatience and irritation of As and Bs.   A statistical contrast was performed to test the hypothesis that Pattern A subjects in the Slowdown treatment showed more behavioral signs of impatience and irritation than did comparable Pattern B subjects. The contrast involved comparing the relative increase in irritation of As and Bs from baseline to a composite score based on scores for each of the other decision-item categories. The results did not achieve an acceptable level of statistical significance, although the means were clearly in the expected direction, that is, 2.6 for As and 1.9 for Bs.

It occurred to us at this point that the observational data might be examined in terms of a more direct index of the subjects' time urgency. The student JAS, it will be recalled, permits computation of a Factor S score, which presumably measures the subject's propensity toward speed and impatience in his everyday activities (see, also, Appendix A). Accordingly, each subject was given an S score and then classified as High S or Low S depending upon whether he scored above or below the median of the distribution of 40 Factor S scores. Table 5.4 presents the behavioral data grouped according to the S-score variable.

The results again indicate a main effect due to the Slowdown variable, $F(1, 36) = 10.37, p = .003$; a repeated-measures effect, $F(4, 144) = 11.98, p < .001$; and an interaction between the two variables, $F(4, 144) = 5.28, p < .001$. Of greater significance was the outcome of a contrast between High S and Low S subjects within the Slowdown treatment. Data for this contrast were the relative increases in impatience and irritation from baseline items to the composite score based on the scores for the other four item categories (*agree, subject shift*, etc.). As expected, High S subjects exhibited a greater increment

TABLE 5.4
Mean Scores of Impatience and Irritation

Experimental group	Decision item categories				
	Baseline	Agree	Subject shift	Confederate shift	Compromise
Control					
High S[a]	8.1	7.5	8.9	8.3	8.0
Low S[b]	7.8	7.7	9.1	8.1	7.8
Slowdown					
High S[b]	7.3	9.6	10.8	10.0	9.8
Low S[a]	7.9	8.6	9.6	9.6	9.8

[a] $N = 8$.
[b] $N = 12$.

in impatience/irritation than Low S subjects, $t(144) = 1.93$, $p < .06$. The mean increase was 1.5 for the Low S group and 2.7 for the High S group. A comparable effect did not occur in the Control treatment, where mean changes in the impatience/irritation index were .32 and .04 for Low S and High S subjects, respectively. A subsequent analysis of the index data was performed only for the *baseline* and *agree* items. High S subjects in the Slowdown condition again showed greater impatience and irritation than comparable Low S subjects, $t(36) = 2.11$, $p < .05$. We may conclude, therefore, that Pattern A subjects, at least those who scored high on speed and impatience, are indeed more irritated than Pattern B subjects when the activities of both are slowed down by another person.

The student JAS also permits computation of a Hard Driving (H) factor score for each subject (see Appendix A). The sequence of statistical analyses reported above was repeated with the median Factor H score substituted for Factor S in classifying subjects. The results did not achieve acceptable levels of significance. High H subjects were not more impatient and irritable than Low H subjects ($p > .20$). This finding confirms our initial expectation and indicates that the time-urgent component of Pattern A is the operative factor in determining differential annoyance reactions to being slowed down.

Other relevant data. The postexperimental attraction scale enabled us to determine whether High S subjects in the Slowdown treatment derogated the confederate more than comparable Low S subjects. Table 5.5 presents the relevant means, where a high score indicates positive evaluation and a low score negative evaluation. Analysis of variance revealed an interaction between Factor S and the Slowdown manipulation, $F(1, 36) = 3.68$, $p < .06$. High S subjects gave a more positive evaluation of the confederate in the Slowdown treatment than in the Control treatment, $t(36) = 2.10$, $p < .05$, whereas a nonsignificant reversal occurred for Low S subjects ($p > .10$). Comparable

TABLE 5.5
Mean Evaluations of the Confederate

Subject	Experimental condition	
classification	Control	Slowdown
High S	24.5	36.9
Low S	31.5	27.9

analyses with A–B and Factor H scores yielded nonsignificant results ($ps >$ .15), although the trend of the evaluation means was in the same direction as reported here for Factor S.

The evaluation results are seemingly inconsistent with the observational data. It would appear that being slowed down produces both greater irritation and greater liking of the confederate in High S subjects. A possible explanation is immediately apparent if we recall that Type As often try to conceal their hostility (see Chapter 3; see, also, Friedman, 1969). It follows that As (and High S subjects as well) would tend to deny dislike of the confederate while at the same time showing behavioral signs of irritation with his delaying tactics. These are, of course, precisely the results obtained in this study.

CONCLUSIONS

We may conclude from the last experiment that subjects with Pattern A traits show greater impatience and irritation when delayed in the execution of their activities than do subjects with Pattern B traits. Taken together with data from the other studies reported in this chapter, it would appear that time urgency is indeed a major facet of Pattern A, with demonstrable effects on the perception of time, timing behavior, and interpersonal relationships. The experimental results also underscore the importance of treating Pattern A behavior as an interplay of predispositions and eliciting environmental circumstances. The behavioral effects produced in our research depended upon As and Bs being confronted with situations designed to elicit differential responses. Without appropriate stimulation, Pattern A and Pattern B subjects would probably have behaved in similar ways.

6

Pattern A and Aggressiveness

A third major facet of Pattern A is hostility and aggressiveness. Excess hostility and aggression are, however, not always easily detected in Type As, for, as we noted in previous chapters, they often keep such affect and reactions under cover. Friedman and Rosenman (1974) suggest that a prime index of the presence of hostility is the tendency to compete with or to challenge other people. They also suggest that there is often a note of rancor and contentiousness in the speech of fully developed Type As.

While there seems to be agreement that As are more hostile than Bs, the judgment is based on clinical observation and data collected in the stress interview for classifying subjects as A or B. The irritation results of the interruption experiment (see Chapter 5) provide some evidence of the aggressiveness of Pattern A subjects, but there is an obvious need for more compelling documentation. An experiment was designed by Charles S. Carver and the author for just this purpose. We reasoned that As would react with enhanced aggressiveness toward another person who impedes and denigrates their efforts to perform a difficult task. By contrast, Bs were expected to show significantly less aggression following a comparable instigation.

THE AGGRESSION EXPERIMENT

Subjects

Male undergraduates were classified as Pattern A if they scored in the upper third of a larger distribution of JAS scores, and as Pattern B if their A–B score was in the lower third of the distribution. Forty-eight subjects completed the experiment, of which 23 were As and 25 Bs. There was the usual random assignment of cases within each A–B group to two experimental conditions. Five additional cases were recruited and then deleted before analysis for the following reasons: (1) three subjects completed the ''tower puzzle'' (see below) in the allotted 3 min; (2) two subjects expressed the belief that the learner was not being shocked.

Procedure

After arriving at the experimental facility, the naive subject and a confederate (ostensibly another subject) were told that they were participating in a learning experiment. The procedure was actually a modification of the Buss aggression paradigm, described in detail elsewhere (e.g., Buss, 1961). The subject was assigned to the teacher role in the paradigm, presumably because he arrived a few minutes before the confederate.

Leaving the confederate seated in the first room, the subject was taken to an adjoining experimental room where the experimenter explained how to present stimuli and record responses in the forthcoming concept learning task. He was shown the ''teacher's console,'' a component in the Buss aggression machine, and told about pressing buttons which would activate a set of four stimulus lights on the ''learner's console.'' He was also given a prearranged schedule which indicated the specific pattern of lights he was to activate on any given trial. The learner (the confederate) would respond to the lights presented on each trial by depressing one of two switches on his console. The subject was instructed to flash a ''correct'' light for each correct response and to deliver shock for each incorrect response. There were 10 shock buttons of graded intensity available to the subject. A wooden partition separated the two consoles.

After explaining the task, the experimenter attached a finger electrode to the subject and gave him shocks from buttons 1 through 5. Button 1 produced a barely perceptible tingling, with shock intensity increasing gradually up to 5. Button 5 was rated by all subjects (on an 8-point scale) as producing ''slightly painful'' to ''definitely painful'' shocks. The impression was given that the shocks continued to increase in intensity so that Button 10 delivered a shock that would be experienced as severely painful. The subject was told he could use any of the shock buttons he wanted during the actual learning trials.

Next, the entire procedure was summarized by the experimenter in order to make certain that the subject understood what he and the confederate would be doing. Emphasis was given to the instruction that he, the subject, would be teaching the confederate a concept by using reward (correct light) and punishment (shock). Following the summary, the experimenter and subject returned to the room where the confederate was waiting.

In the No Instigation condition, the experimenter said the experiment was ready to begin, and then both confederate and subject were escorted back to the room with the aggression machine. After a brief explanation to the confederate of his role as "learner," the experimenter attached the shock electrode to the confederate's finger. He then told the subject to begin the learning trials and immediately left the room.

In the Instigation condition, the experimenter told the subject and confederate to remain in the first room—the one without the aggression machine; he then pointed out that one of the purposes of the study was to see how learning a concept influenced subsequent teaching of another concept. Half of the subjects who were to be teachers in the learning session, the experimenter explained, were being asked to work on a perceptual-motor task called the "tower puzzle" (Fenigstein & Buss, 1974). The puzzle consisted of a wooden base with three dowels projecting upward. Seven wooden disks of varying diameters were stacked in the form a pyramid on one of the dowels. The subject's task was to move the stack of disks to one of the remaining two dowels while adhering to two rules: (1) he could move only one disk at a time; (2) he could not place a larger disk on top of a smaller one. The experimenter then stated that he had to see the departmental secretary and, turning to the confederate, asked him to time the subject on the puzzle while he was away. The confederate was given a stopwatch and cautioned not to help the subject in any way.

When the experimenter left the room the confederate proceeded to deliver a prearranged series of denigrating remarks. He began by stating that he had seen the puzzle before, that it was very easy, and the subject should have no trouble completing it. The puzzle was, in fact, complex and difficult. An individual could complete it in 3 min only if he had considerable prior experience. As the subject worked on the puzzle, the confederate made these comments:

I don't know what's taking you so long; it's not that difficult.
The next move is obvious. . . . Well, I *thought* it was obvious.
Hurry up, or you'll never get finished.

When 3 min had elapsed, the confederate said: "I don't know how you're going to teach me, if you can't even do this simple thing." In short, Instigation subjects were exposed to the following: (1) negative comments from the confederate; (2) high time pressure to finish the puzzle. Both procedures were deliberately used in what amounts to a confounded manipulation in order to maximize the likelihood of observing A–B differences in aggression.

After the instigation manipulation was complete, the experimenter returned and led both subject and confederate to the experimental room with the aggression machine. As in the No Instigation condition, the experimenter left the room immediately after attaching the shock electrode to the confederate and giving him a brief explanation of the learning task.

Measurement of the dependent variable.   In both experimental conditions, the subject and confederate were unable to see one another once they were seated behind the wooden partition separating their consoles. The confederate opened a trapdoor on his console that disconnected the shock circuit and exposed a ''Nixie'' tube enabling him to read off numbers corresponding to the shock button being pressed by the subject. By following a prearranged list of ''correct'' and ''incorrect'' responses, the confederate caused the subject to deliver shock on 35 of the learning trials. The level of each of these shocks (that is, the shock-button number) was recorded by the confederate. These data constituted the principal measure of aggression used in the study.

Postsession.   After completion of the learning session, the subject filled out a short postexperimental questionnaire. An interview and debriefing completed the experimental procedure.

Results

Shock-intensity data were analyzed as the mean level delivered by each subject over the 35 shock trials. Figure 6.1 presents these results for the four

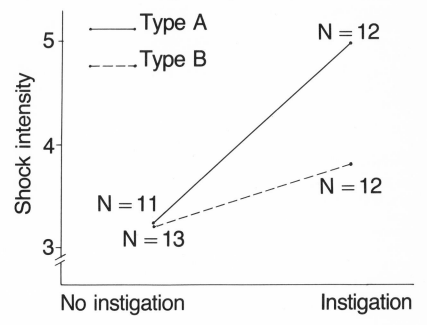

FIGURE 6.1   Mean shock intensities.

experimental groups. Analysis of variance revealed that mean shock intensity in the Instigation condition was reliably higher than in the No Instigation condition, $F(1, 44) = 7.31$, $p < .01$. However, as Figure 6.1 indicates, the principal source of this effect was the high level of shock delivered by Pattern A subjects in the Instigation treatment. Individual contrasts (using the error-mean-square from the analysis of variance) revealed that Instigation As delivered higher levels of shock than did their counterparts in the No Instigation treatment. While the interaction did not achieve statistical significance ($p > .15$), nevertheless individual contrasts revealed that Instigation As delivered higher levels of shock than did their counterparts in No Instigation ($p < .01$), whereas Type Bs in the Instigation treatment did not shock at a reliably higher level than No Instigation Bs ($p > .30$). The difference between As and Bs in the Instigation condition approached significance at less than the .08 level.

The instigation manipulation might be expected to produce differences in subjective liking of the confederate, although the tendency of As to suppress hostility might militate against detecting such differences. Nevertheless, subjects were asked the following question in the postexperimental questionnaire: "In your opinion, how likeable a person is the learner [confederate]?"; 1 represents "not at all likable," and 7 represents "very likable." Instigation subjects rated the confederate as significantly less likable than did No Instigation subjects [Ms = 4.13 and 5.18, $F(1, 44) = 6.18$, $p < .02$]. As with the shock-intensity results, this effect was largely attributable to the difference between Instigation and No Instigation As ($p < .03$). There was no difference in mean ratings between conditions for the Bs ($p > .25$).

Discussion

The shock results support initial predictions. Pattern A subjects responded to the threat implicit in the Instigation procedure with aggression directed toward the instigator; Pattern B subjects did not react with comparable aggressiveness. Since there was no difference between As and Bs in the No Instigation treatment, we may tentatively conclude that the potential for hostility and aggression characteristic of Pattern A is elicited only when an appropriately challenging situation confronts the individual. Type As are not uniformly more aggressive than Type Bs; they become so in response to a specific set of circumstances which threaten their sense of task mastery. It should also be noted that Bs are not uniformly nonaggressive. There are conditions sufficiently provocative to arouse aggression in Bs. Indeed, three Pattern B subjects in the Instigation treatment delivered a substantial amount of shock to the confederate.

Ratings of the confederate's likability were consistent with the aggression results. Pattern A subjects in the Instigation condition reported that the confederate was less likable than did their counterparts in No Instigation. These data may be interpreted in the same terms as the shock-intensity results; on the other hand, they may reflect a dissonance reduction process in which the group that delivered the most shock rated the confederate as least likable. In either case, it is worth noting that the instigation procedure was successful in eliciting aggressive responses on both behavioral and subjective measures. This finding takes on added significance in view of our previous results indicating a tendency on the part of As to suppress aggressive and hostile feelings (see Chapter 5). Taken together, the shock intensity and liking data provide evidence for the aggression component of Pattern A.

CONCLUSIONS

The research reported up to this point provides systematic documentation for the three principal components of Pattern A behavior and, in so doing, presents evidence for the construct validity of the student JAS. Additional validity data can be found, it will be recalled, in Appendixes C and D. Appendix C contains correlations between the student JAS and standardized psychological tests; Appendix D describes associations between the JAS and traditional risk factors for CHD (for example, certain college-student As have reliably higher serum cholesterol levels than their Type B counterparts). We are now prepared to move to a different and more theoretical set of issues, namely, the interplay of Pattern A and uncontrollable stress. The explication of this relationship is, of course, the major theme of this monograph, and the next four chapters report relevant experimentation.

7
Pattern A
and Initial Exposure
to Uncontrollable Stress

A more genotypic approach to the data presented in Chapters 4 through 6 suggests, in our view, a general consistency in the array of empirical facts. It appears that Type As exert greater effort than Type Bs to master events which they appraise as a threat to their sense of environmental control. In contrast to Bs, Type As work hard to succeed, suppress subjective states (like fatigue) that might interfere with task performance, exhibit rapid pacing of their activities, show little tolerance for interruption, and express hostility after being harassed in their efforts at task completion—all, we submit, in the interests of asserting control over environmental demands and requirements. We would also suggest that these demands must be at least minimally stressful, for the possibility of failure and loss of esteem was inherent in most of our experimental situations. Pattern A behavior might thus be conceptualized as a characteristic style of responding to environmental stressors that threaten the individual's sense of control. Type As are engaged in a struggle for control, whereas Type Bs are relatively free of such concerns and, hence, free of characteristic Pattern A traits.

Psychological stress was defined earlier (Chapter 2) as involving a cognitive appraisal process in which the individual anticipates harm or injury from some event. An environmental stressor is, therefore, any external stimulus which is judged to threaten the individual's physical and/or psychic well-being. The concept of uncontrollability may be defined as the perception of a noncontingency between responding and reinforcement (cf. Seligman, 1975). When a response will not determine what an individual gets, the outcome is considered uncontrollable. By contrast, controllability involves the perception that responses do in fact determine outcomes, that a contingency exists between the two variables. An uncontrollable stressor is, then, a potentially harmful stimulus which the individual can neither escape nor avoid. A controllable stressor is a harmful stimulus which can be avoided by appropriate instrumental responses.

The initial reaction of Type As to an uncontrollable stressor may be termed *hyperresponsiveness,* since it is assumed to reflect a concerted effort to assert control over the stimulus. Despite these efforts, however, the Type A individual comes to learn through extended experience with the stressor that he cannot escape and/or avoid the unpleasant stimulation. When he becomes convinced of his lack of control, the Type A will cease trying to master the event and show *hyporesponsiveness* compared to his Type B counterpart. The experiments reported in this chapter provide successive tests of derivations from the hyperresponsiveness part of the hypothesis. Chapter 8 is concerned with research pertaining to hyporesponsiveness.

REACTIONS TO AN UNCONTROLLABLE STRESSOR: EXPERIMENT I

The basic paradigm for this and the following experiment is based on a modification of procedures used in learned-helplessness research (e.g., Seligman, 1975). Subjects are exposed to controllable or uncontrollable stimuli during what is called a pretreatment phase of the study. For example, loud noise is delivered to subjects who are seated in front of some manipulandum, say, a button-pressing task. All subjects are led to believe that there is something they can do with the manipulandum that will terminate the sound. A designated pattern of responses does in fact permit escape for half of the cases (Escape pretreatment); for the other half, the circuitry is disconnected so that responding cannot lead to noise termination (No Escape pretreatment). After some period of exposure to pretreatment, all subjects are introduced to what may be called the test phase of the study. Subjects work on a new task, but this time *everyone* can escape from the noise. Subjects who were in Escape pretreatment are expected to learn the correct pattern of escape responses in the test phase more quickly than those who were pretreated with No Escape. The latter group are said to be helpless because they learned in pretreatment that a noncontingency exists between responding and reinforcement. Learned expectations of noncontingency are assumed to generalize from pretreatment to the test phase, where they are manifest in retarded learning of the escape response.

The theoretical basis of learned helplessness is somewhat more complex than this, but the essential elements of the paradigm are as described above. Modifications of the paradigm have been used by a number of investigators. Glass and Singer (1972), for example, have shown that exposure to an uncontrollable stressor leads to a dampening of performance on subsequent nonstressful tasks. Having experienced helplessness during the first part of an experiment, subjects experience a decrement in motivation to master tasks introduced in the second part of the study—even when those new tasks are not stressful and entirely different from the first task.

A learned-helplessness model, then, suggests that exposure to an uncontrollable stressor results in passivity and impaired learning and performance. However, closer examination of the parameters affecting the model indicates that this may not always be the case. If a person expects to control events that are important to him, finding those events to be potentially uncontrollable should constitute a threat to his sense of control (Wortman & Brehm, 1975; Thornton & Jacobs, 1972). In other words, among individuals who are accustomed to exerting control, for example, Pattern A individuals, initial exposure to uncontrollable stimuli (that is, the first few trials) should lead to increased motivation to assert and maintain control. However, despite this enhanced motivation, the individual eventually learns through extended exposure to uncontrollability that he cannot influence the stressful stimuli confronting him. When he becomes convinced of his inability to exert control, the individual gives up and shows the learned-helplessness effects described earlier.

The foregoing line of thought conforms nicely to our previous discussion of differential responses of As and Bs to uncontrollable stress. The hyperresponsiveness of As might be expected to occur immediately after exposure to a few trials of inescapable noise. In comparison to Bs, Type As should experience an initial increment in motivation to master a nonnoise task administered after inescapable noise stimulation. This increase in motivation is presumed to facilitate reassertion of environmental control following its loss during noise exposure. Given the importance of uncontrollability in this formulation, we would not expect pretreatment with escapable noise to produce similar A–B differences on a subsequent task.

Enhanced motivation to control events may improve or dampen actual performance, depending upon the nature of the task given to the subject after pretreatment. Consider the choice RT procedure using the long foreperiod (see Chapter 5). It will be recalled that Pattern A subjects showed significantly longer RT latencies than Pattern B subjects, presumably because of their inability to sustain the patience needed to remain alert during the relatively long preparatory interval. However, we might expect improvement in choice RT (that is, shorter response latencies) if the task were administered after brief exposure to inescapable compared to escapable noise. The logic of this prediction is that prior experience with uncontrollable stress enhances the motivation of As to master subsequent tasks. Since most subjects recognize the importance of avoiding distraction during the RT foreperiod, it is not unreasonable to expect As to contain their impatience in order to respond as quickly as possible to the signal light. This is, after all, the instruction given to all subjects. Type As should, therefore, accelerate their speed of response if a brief experience with uncontrollability does indeed potentiate their motivation to control. Type Bs, by contrast, should remain relatively unaffected by pretreatment since they are assumed to be less responsive to the incentive of environmental control.[1]

Design

The foregoing line of thought was tested in an experiment designed by David Krantz and the author. Controllability was manipulated in the first phase of a two-part study. All subjects were exposed to 12 bursts of 100-dB(A) noise.[2] Half of the cases were able to escape by an appropriate series of lever-pressing responses (Escape pretreatment), whereas the other half were unable to terminate sound (No Escape pretreatment). Within each of these conditions, half of the subjects were As and the other half Bs. The test phase of the study consisted of a choice RT task identical to the one used in the long foreperiod condition of the RT study reported in Chapter 5. The principal dependent measure consisted of response latencies averaged across RT trials. It was expected that Pattern A subjects would have shorter latencies than Pattern B subjects following No Escape pretreatment, whereas the reverse effect would occur following Escape pretreatment. The latter half of the prediction was based on the earlier finding that Bs were faster than As on choice RT, at least where the foreperiod was relatively long. It was not expected that exposure to escapable noise would alter the superior performance of the Bs. In short, the major prediction took the form of an interaction between the A–B classification and the escapability–inescapability manipulation.

Subjects

Twenty Type A and 20 Type B college students participated in this study (see Appendix A). Subjects in each A–B category were randomly assigned to the two experimental conditions.

---

[1] An early attempt to test these predictions resulted in equivocal findings. The test-phase used a number-comparison test (French, Ekstrom, & Price, 1963) which proved to be too simple for college-student subjects. In consequence, we were unable to detect systematic acceleration of performance on the test in As compared to Bs, after both groups were exposed to uncontrollable pretreatment.

[2] Twelve trials of noise were arbitrarily selected as constituting brief exposure to an uncontrollable stressor. The decision was dictated by previous research (e.g., Hiroto, 1974), as well as by experimentation reported in the next chapter indicating that prolonged exposure (say, 30 noise bursts) produces learned-helplessness rather than facilitation effects.

Apparatus

In pretreatment, a 3000 Hz tone generated by an audio oscillator set for 100 dB(A) was delivered to the subject. There was a total of 12 noise bursts. The sound was presented over earphones and decibel level was measured at the earphones. The oscillator output for each subject in the Escape pretreatment was recorded on audio tape for later delivery to a yoked subject assigned to the No Escape condition. The audio tape was played back through a voice key connected to the oscillator. This procedure equated pretreatment conditions for duration and intermittency of noise bursts. Each of the noise trials actually averaged about 4.5 sec in duration. Intertrial intervals varied randomly from 15 to 25 sec with a mean of 20 sec.

The subject's *pretreatment* response unit consisted of a wooden box containing six spring-loaded switches. A green light built into the panel signaled successful termination of the noise. In the *test phase* of the experiment, subjects worked at the reaction-time task described in Chapter 5.

Procedure

When the subject arrived at the laboratory, he was told that the study was concerned with his ability to solve problems, ranging from purely mental tasks to tasks involving both mental and motor activity. He was told further that in the first part of the study he would be asked to solve a psychomotor problem under distracting and somewhat stressful noise conditions. The pretreatment response unit was then moved in front of the subject, and the experimenter explained that future instructions would be given from a tape recording. He left the laboratory chamber, entered the observation room, and activated the tape-recorded instructions given below.

Pretreatment phase.   All subjects heard the same instructions:

> Listen to these instructions carefully. I am not allowed to give you any information other than what I give you now. Please listen carefully and do not ask any questions. From time to time, a relatively brief noise will come on. There will be a series of such noise bursts. When each one comes on, there is something you can do to stop it. Look at the green light on the box in front of you. If you find the way to stop the noise, the green light will flash on . . . If you are unable to stop the noise, the green light will not flash on. You will have stopped the noise *only* when the green light comes on. Taking the earphones off or dismantling the apparatus is not the way to stop the noise.
>
> There is a combination of six switches that you can press to terminate

the noise. You have to press all six switches. It is up to you to figure out the correct combination of switches. Most people need only a few trials to figure out the combination. However, we are going to give you a total of 12 trials on this task.

In the Escape condition, the subject was able to terminate each noise burst by pressing all six switches in any order. The green light flashed on when the switches were pressed correctly. Both noise and light terminated .1 sec later. These procedures were designed to assure that Escape subjects received at least several seconds of noise on each trial and, in addition, were aware of their successful termination of a given noise burst. The noise ended automatically after 8 sec if the subject did not make the required response. Subjects in the yoked No Escape condition were unable to terminate the noise. The six switches on the response unit were not connected to the sound-stimulus circuitry.

After pretreatment, the experimenter reentered the laboratory chamber, removed the headphones, and asked the subject to complete a brief questionnaire.

Test phase.   After completing the questionnaire, the subject was moved over to the choice RT apparatus located on a different table in the same room. He was told that the next task involved performance under normal test conditions without noise. As in the earlier study (see Chapter 5), the subject was instructed to release the key opposite to the signal light in order to make the correct response and stop the timer. He was told to respond as quickly as possible without making errors.

There were 51 stimuli—4 trials constituting practice, followed by 47 experimental trials.[3] Of the 47 trials, 24 were for the right signal light and 23 were for the left light on the RT apparatus. The alternation between left and right was random. Intervals between ready signal and stimulus light were randomized, ranging from 4 to 9 sec. The signal light went off contiguous with the onset of the stimulus light. Intertrial intervals were random, ranging from 4 to 9 sec.

Results

Effectiveness of the experimental manipulations.   The Escape–No Escape pretreatment was successful in inducing differential perceptions of uncontrollability. In the questionnaire administered after pretreatment, subjects were asked, ''How much control did you feel you had over the termination of

[3] Through an oversight, the tape was programmed for 47 rather than the originally intended 48 trials.

the noise?''; 7 represents ''complete control,'' and 1 represents ''no control at all.'' Analysis of variance of responses to this item revealed an Escape–No Escape main effect $[Ms = 4.8$ and $1.7; F(1, 36) = 61.45, p < .001]$ and no other significant terms $(ps > .65)$.

Additional information regarding perceptions of pretreatment comes from a postexperimental question asking subjects to indicate, ''in percentages of total responsibility,'' which of four factors determined their ''degree of success and failure'' in terminating the noise. The four factors were: ''your own ability''; ''your own effort''; ''difficulty of the task''; ''chance.'' Analysis of the percentage responses for each factor revealed that only ''effort'' produced significant differences between Escape and No Escape. The mean percentages were 37.3 and 16.2; $F(1, 36) = 8.06, p < .01$. There was no A–B main effect or interaction $(ps > .60)$. The ''ability'' factor was assigned an average responsibility of about 20% by all four experimental groups, and ''chance'' was similar with averages of about 25%. On the other hand, ''task difficulty'' produced a marginal Escape–No Escape main effect $[Ms = 18.2\%$ and $29.8\%; F(1, 36) = 2.84, p < .10]$.

To sum up, the Escape–No Escape manipulation proved successful as measured by retrospective ratings of perceived control. The attribution-of-responsibility question indicates that No Escape subjects blame uncontrollability on their own relative lack of motivation and, to some extent, on the difficulty of the task. While these perceptions may reflect nothing more than rationalization for failure to escape, nevertheless we would expect No Escape As, in contrast to Bs, to increase their efforts to master the test phase task and thus reassert control over their environment. Let us turn to the data relevant to this prediction.

Test phase effects.   Figure 7.1 presents the RT latencies (in milliseconds) averaged over the 47 RT trials for each of the four experimental groups.[4] It is obvious that As were faster than Bs following No Escape pretreatment, whereas the reverse occurred after Escape pretreatment. Analysis of variance confirmed this observation, for the only significant term was the predicted interaction between the A–B variable and Escape–No Escape, $F(1, 36) = 8.78, p < .005$. A subsequent contrast indicated that the difference between As (446.0 msec) and Bs (506.1 msec) in No Escape was statistically significant $(p < .03)$. The reverse difference in Escape $(Ms = 479.2$ and 433.7 msec) approached significance at the .08 level—precisely the level obtained for As and Bs without pretreatment (see Chapter 5). The difference between As in Escape and No Escape did not attain significance $(p > .15)$, whereas the comparable comparison for Bs was statistically reliable $(p < .01)$.

---

[4]Incorrect responses or no responses were not included in the computation of average RT latencies.

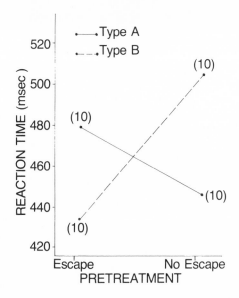

FIGURE 7.1   Mean reaction times. (Group sizes in parentheses.)

The RT data for the first 10 trials was also analyzed. The results indicated an interaction between the A–B factor and escapability–inescapability, $F(1, 36) = 10.33$, $p < .01$. Individual comparisons indicated that As in No Escape were faster than their counterparts in Escape ($Ms = 438.2$ and 493.2, $p < .07$), whereas Bs showed just the opposite effect ($Ms = 519.0$ and 427.8, $p < .01$). The other two contrasts were virtually identical to those reported for the entire 47 trials, although the difference between As and Bs in Escape was clearly significant in this analysis ($p < .05$).

Discussion

This experiment suggests that choice reaction-time responses are potentiated in Pattern A subjects relative to Pattern B subjects by brief exposure to an uncontrollable noise stressor. Type As normally have difficulty with a choice RT task involving long foreperiods, probably because their impatience with delay causes distraction and consequent interference with rapid responding (see Chapter 5). However, the threat inherent in exposure to uncontrollable stress appears to have motivated Type As to restrain their customary impatience and thus respond rapidly to the signal light in the RT task. Type Bs, in contrast, appear to have experienced a decrement in motivation–at least their RT performance was impaired by prior uncontrollability. In short, Pattern B subjects gave up efforts at mastery, whereas Pattern A subjects tried harder to do well, presumably in the interests of reasserting environmental control.

One might characterize the hyporesponsivity of the Bs as indicative of helplessness, which, it will be recalled, is predicted for As only after a prolonged experience with uncontrollable stimulation. While it is tempting to suggest that Bs have a lower threshold for helplessness, such an inference is unwarranted in view of data presented in later chapters. Suffice it to say here that we have confirmed initial predictions about the hyperresponsiveness of As compared to Bs after both groups are threatened with loss of control over an environmental stressor. Pattern A subjects show subsequent behaviors that are indicative of increased motivation to assert control.

The results reported here call for conceptual replication. We have documented the effects of uncontrollability on later task performance, where responding faster was the explicit criterion of mastery. The next experiment, also conducted by David Krantz and the author, examines the effects of uncontrollability on subsequent task performance, where delayed responding was the criterion of success.

REACTIONS TO AN UNCONTROLLABLE STRESSOR: EXPERIMENT II

An uncontrollable event was defined in terms of noncontingency between instrumental responding and reinforcement. The applicability of this definition is clear in the case of inescapable noise, but experience with noncontingent reinforcement on cognitive problems is also an instance of uncontrollability. Random delivery of positive and negative reinforcement (that is, "correct" or "incorrect" evaluations) for efforts to solve, say, a series of concept-formation problems, implies that the probability of being correct is independent of the subject's responses. Previous research has documented a similarity in behavioral effects attributable to uncontrollable physical stressors and noncontingent reinforcement on cognitive problems (e.g., Dweck, 1975; Glass & Singer, 1972; Roth & Kubal, 1975; Seligman, 1975). Moreover, a recent study suggests that reactions to noncontingent reinforcement are a result of the subject's learning that he cannot control his reinforcements, not an affective response to failure (Cohen, Rothbart, & Phillips, 1976). Thus, failure may be seen as a correlate of responses to uncontrollability (either facilitation or giving up), but not as their cause.

The logic of the experiment described next is that relatively short exposure to noncontingent reinforcement on a concept formation problem will threaten a subject's sense of control in much the same way as an inescapable physical stressor. Given the previous line of thought concerning Pattern A and uncontrollable stress, it was expected that this type of uncontrollability would lead As to increase their motivation to master a subsequent test-phase task. The task chosen for this purpose was the DRL procedure described in Chapter 5.

Recall that the DRL performance of As was inferior to that of Bs, presumably because they were unable to sustain the frustration of delaying their responses. However, we might expect substantial improvement in DRL if it were administered following noncontingent reinforcement on a prior task. After several trials with a DRL schedule, most subjects appear to recognize that only delayed responses result in reinforcement. Type As should therefore reduce rather than accelerate their rate of responding if noncontingency does indeed enhance their motivation to succeed and thus control their environment. By contrast, the DRL performance of Type Bs should remain unaffected by prior noncontingency, or possibly be dampened, as we observed in the previous choice RT study.

Overview

Contingency of reinforcement was manipulated in the first phase of a two-part study. Subjects worked on a pair of four-dimensional stimulus patterns used in previous research (Hiroto & Seligman, 1975).[5] Each of the four dimensions had two associated values: (1) letter (*A* or *T*); (2) letter size (large or small); (3) border shape surrounding the letter (circle or square); (4) border texture surrounding the letter (dashed or solid). In the contingent or Soluble condition, one value of one of the dimensions (e.g. circle) was always correct. In the noncontingent or Insoluble condition, no value was treated as consistently correct. The test phase of the study consisted of performance on the DRL task.

Subjects

Forty-five male undergraduates participated in the study. They all completed the student JAS at the end of the experimental session. Those scoring above the sample median were designated As, whereas those scoring below the median were treated as Bs.

---

[5] Two problems were selected for use in this experiment on the assumption that this number constituted brief exposure to noncontingent reinforcement. The decision was dictated by the fact that learned helplessness has been produced with four of the dimension problems (Hiroto & Seligman, 1975; see also Chapter 8). Since we wished to maximize the likelihood of obtaining facilitation, two rather than four problems were used in this study.

Procedure

Each subject was told that the experiment was concerned with his ability to solve a variety of problems ranging from mental tasks to tasks involving both mental and motor activity. Two sets of dimension problems, plus a shorter sample set, were then presented in a small booklet. Each problem consisted of 10 pairs of stimulus patterns composed of four dimensions, as described in the Overview section. The sample problems were composed of five dimensions, letter color being added to the four other dimensions. The following instructions introduced the task:

> We will begin with a set of tasks called dimension problems. Later you'll be looking at cards like this one. Note that each card has two stimulus patterns . . . composed of five different dimensions. There are specific values associated with each dimension. . . .

The experimenter proceeded to describe each dimension and each value, for example, large or small letter, circular or square border shape. The instructions continued as follows:

> Each pattern has one value from each of the . . . dimensions. I have chosen one of the values as correct. The idea is for you to find out this value. Look at each card and choose which side, left or right, you think contains the correct value. I'll tell you if your choice was correct or incorrect. In this way, you can eliminate the incorrect values in just a few trials. The object is to figure out the correct value so as to choose the correct side as often as possible. At the end of a series of trials, I'll ask you to tell me the correct value.

Next, five trials of the sample problem were presented. This part of the procedure clarified the task of finding the "correct" value. After the sample trials were complete, the experimenter summarized the instructions and told the subject to give his responses out loud so they could be heard over the intercom system in an adjoining room where the experimenter would be seated. The experimenter left the room and signaled the subject to begin work on the first of the two dimension problems.

The stimulus patterns in the test series were composed of four dimensions, as noted earlier. The two different problems were presented in blocks of 10 trials each. At the end of each trial, the subject was asked to choose the side of the card he thought contained the "correct" value. Subjects in the Insoluble condition received a prearranged random schedule of "correct" (C) and "incorrect" (I), regardless of which side was chosen. The schedules of reinforcement were (a) C–I–I–C–C–I–I–C–C–I for the first problem and (b) I–C–I–C–C–I–C–I–C–I for the second problem. In addition, Insoluble subjects were told, "That's the wrong answer," when they were asked to identify the correct value at the end of each of the dimension problems. *This statement was said with emphasis, as was the successive feedback of "correct" and "incorrect."*

Subjects in the Soluble condition were given contingent reinforcement after each trial, thereby allowing them to deduce the correct value before the end of a 10-trial set. They were also informed, "That's the right answer," when asked to identify the correct value at the end of 10 trials. Emphasis was given to this statement, as in the Insoluble condition. A "correct" value was arbitrarily selected for each problem for use with all subjects in the Soluble treatment. In a few cases, Soluble subjects guessed incorrect values. They were still told they were correct, and all subjects in this study appeared to believe the experimenter.

Both Soluble and Insoluble subjects worked on each problem giving their guesses after each trial. If a guess was not made voluntarily after 10 sec, the experimenter asked for the subject's choice. This exchange was relatively infrequent, since subjects rarely delayed longer than 10 sec before giving their answers. At the end of the tenth trial of each problem, subjects announced their guess as to the correct value dimension. After receiving a "correct" or "incorrect" response from the experimenter, they were told: "Go on to the next problem. You do not know at this point if I have chosen a different value for this new problem. I will continue telling you if you are correct or incorrect."

DRL task.   After completion of the two dimension problems, the experimenter reentered the laboratory and began the test phase of the study. He moved the DRL apparatus in front of the subject and told him that the next set of instructions would be delivered from a tape recording. The subject was informed that he had an opportunity to earn money based on his performance on the new task. The experimenter then returned to the observation room and played taped instructions adapted from the previous DRL study (see Chapter 5).

Subjects were tested for 45 min on the DRL schedule. The number of responses during the session were recorded on a digital printer located in the observation room. These data were subsequently grouped into two categories: (1) number of responses in the reinforced (20–25-sec) interval; (2) the number of responses occurring outside of this interval. These data formed the basis for calculating a measure of percentage of reinforcement—our major dependent variable.

Postsession.   At the end of the DRL trials, the experimenter returned to the laboratory and administered a postexperimental questionnaire. Included were several items measuring the effectiveness of the experimental manipulations.

Results

Effectiveness of the experimental manipulations.   The solubility–insolubility procedure appeared to be successful in inducing differential perceptions of loss of control. Two items from the postexperimental questionnaire provide the relevant data. Subjects responded to the question, "To what extent did you believe that you could not solve the [dimension] problems?"; 6 represents "definitely believed I could *not* solve them," and 1 represents "definitely believed I could solve them." The only significant term in the analysis of variance of these data was the expected Insoluble–Soluble main effect, $F(1, 41, = 8.35, p < .01$. Insoluble subjects also rated themselves as having been less "successful at solving the dimension problems" than did Soluble subjects, $F(1, 41) = 195.03, p < 001$. There were also no A–B differences or interactions on this item.

DRL effects.   The pertinent data consist of the total percentage of reinforcement [(number of reinforced responses/total number of responses) × 100] for the 45-min DRL session. Figure 7.2 presents the group means for this score. The interaction is remarkably similar to the one depicted in Figure 7.1 for choice RT latencies, except the criterion here is a delayed response, whereas a fast response was considered correct in the previous study.

Analysis of variance of the data depicted in Figure 7.2 revealed that the observed interaction was statistically significant, $F(1, 41) = 5.81, p < .02$. Subsequent contrasts using the error-mean-square from the analysis of variance indicated that Insoluble As received a greater percentage of reinforcement than did Soluble As ($p < .08$). While not approaching statistical significance, Soluble Bs tended to obtain somewhat more reinforcement than Insoluble Bs ($p > .11$). Individual contrasts also showed that Soluble As performed more poorly than Soluble Bs ($p < .05$). This effect replicated the findings reported in Chapter 5, where As and Bs worked on the DRL task without previous exposure to soluble and insoluble pretreatment.[6]

Error distributions.   Analysis of the number of responses occurring within the time segment prior to the 20–25-sec reinforcement period ("undershoots") revealed a significant Solubility–Insolubility by A–B interaction,

---

[6]One Pattern A subject in the Soluble condition had particular difficulty with the pretreatment stimulus patterns and answered incorrectly on both problems. He was told that he was correct in accordance with our usual procedure. It is doubtful that he believed this feedback, however. Analysis of the scores for total percentage of reinforcement was therefore repeated with this case deleted from the Soluble cell. The interaction term was again significant, $F(1, 40) = 7.24, p < .01$, and the contrast between Soluble and Insoluble As reached statistical significance at less than the .05 level.

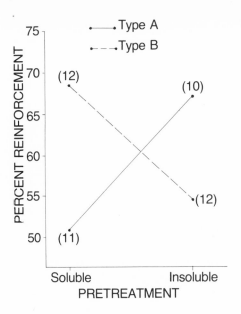

FIGURE 7.2   Percentage of reinforcement over the total DRL session. (Group sizes in parentheses.)

$F(1, 41) = 5.42$, $p < .03$. Soluble As had a greater percentage of "undershoots" (41.8%) than Soluble Bs (24.2%), Insoluble Bs (38.4%), and Insoluble As (27.9%). There were no differences between experimental groups in the number of responses occurring during the period following the reinforcement interval ("overshoots"). It would appear, then, that the inferior performance of Soluble As can be attributed to their inability to wait long enough after reinforcement. This is similar to the result obtained in the earlier study (see Chapter 5), although there the A–B difference in "undershoots" occurred specifically in the 10– to 20-sec interval.

Discussion

This experiment indicates that enhanced performance among As occurred after noncontingent compared to contingent reinforcement, even though such behavior required suppression of inferred impatience with a DRL schedule. The previous RT experiment also indicated a direct relationship between uncontrollability and Pattern A. In that study, however, acceleration of response rather than deceleration was the criterion of task mastery. Taken together, the two experiments suggest that Pattern A behavior emerges in the presence of a particular eliciting situation, namely, a threat to environmental control. This conclusion is consistent with the notion of Pattern A as a strategy for coping with uncontrollable stress; enhanced performance reflects an attempt to assert and maintain control in the face of its threatened loss.

There is a seemingly plausible alternative to this interpretation, at least for the DRL data. It might be argued that it is misleading to treat the noncontingency manipulation as an instance of loss of control, and that it is simpler to call it failure even though it has effects on feelings of control. It could then be argued that the behavior of Pattern A subjects is explicable in terms of the dual constructs of need for achievement (n Ach) and fear of failure (f Fai). Indeed, Atkinson (1957) and Weiner (1972) have developed theoretical models which propose that success depresses the performance of individuals high in resultant achievement motivation (that is, high n Ach and low f Fai), whereas failure increases their achievement strivings. A reverse set of predictions are made for individuals low in resultant achievement motivation (low n Ach and high f Fai). The applicability of this line of thought to the DRL results is obvious if we assume that Type As are individuals with high resultant motivation to succeed.

The assumption is not warranted by the facts, however. The correlation between student JAS scores and n Ach is of the order of .15, and f Fai is virtually unrelated to the student JAS (see Appendix C). It would appear, then, that Pattern A may not be an alternative label for high n Ach and low f Fai. Type As are hard-driving individuals, but their achievement motivation reflects something more than just drive for success. It can still be argued, of course, that the noncontingency manipulation induced feelings of failure and that As and Bs simply respond differently to this affective state. But such an ad hoc explanation becomes hard to distinguish from loss of control, which can account for the DRL data as well as the results obtained in the RT experiment.

Another alternative to an uncontrollability interpretation of Pattern A behavior suggests that Insoluble As in the DRL study became discouraged, responded slower, and therefore earned more reinforcements. This explanation makes the somewhat unreasonable assumption that when Insoluble As delayed their responses, they managed to locate the bulk of them precisely in the critical reinforcement interval. An equally plausible assumption is that when a subject becomes discouraged with DRL, he gives up and makes more "overshoot," or even "undershoot," responses. Recall that there were no differences between experimental groups in "overshoots" and that it was Soluble As, not Insoluble As, who showed the greatest percentage of "undershoots." Moreover, a discouragement explanation for the RT data is clearly inapplicable; No Escape As increased rather than decreased their speed of response in that study.

There is still another alternative to the uncontrollability explanation. Frustration may have been experienced to a greater extent in the uncontrollable than in the controllable conditions of both studies. Since frustration is usually interpreted as energizing motivation (e.g., Amsel & Roussel, 1952), Insoluble (or No Escape) As could have exhibited enhanced performance because they were more frustrated than their Type B counterparts. There are several difficulties with this explanation. First, both experiments failed to reveal an A–B by Treatments interaction for postexperimental ratings of frustration ($ps > .10$). Second, frustration should have produced an increase rather than a decrease in DRL response rate; indeed, there is evidence that high levels of arousal interfere with DRL performance (Singh, 1971). Third, one can choose to interpret the results—particularly those of the RT experiment—in terms of the energizing effects of frustration, but then the explanation proposes what is tantamount to a *general mechanism* which might mediate the impact of uncontrollability on Type A subjects. Precise specifications of such a mechanism are not available at this time.

ADDITIONAL DATA ON THE HYPERRESPONSIVENESS OF TYPE A SUBJECTS TO UNCONTROLLABLE STIMULATION

The preceding experiments suggest that Pattern A characteristics reflect a hyperresponsive style of coping with uncontrollable environmental stressors. Further support for this generalization can be gleaned, we believe, from studies of Pattern A performance on partial reinforcement schedules. While such procedures are usually challenging rather than stressful (that is, they emphasize the potential for reward rather than harm), nevertheless they can be construed as at least moderately stressful. For nonreinforcement on such schedules is tantamount to failure on an achievement-related task, and in these terms partial reinforcement constitutes a threat to the individual's self-esteem.

Schedules of partial reinforcement can also be manipulated so as to vary in terms of perceived uncontrollability. Consider these two schedules: (1) reinforcement occurs consistently after every fifth button press, that is, a fixed-ratio schedule (FR/5); (2) reinforcement occurs randomly such that, on the average, the subject receives reward after every five button presses, that is, a variable-ratio schedule (VR/5). Since VR/5 contains no immediately discernible contingency between responding and reinforcement, it should be perceived as more uncontrollable than FR/5. To the extent that both schedules are experienced as threatening (as just discussed), we might interpret differences in performance on VR/5 compared to FR/5 in terms of the dual notions of stress and uncontrollability.

Given the preceding line of thought, as well as the more general assumption that As try harder than Bs to assert control, we might expect As to reach an acquisition criterion more quickly than Bs in VR/5. By contrast, both types of subjects should respond at about the same rate in FR/5. These predictions were given explicit test in the next experiment and its replication. The original study was designed and conducted by James W. Pennebaker and the author; the replication was conducted in collaboration with Karen Matthews.

Design and Subjects

Male undergraduates pressed a button in order to earn nickels dispensed through a coin chute. A VR/5 condition reinforced subjects on a random basis which averaged to a nickel for every five responses. An FR/5 condition consistently provided reinforcement after every fifth button press. Acquisition was arbitrarily defined as earning 31 nickels. Half of the cases ($N = 20$) in each treatment were As, while the other half ($N = 20$) were Bs (see Appendix A).

Apparatus

The subject's response unit consisted of the following components: a counter, indicating number of nickels earned, was located in the center of a wooden panel; a nickel chute projected from beneath the panel; a nickel dispenser, which held and dispensed coins, was located behind the panel; and a response button was attached to the right side of the panel. To the left of the panel stood a vertical coin holder suitable for stacking nickels. The holder was graduated in terms of dollars of nickels up to $5.00. *Note that a high-intensity lamp illuminated the apparatus in an otherwise darkened chamber.* Number of responses and cumulative reinforcements (nickels) per 5 sec were automatically recorded throughout the session.

Procedure

Each subject was told the following:

This is an experiment dealing with various types of reinforcement schedules on learning. I am comparing this study with one I ran last spring with females to see if I get comparable results with males . . . By pressing this button appropriately you will be rewarded with nickels. The nickels that you get are yours to keep. In other words, the more efficiently you push the button, the more nickels you will earn, and the more money you will have to take home.

The experimenter then explained that the subject was to remove each nickel as it fell into the chute and place it in the nickel holder. It was also pointed out that the counter registered how many nickels were earned at any given point in time.

In order to dispel any curiosity about hidden "tricks" involved in getting nickels, all subjects were told:

> You will earn the nickels only by pressing the button. No other behavior is involved in this experiment except button-pressing. I tell you this because I've had people try to take the button apart, reach around behind the machine, and so forth. . . .

In the FR/5 treatment, subjects were reinforced with a nickel after every fifth button press. In VR/5, reinforcements were delivered randomly between 1 and 12 button presses. On the average, however, there were five responses for each reinforcement, thereby yielding an 11% probability of reward following a given response. The variable-ratio schedule was determined by a random-number generator. Subjects in both VR/5 and FR/5 received 31 nickels, the criterion of acquisition selected for the study. Total time (in seconds) to earn the 31 nickels was the principal dependent measure.[7]

San Francisco Replication

For reasons of external validity, it seemed desirable to replicate some aspects of the study with an adult sample of subjects. Accordingly, we conducted an additional experiment using only the VR/5 treatment from the original design. A variety of logistical problems made it impossible to replicate both FR/5 and VR/5.

Subjects.   Sixty-two male subjects completed the study. They ranged in age from 40 to 50 years. The median income was about $15,000 per annum, and all were federal employees working for the post office, NASA, or some related agency in the San Francisco Bay area. The majority (67%) had attended college. All subjects had completed the adult JAS, as well as the stress

---

[7] A brief period of extinction, in which no reinforcements were delivered, followed acquisition of the thirty-first nickel. Total number of button presses were recorded for all subjects. The results indicated that in VR/5, As made a higher number of responses than Bs during 1 min of extinction ($p < .01$), whereas there was no A–B difference in FR/5 ($p > .10$). Since we were unable to obtain this effect with adult subjects in the replication described next (the A–B difference for extinction in VR/5 yielded a significance level of .20), we do not discuss the student extinction data in this book. But even if the replication had been successful, we would expect, for reasons discussed in Chapters 8 and 9, substantial decrements in response among As if the extinction period were extended for a longer period of time. Indeed, button-pressing results interpretable in such terms are reported in Chapter 9.

interview. Pattern A classification was therefore possible on the basis of each of these measures.

Procedure. Specific instructions for the reinforcement task were essentially the same as those used with the college students. However, a few changes were necessary in order to motivate more sophisticated adult subjects. Therefore, emphasis was placed not on earning money but on getting as many nickels as possible, since this signified superiority to other subjects who would work on the same task.

Results

Evidence pertaining to perceived uncontrollability. All subjects in the original (college-student) experiment were asked to respond to the following rating scale in a postexperimental questionnaire: "To what extent did you feel your success or failure in earning nickels was under your own control?"; 1 represented "not under my control at all," and 7 represented "completely under my control." Analysis of variance of these data revealed that the mean response for FR/5 subjects (3.3) was greater than the mean for VR/5 subjects (2.4) at the .08 level. However, the results also indicated that while Bs in VR/5 reported less control than Bs in FR/5 ($Ms = 1.6$ and $4.0, p < .01$), type As reported about the same amount of felt control in both conditions ($Ms = 3.1$ and 2.9). We return to this result later in this chapter.

Acquisition effects. Table 7.1 shows the average number of seconds required by subjects to reach the acquisition criterion of 31 nickels. In the original experiment, it is clear that As in VR/5 reached criterion more quickly than their Type B counterparts, whereas no difference occurred between the two types of subjects in FR/5. Analysis of data in the first row of Table 7.1 yielded a significant A–B main effect, $F(1, 36) = 5.25, p < .03$, and an interaction between VR/5–FR/5 and the A–B variable, $F(1, 36) = 4.39, p = .04$.[8] Individual comparisons showed a significant difference between As and Bs in VR/5 ($p < .01$) but not in FR/5 ($p > .20$). Note also that the sluggishness of Bs in VR/5 was reflected in a reliable difference for these subjects between VR/5 and FR/5 ($p < .05$). There were no other significant differences between individual cell means ($ps > .20$).

---

[8] A similar pair of effects were obtained when the analysis was done on mean number of responses per 5-sec intervals averaged across acquisition trials. The time measure was selected for presentation here because of contamination of the button-press data; that is, there were forced delays in the subject's responding due to his having to stack nickels and wait for the coin to come down the chute. In Chapter 10, we present a partial-reinforcement experiment in which such delays were eliminated. Mean number of button presses were used as the principal dependent measure in that study.

TABLE 7.1
Mean Number of Seconds to Reach Acquisition

Study	Experimental group			
	FR/5, A	FR/5, B	VR/5, A	VR/5, B
Original experiment (students)[a]	275.4	280.2	248.4	349.2
San Francisco replication (adults)[b]	—	—	230.8[c]	294.3

[a] The cell Ns are 10.
[b] The cell Ns are 26 and 36, respectively.
[c] Classification of subjects was based on the adult JAS, with those scoring above the standardized mean of 0.0 being treated as As and those scoring below as Bs (see Chapter 3 and Appendix A).

The A–B difference in the variable-ratio treatment also occurred in the replication with adult subjects. Analysis of the second row of Table 7.1 revealed the expected effect, that is, time to the acquisition criterion was again shorter for As than Bs $[t(60) = 2.61, p = .01]$. These data were reanalyzed in terms of an A–B classification based on the stress interview. Six cases diagnosed as Type X (see Chapter 3) were eliminated from analysis. The mean times (in seconds) to a criterion of 31 nickels were 247.6 for As and 303.0 for Bs $[t(54) = 2.04, p < .05]$. Clearly these results are virtually identical to those obtained with the adult JAS as the basis for A–B classification.

Discussion

The results of the two experiments indicate that Pattern A subjects, whether college students or working adults, reached an acquisition criterion more quickly than Pattern B subjects when both groups were trained on a variable–ratio schedule. There were no individual differences in speed of acquisition on a fixed-ratio schedule. These results might be explained in terms of differences in amount of frustration (cf. Amsel & Roussel, 1952). A similar alternative was discussed in connection with the two previous experiments in this chapter. A principal difficulty with the frustration interpretation of our acquisition results is the lack of differential perceptions of frustration in As and Bs. On a postexperimental questionnaire, both groups in the adult sample reported feeling equally frustrated by VR/5 $(p > .20)$. In the college sample, Type Bs tended to report greater frustration (on a 7-point rating scale) than Type As, irrespective of the reinforcement schedule $(Ms = 3.4$ and $2.6, p = .07)$.

An alternative possibility is that As and Bs were equally frustrated by the variable-ratio schedule (which was more frustrating than the fixed-ratio schedule), but As reacted with enhanced button pressing whereas Bs tended to give up efforts at responding. This type of explanation is, however, similar to the line of thought which emphasizes perceived uncontrollability as the motivating factor in producing acquisition effects. It can thus be argued that Pattern A subjects exerted greater efforts than Pattern B subjects because the variable-ratio schedule was experienced as an uncontrollable stimulus. By contrast, the FR/5 schedule was controllable and therefore A–B differences did not appear.

The postexperimental ratings of control provide some support for this interpretation. Recall that the VR/5 schedule was perceived as more uncontrollable than the FR/5 schedule. While Type Bs were primarily responsible for this difference (As actually reported the same amount of felt control in VR/5 and FR/5), it should be noted that control ratings were made at the end of the study. Thus, the absence of a VR/5–FR/5 difference for Type As may reflect nothing more than a veridical perception of their superior acquisition performance.

Our tentative conclusion, then, is to interpret A–B differences in acquisition in terms of the greater uncontrollability of the variable-ratio schedule compared to the fixed-ratio schedule. To the extent that these reinforcement schedules were somewhat stressful for our subjects, as suggested earlier in this section, the VR/5–FR/5 research provides further support for the idea that, compared to Bs, As react to uncontrollable stress by increasing their efforts to assert control.

SUMMARY AND CONCLUSIONS

The four experiments reported in this chapter lend some credence to the general hypothesis that Pattern A characteristics reflect a style of response aimed at achieving and maintaining control over environmental stressors. It was previously suggested, however, that Type As will stop asserting control when they become convinced that the stressful event is in fact uncontrollable. Such an effect might have occurred in the RT or DRL studies if, for example, subjects had experienced a much longer series of uncontrollable stimuli during pretreatment. In other words, amount of exposure to uncontrollability may determine whether facilitation or giving up (helplessness) responses will occur (cf. Roth & Kubal, 1975; Wortman & Brehm, 1975). While the initial reaction of Pattern A individuals is to assert control, extended experience with uncontrollability is presumed to lead to more passive behavior in As than in Bs. The research reported in this chapter provided evidence for the hyperresponsiveness part of this hypothesis. The next chapter is specifically concerned with hyporesponsiveness.

8
Pattern A
and Extended Exposure
to Uncontrollable Stress

Previous research has shown that behavioral response to aversive stimuli depends on the individual's history of success or failure in controlling his environment (e.g., Glass & Singer, 1972). Seligman (1975) has proposed a learned-helplessness hypothesis, as described in the last chapter, to account for this phenomenon. To recapitulate, the theory states that uncontrollable pretreatment results in learning that instrumental responding is independent of outcomes. Such learning interferes with subsequent performance because low expectations of reinforcement depress response initiation, and there is proactive impairment of learning the association between responding and reinforcement. A number of studies have confirmed this line of thought with both humans and infrahuman species (e.g., Glass & Singer, 1972; Hiroto, 1974; Roth & Kubal, 1975; Seligman & Maier, 1967).

The last chapter showed that frustration of efforts at control elicited more subsequent controlling behavior in As than in Bs. Other results indicated that, compared to Bs, Type As reacted to uncontrollability with enhanced responding designed to assert control. However, direct coping responses of this kind must, in the long run, prove ineffective with uncontrollable stimuli. Extended exposure to uncontrollability should thus lead to the perception of a noncontingency between responses and outcomes, in which case the individual may be expected to give up efforts at control and experience learned helplessness. These effects should be greater in Pattern A than in Pattern B individuals, since As are assumed to experience lack of control over a stressor as more threatening than Bs. While Type As may increase their efforts at control when threatened with its loss, nevertheless we should observe greater helplessness in As than in Bs when exposure to uncontrollable stimulation finally convinces them that they cannot in fact exert control.[1] Wortman and Brehm (1975) have

---

[1] Recall that college-student As showed a greater level of responding than their Type B counterparts during a 1-min extinction period following a VR/5 training schedule (see footnote 7 in Chapter 7). We would expect such a difference (assuming it is indeed reliable) to disappear if extinction were extended for a longer period of time.

recently proposed a similar line of thought in which initial reactions to uncontrollable events take the form of increased efforts to control (that is, facilitation), whereas extended exposure leads to helplessness.

The learned-helplessness paradigm was used to test our notions about Pattern A and prolonged uncontrollability in the study described next (see Krantz, Glass, & Snyder, 1974, Experiment I). Assuming that Type As feel more helpless than Type Bs after extended uncontrollable pretreatment, we may expect As to show greater interference with later escape and/or avoidance learning than their Type B counterparts. Controllable pretreatment should have minimal impact on the subsequent learning of the two types of subjects, although the hard-driving characteristic of the Type A might result in somewhat superior learning. Since previous research (Thornton & Jacobs, 1971) suggests that learned helplessness is potentiated by high as compared to moderate levels of stress, we incorporated a stress-level manipulation as an explicit component of the experimental design. However, as we shall see later, the results indicated a more complex relationship in which the magnitude of stress mediates the nature of the reaction of As and Bs to uncontrollable stimulation.

LEARNED HELPLESSNESS: EXPERIMENT I

Overview

Subjects were exposed to loud or moderate noise in an effort to induce differential degrees of stress. Thirty-five noise bursts, rather than the 12 used in the first study reported in Chapter 7, were administered to each subject. Since previous research shows that 35 inescapable noise trials lead to learned helplessness (e.g., Hiroto, 1974), we decided to treat this number as constituting extended uncontrollability in this study. Half of the subjects within each stress-level condition were unable to escape from noise (No Escape condition), whereas the other half could affect termination by manipulating two rotary switches (Escape condition). Approximately half of the cases in each treatment were Type As, and the other half were Type Bs. After the pretreatment phase, subjects were exposed to the same intensity of noise received in the first part of the experiment. All subjects in this test phase could escape or avoid the noise bursts by making an appropriate response with a shuttle box lever. The major dependent variables were measured in the test phase and included such indices as number of trials to a criterion for escape and/or avoidance learning.

Subjects

Sixty male undergraduates were randomly assigned to the experimental conditions. (Four additional cases were not included in the results: one because of equipment failure, and three because of their suspicions of the experimental manipulations.) Subjects were classified as A or B, depending upon whether they scored above or below the sample median for the student JAS. The test was administered to most of the subjects at the end of the experimental session.

Apparatus

In pretreatment, the subject's response unit consisted of a 16 × 18 × 6-inch wooden box in which two spring-loaded rotary switches were located. Large knobs were attached to the rotary switches. Red and green signal lights were also built into the box. The red light was activated simultaneously with the acoustic stimulus and remained on for the duration of a trial. The green light signaled a correct response.

In the test phase, the response unit was a modified "Manipulandum Type-S" human shuttle box (Turner & Solomon, 1962). The unit contained a 1½-inch handle mounted on a sliding wooden block embedded in a channel in the box. A hidden relay was located at each side of the channel. Moving the handle left or right from one end of the box to the other terminated all circuits. Hunter clock counters recorded all response latencies to the nearest .01 sec.

A tape recorder delivered a 3000-Hz tone generated by an audio oscillator set for 107 dB(A) (High Stress) or 78 dB(A) (Moderate Stress). The sound was presented over earphones. The oscillator output used with each Escape subject was recorded on audio tape for later delivery to a yoked subject assigned to a comparable No Escape condition. In other words, subjects in High Stress–No Escape conditions were yoked to those in High Stress–Escape conditions, whereas subjects in Moderate Stress–No Escape were yoked to those in Moderate Stress–Escape. This procedure equated each set of Escape and No Escape treatments in terms of duration and intermittency of noise.

Physiological Recording

Palmar skin conductance was measured with a Beckman Type R Dynograph recorder and a Type 9844 Skin Conductance coupler. Beckman biopotential electrodes were placed on the volar surface of the middle segment of the first and third fingers of the subject's nonpreferred hand. A ground electrode was placed on the wrist of the same arm.

Procedure

The study was presented to each subject as being concerned with the effects of noise on human physiology. A 3-sec sample of noise appropriate to the subject's stress condition was then delivered over earphones. After this, the phones were removed and an option to leave was given to the subject. All subjects elected to stay in the experiment. Electrodes were then attached and the subject relaxed for 10 min.

Next, the experimenter reentered the laboratory chamber and explained that the subject would be working on some tasks as he listened to noise. The headphones were put in place, and the pretreatment response unit was moved in front of the subject. The experimenter then returned to the observation room and activated tape-recorded instructions.

Pretreatment phase.   All subjects listened to instructions similar to those used in the noise experiment reported in Chapter 7.

In Escape conditions, subjects could terminate each noise burst by rotating two knobs on the response unit (in any order) as far as they could go, that is, approximately 270 degrees. The green light appeared when the knobs were correctly rotated. Both noise and light terminated 0.5 sec later. These procedures were designed to assure that Escape subjects received at least several seconds of noise on each trial and were aware of their successful termination of a noise burst. The noise ended automatically after 8 sec if a subject did not make the required response. The 35 noise trials ranged from 2 to 8 sec per trial, with a mean duration across conditions of 5.3 sec. Intertrial intervals varied randomly from 15 to 33 sec, with a mean of 20 sec.

Subjects in the two yoked No Escape conditions were unable to terminate noise because the rotary knobs were unconnected to the stimulus circuitry. However, the pretreatment instructions led them to believe that noise termination was possible—precisely the instructions given to Escape subjects.

After pretreatment, the experimenter reentered the laboratory chamber, removed the headphones, and asked the subject to complete a brief questionnaire asking for ratings of noise unpleasantness and feelings of control over noise termination.

Test phase.   The test-phase response unit was moved in front of the subject. He was told to put on the headphones and wait for further instructions. The experimenter returned to the observation room and activated taped instructions heard as follows:

You will be given some trials in which noise will be presented to you at different intervals. Now here is the important part, and I want you to listen carefully. Whenever you hear the noise come on, there is something you can do to stop it. What you do is really up to you to figure out. There is a solution to the problem, and if you figure it out the noise will stop. Therefore, the amount of unpleasantness you receive is dependent on *your* skills and ability to find a solution to the problem. You are potentially in control of the situation.

The test phase of the study consisted of 18 10-sec trials. The white light was automatically activated 5 sec prior to each of the noise bursts. An avoidance response was possible during this foreperiod. The signal light terminated contiguous with onset of noise. Subjects were exposed to the same level of noise delivered during pretreatment, that is, the High-Stress group received 107-dB(A) noise and the Moderate Stress group received 78-dB(A) noise.

A correct response avoided or terminated noise instantaneously for a given trial. The response was to slide a handle to the left or to the right so as to touch the side of the shuttle box most distant from the position of the handle at the beginning of that trial and then move it back to touch the other side of the box. This sequence of movements terminated the trial and stopped the counter. An avoidance response terminated the signal light, and noise was not heard on that trial. An escape response terminated noise at any time after noise onset. If a response was not made within 10 sec, the noise automatically stopped and a latency of 10 sec was recorded for that trial.

Postsession.   After the test phase, a questionnaire was completed similar to the one given after pretreatment. Subjects were then questioned about their perceptions of control over noise during pretreatment and test phases of the study. Sixty percent of the No Escape subjects reported feeling little control during pretreatment because of their inability to find a way of terminating noise. The remaining No Escape subjects suggested that lack of control may have been due to the fact that there was no way of actually escaping from noise.

Dependent Variables

Five major response variables were used to measure helplessness-induced interference with escape–avoidance learning in the test phase of the experiment. These were (1) response latency, where an appropriate response in less than 5 sec (that is, prior to noise onset) constituted an avoidance, and response latencies between 5 and 10 sec were defined as escape responses; (2) number of escape responses over the 18 test trials; (3) number of avoidance responses; (4) number of escapes plus avoidances; (5) trials to criterion for escape and/or avoidance learning, defined as three consecutive escape and/or avoidance responses.

Results

Effectiveness of the stress-level manipulation. The two levels of noise intensity appeared to be successful in inducing high and moderate levels of stress. Support for this conclusion comes from ratings of noise unpleasantness on a scale ranging from 6 ("very unpleasant") to 1 ("not at all unpleasant"). High Stress subjects rated the noise as more unpleasant than Moderate Stress subjects after both pretreatment and test phases of the study. The means for post-pretreatment were 4.5 and 2.3, $F(1, 52) = 54.06, p < .001$; for post–test phase, the means were 4.3 and 2.3, $F(1, 52) = 33.06, p < .001$. There were no reliable differences between Escape and No Escape treatments in both analyses ($ps > .20$). There were also no A–B main effects ($ps > .20$) or interactions between this variable and either of the experimental factors ($ps > .20$).

Additional data assessing the effectiveness of the stress manipulation comes from the automatic measurements made during pretreatment; namely, the magnitude of phasic skin conductance reactions (SCR), where the maximum SCR to each of the 35 noise bursts was measured in log (base 10) of conductance-change units. These data were blocked into seven groups of five trials each and subjected to a repeated-measures analysis of variance (the A–B factor by High–Moderate Stress by Escape–No Escape by Trial Blocks). There was a significant main effect for the Stress Level variable ($Ms = 2.57$ and 2.24), which supports the assumption that noise produced differential levels of stress, $F(1, 52) = 11.51, p < .002$. There was also a reliable Trial-Blocks term, $F(6, 312) = 16.36, p < .001$, which may be interpreted as reflecting autonomic adaptation to successive noise stimuli (cf. Glass & Singer, 1972).

The analysis also revealed a lower mean SCR for No Escape subjects than for Escape subjects $[Ms = 2.14$ and 2.68; $F(1, 52) = 31.17, p < .001]$. A principal source of this difference was an exceptionally low level of reactivity in the Moderate Stress–No Escape condition ($M = 1.91$). Closely related to these results was a significant Escape–No Escape by Trial Blocks interaction, $F(6, 312) = 6.62, p < .001$. It appears that SCR diminished more rapidly for the No Escape than the Escape group. Both of these effects can probably be interpreted as electrodermal correlates of decreased task motivation in helpless subjects (discussed next). Similar results have been obtained in a recent study by Gatchel and Proctor (1976).

Effectiveness of the helplessness manipulation. The Escape–No Escape treatment was successful in inducing feelings of helplessness and lack of control. Self-ratings of helplessness were made on a 6-point scale immediately after the test phase of the study. Subjects in the No Escape condition reported feeling significantly more helpless during the experiment than those in the Escape condition [$Ms = 3.6$ and 2.7; $F(1, 52) = 4.48, p < .04$]. There was no evidence of other significant main effects or interactions. It should also be noted here that No Escape subjects, irrespective of their A–B classification, behaved in a helpless fashion during the test phase. Several cases sat dejectedly throughout the test series and passively listened to the noise bursts. However, most subjects engaged in "superstitious" and other behaviors aimed at escaping from noise.

Subjects also responded to the question, "How much control did you feel you have over termination of the noise?"; 6 represented "complete control," and 1 represented "no control at all." These ratings were made after pretreatment and again after the test phase, although the item referred in both cases to the subject's experience during pretreatment. For post-pretreatment, Escape subjects reported more control over noise offset than No Escape subjects [$Ms = 4.4$ and 1.3; $F(1, 52) = 79.08, p < .001$]. There were no A–B main effects ($p > .40$) and no interactions with the other variables ($ps > .20$).

The Escape–No Escape result was understandably weaker after the test phase ($Ms = 5.0$ and 3.9), since most No Escape subjects eventually learned the escape response. However, a separate analysis of the post-test-phase ratings showed a reliable effect due to the Escape–No Escape manipulation, $F(1,52) = 5.26, p < .02$. There was, in addition, an A–B main effect, $F(1, 52) = 3.99, p < .05$, and an A–B by stress-level interaction, $F(1, 52) = 4.24, p < .05$. Subsequent examination of individual cell means revealed that the latter effects were attributable to a low rating of control by Type Bs in Moderate Stress–No Escape ($M = 2.1$), which was significantly lower ($p < .02$) than the mean ratings for Type As in that cell ($M = 5.1$). This result may reflect nothing more than a veridical perception by Bs that they gave up in Moderate Stress–No Escape, but it is also possible that As engaged in some type of distortion which led to denial of lack of control. We will return to the issue of denial later in this chapter.

To sum up, the stress-arousal manipulation proved successful as measured by retrospective ratings of subjective unpleasantness and phasic skin conductance reactivity during pretreatment trials. Self-rating results showed that the Escape–No Escape manipulation was also effective, insofar as it induced feelings of helplessness and lack of control over the noise.

Test phase results. Analyses of variance were conducted on each of the five response variables sensitive to helplessness-induced interference effects. The most impressive results occurred with number of trials to criterion for

TABLE 8.1
Mean Number of Trials to Criterion for Escape and/or
Avoidance Learning[a]

Condition	Escape	No Escape
High Stress, Pattern A	6.3 ($N = 9$)	12.7 ($N = 9$)
High Stress, Pattern B	7.2 ($N = 6$)	8.7 ($N = 6$)
Moderate Stress, Pattern A	7.7 ($N = 7$)	8.5 ($N = 6$)
Moderate Stress, Pattern B	9.0 ($N = 8$)	20.1 ($N = 9$)

[a] Comparisons between cell means were conducted using the error-mean-square from the three-way analysis of variance. These comparisons revealed a number of significant differences ($p < .05$ or better), including those between the following cell means: (1) 12.7 and 6.3; (2) 20.1 and 9.0; (3) 20.1 and 8.7; (4) 20.1 and 8.5. The differences between 12.7 and 8.5 and between 9.0 and 7.2 were not statistically significant ($ps > .20$).

escape and/or avoidance learning. Table 8.1 presents the relevant mean scores on this variable. These data show an Escape–No Escape main effect, $F(1, 52) = 8.91$, $p < .01$, a significant Stress Level by A–B interaction, $F(1, 52) = 5.91$, $p < .02$, and a significant triple interaction, $F(1, 52) = 5.26$, $p < .02$. This last term indicates that under moderate levels of uncontrollable stress, Type A subjects take fewer trials to learn the escape and/or avoidance response than Type B subjects. Just the opposite occurs in the High Stress condition, although the A–B difference is less pronounced. While there are minimal differences between Pattern A and Pattern B subjects under controllable noise conditions, there is the expected tendency for As to show better learning than do Bs under both levels of stress.

The foregoing pattern of results was obtained with three of the other four response variables used in this study. Only "number of avoidances" failed to show a reliable effect attributable to the A–B factor. A detailed description of these results can be found in Krantz et al. (1974).

Discussion

Examination of Table 8.1 shows that Pattern A subjects react to uncontrollable stress of moderate intensity by attempting to escape from the stressor, just as they do with controllable stress. By contrast, Pattern B subjects give up in the face of a moderately aversive uncontrollable stressor. The difference between the cell means of 20.1 and 9.0 is statistically significant at less than the .05 level. The picture changes with an increment in stress level. The Pattern A individual shows a decrease in escape responses relative to his performance under controllable stress ($p < .05$). The Pattern B individual performs at about the same level in both Escape and No Escape conditions. These results are indeed surprising. Initial expectations called for an interaction between the A–B variable and controllability–uncontrollability, but the data suggest a more complex relationship in which stress level somehow mediates the reactions of As and Bs.

A seemingly obvious approach to interpreting our results would be to invoke the concept of autonomic arousal, that is, As are simply more aroused than Bs (e.g., Fiske & Maddi, 1961). Unfortunately, the A–B variable failed to show reliable associations with the skin conductance measures collected in pretreatment. There was no indication of a consistent pattern of autonomic arousal that might account for the interaction of stress level, inescapability, and the A–B variable. Subjective reports of arousal were also inadequate for purposes of interpretation. Recall that both Pattern A and Pattern B subjects agreed in their assessments that 107-dB(A) sound was more unpleasant than 78-dB(A) sound.

It is possible that differences in arousal reactions of As and Bs were not detected in our experiment because of insufficient sampling of autonomic channels and/or dimensions of subjective discomfort. On the other hand, published research has failed to detect A–B differences on other channels such as heart rate (e.g., Friedman, Rosenman, & Brown, 1963), and studies in our own laboratory have been singularly unsuccessful in producing A–B differences in heart-rate and finger-vasoconstriction responses to high-intensity periodic and aperiodic noise. The possibility exists, of course, that electrophysiological measurements of this kind are insensitive to A–B differences in autonomic reactions to uncontrollable stress. It is also possible that the conditions under which our physiological readings were taken were not appropriate for detecting A–B differences. However, since other types of arousal measurements were not taken from our subjects, we cannot seriously explore the usefulness of such data at this time. The measurements we did take, and the conditions under which they were taken, failed to support the viability of differential arousal as an explanation of why Type B subjects showed greater learned helplessness in the Moderate Stress condition, whereas Type As exhibited greater helplessness in High Stress.[2] A cognitive interpretation is, therefore, proposed in the next section.

A COGNITIVE INTERPRETATION OF LEARNED-HELPLESSNESS EFFECTS

A number of investigators (e.g., Langer, 1973) have suggested that people tend to distort cues signifying lack of environmental control; we all tend to avoid the negative consequences that often accompany the perception of having no control. Since Pattern A individuals are presumably more concerned than

---

[2] Comments on an arousal explanation can also be found in Chapter 12, where by way of conclusion we again suggest that such an approach does not provide a coherent interpretation of the range of data reported in this monograph.

Pattern B individuals about maintaining control (and avoiding its loss), we might expect As to be more prone to such perceptual distortions. Indeed, when uncontrollability cues have low prominence and do not compel attention, Type As should find it relatively easy to deny lack of control. Under these circumstances, As may engage in minimal activity directed toward asserting control and, perhaps, make attributions aimed at enhancing their sense of mastery. If, on the other hand, uncontrollability cues are a salient feature of their environment, As should experience considerable difficulty in ignoring their presence and thus exert enhanced efforts at control.

We recognize that the notion of cue prominence of salience is vague and imprecise. It is admittedly difficult to define, a priori, when a stimulus is above or below a threshold of salience for a given individual. However, since the salience concept had heuristic value in our research, we will attempt to define it here as precisely as possible. Following Schachter and Rodin (1974), cue salience refers broadly to "those stimulus or stimulus-field properties which compel or attract a subject's attention." At the most basic level, the concept could be defined in terms of the physical intensity of the stimulus, but other properties such as novelty, unpredictability, and the relationship to other elements in the stimulus field obviously play an important role in compelling attention. In these terms, a cue signaling uncontrollability would be one which attracts the subject's attention, as, for example, loud rather than soft inescapable noise, or undeniable failure on a task as opposed to failure that might be attributed to the effects of chance factors.

We suggested above that As distort uncontrollability cues that are low in salience but are unable to do so when cues are prominent and not easily ignored. The assumption is that any uncontrollable stimulus above a given threshold is more likely to elicit an escape response from a Type A than from a Type B subject. It might be expected, therefore, that As are more responsive than Bs only to salient uncontrollability cues; when cues are weak, As will actually respond less strongly than Bs because the possibility of lack of control is distorted, or at least not effectively encoded.[3]

---

[3] The uncontrollability-salience hypothesis is similar to a cue-salience explanation proposed by Schachter to account for the heightened responsiveness of obese compared to normal individuals (Schachter & Rodin, 1974). It is only to stimuli high in salience that the obese are more responsive than are normal subjects. Moreover, hyperreactivity to external cues appears to characterize not only the eating behavior of obese individuals, but behaviors unrelated to food as well. Our own version of cue salience differs in this respect, for we only propose that As are hyperresponsive to uncontrollability cues. Subsequent research may suggest a broader interpretation, and Krantz (1975) has indeed detected a few behavioral similarities between obese and Pattern A individuals in a recent series of laboratory experiments. On the other hand, there is little evidence of a direct correlation between obesity and Pattern A, either for adult males (Friedman, 1969) or college-age males. We have computed correlation coefficients for six of our experiments in which obesity and Type A scores were available. An index of obesity—percentage-of-weight deviation (see Schachter & Rodin, 1974)—correlated near zero with the student JAS (rs ranged from .00 to +.11).

It is probably safe to assume that systematic variations in noise intensity are analogous to variations of cue salience [at least one study has documented the validity of such a construction (Pliner, 1974)], in which case lack of control will be more salient for As in high- than moderate-noise pretreatment. Type As should thus experience a greater threat to their sense of control in the high-noise condition and exert greater efforts to locate control-relevant cues. This enhanced activity should lead, in turn, to a stronger certainty that nothing can be done about terminating noise. This expectation might be reflected in eventual extinction of escape attempts during pretreatment, but in any case it should transfer to the test phase of the learned-helplessness paradigm, where it appears as a decrement in response initiation. The final prediction was, of course, confirmed by data from the high-noise condition of the learned-helplessness study.

A similar logic might explain the relative absence of helplessness effects among As in the moderate-noise condition. Assume that Type As did not effectively encode the noncontingency between responses and noise termination. Evidence for this assumption comes from the fact that As in Moderate Stress–No Escape reported more felt control than their Type B counterparts, at least after the test phase of the study. This result may indicate that As were denying the uncontrollable nature of the noise. In consequence, we would expect As to show a lower level of responding during pretreatment and thus fail to develop expectations of uncontrollability. Without these expectations, there might be relatively little evidence of depressed escape behavior on the subsequent test-phase task—precisely the effects obtained in our experiment.

To recapitulate, Pattern A subjects showed depressed response initiation after exposure to uncontrollable loud noise relative to their escape behavior following controllable noise of comparable intensity. Pattern B subjects, by contrast, showed learned helplessness only after uncontrollable noise of moderate intensity. Making the assumption that variations in noise intensity correspond to variations in salience, we propose a cue-salience explanation of this interaction. Type As respond initially to uncontrollability cues of high salience with enhanced efforts at control. Therefore, they learn that a noncontingency exists between responses and outcomes, and this leads to expectations of no control which generalize to the test phase of the learned-helplessness paradigm. When uncontrollability cues are low in salience, As exert less effort than Bs at achieving control, less effectively encode the fact of noncontingency, and hence fail to show subsequent learned helplessness.

LEARNED HELPLESSNESS: EXPERIMENT II

The foregoing line of thought was given explicit test in an experiment conducted by Jack F. Hollis and the author. It was essentially a replication of the previous learned-helplessness experiment, except pretreatment consisted of contingent and noncontingent reinforcement on the same cognitive tasks used in the second study reported in Chapter 7. Four dimension problems instead of two were used in the Hollis study, on the assumption that noncontingent reinforcement on all four constituted more extended exposure to uncontrollability. Previous research (e.g., Hiroto & Seligman, 1975) has, in fact, documented learned helplessness following pretreatment with noncontingency on the four dimension problems.

Salience was manipulated orthogonally in the experimental design. A non-noise procedure was used for this purpose in order to avoid the potential confound inherent in treating noise intensity as a variation of salience. Noise may produce differences in emotional arousal along with differences in salience. Learned helplessness effects were also measured under nonnoise conditions with still another cognitive task, that is, anagrams.

An A–B × salience × uncontrollability interaction in this study would replicate previous results and, in so doing, provide empirical support for the idea that salience of uncontrollability cues does indeed mediate the learned-helplessness effects observed in Type A and Type B subjects. The specific prediction was that As would show helplessness after exposure to salient uncontrollable events (pretreatment), but not after similar exposure under conditions of low salience. By contrast, Pattern B subjects were expected to manifest learned helplessness only after uncontrollable pretreatment of low salience.

Subjects

Thirty-two Type A and 32 Type B college females participated in the study. (The A–B classification was based on a median split as described in Appendix A.[4])

Design

Half of the subjects in each A–B category were randomly assigned to a noncontingent, or Insoluble, condition; the other half were placed in a contingent, or Soluble, condition. Within each of the treatments, half of the cases

[4]Several additional cases were eliminated from the study for the following reasons: (a) four subjects did not understand or follow instructions for the dimension task and the anagrams task; (b) two subjects suspected the true purpose of the study; (c) three subjects in the Soluble condition missed all of the dimension problems. The eliminated cases were about evenly distributed across experimental groups.

listened to the experimenter evaluate their performance on the series of four dimension tasks (Low Salience). The remaining subjects not only listened to these evaluations but, in addition, kept a written record of the evaluations (High Salience). After pretreatment, subjects were asked to work on a series of five-letter anagrams that served as the principal test for learned helplessness. All anagrams in this test phase of the study could be solved.

Procedure

After the subject was seated in the laboratory, instructions were given for the dimension task—the pretreatment phase of the study. These instructions were virtually identical to those described for Experiment II in Chapter 7.

After the preliminary instructions and some practice trials, the dimension problems in the test series were presented to the subject. Four different problems were administered in blocks of 10 trials each. At the end of each trial, the subject was asked to choose which side of the card he thought contained the "correct" value. As in the earlier study, subjects in the Insoluble conditions received a predetermined schedule of "correct" (C) and "incorrect" (I), regardless of which side was chosen. The schedule of reinforcements were: (a) C–I–I–C–C–I–I–C–C–I for the first problem; (b) I–C–I–C–C –I–C–I–C–I for the second problem; (c) I–C–I–C–I–C–C–I–C–I for the third problem; and (d) C–I–C–I–I–C–I–C–I–C for the last problem. In addition, Insoluble subjects were told, "That's the wrong answer," when they were asked to identify the correct value at the end of each of the four dimension tasks.

Subjects in the Soluble conditions were given contingent correct and incorrect evaluations after each trial. They were also informed, "That's the right answer," when asked to identify the correct value. The criterion for learning was identification of the correct value for three or more of the four problems. Only eight cases gave an incorrect value as their final answer on any of the problems. Five of these subjects were incorrect on one or two of the four problems, and the experimenter still told them they were "right." These cases were retained in the study. Another three subjects gave incorrect final answers on all four problems and, moreover, reported that they were unconvinced when the experimenter said they were correct. These cases (two Bs and one A) were eliminated from the study, as indicated in footnote (4).

Salience manipulation.   Half of the subjects in the Soluble and Insoluble conditions received evaluative feedback from the experimenter as described above (Low Salience condition). The remaining subjects were assigned to a condition in which efforts were made to enhance their awareness of contingency and noncontingency (High Salience condition). These subjects were required to keep a written record of "correct" and "incorrect" answers. They were provided with a tally sheet consisting of 10-line columns, headed "correct" and "incorrect," for each of the four sets of dimension problems. The sheet also contained the words, "right" and "wrong" next to each of the four pairs of columns. Checkmarks were to be placed in one or the other column for each of the 10 trials of a given problem. These tallies corresponded to whether the subject's choices were correct or incorrect according to the experimenter. Subjects were also told to circle "right" or "wrong" at the end of each pair of columns, depending on whether or not they had finally guessed the right value. This procedure made it relatively simple for subjects to see how they were doing on the problems throughout the session, thereby enhancing their perceptions of contingency or noncontingency.

Test phase.   After completion of the pretreatment task, the experimenter returned to the laboratory and collected the booklet of dimension problems. The instructions for the test phase of the study were then delivered. They were adapted from Hiroto and Seligman (1975) as follows:

> You will now be asked to solve some anagrams. As you may know, anagrams are words with the letters scrambled. The problem for you is to unscramble the letters so that they form a word. Use all the letters to form a word, and do not look back through previous words as you work through the series of anagrams. When you find a word for a given anagram, tell me what it is over the intercom system. Now there could be a pattern which will enable you to solve the anagrams, but that's up to you to figure out. I can't answer any questions now. After the experiment is over, I'll answer all questions. I will not be telling you this time whether your solutions are right or wrong.

> The subject received a stack of 20 index cards on which the anagrams were printed. The experimenter then reentered the observation room and signaled the subject to begin work. Time to solution for each anagram was recorded to the nearest second. After solving a given anagram, the subject announced his solution and proceeded to the next card. Subjects were not told there was a time limit on each anagram, but if they exceeded 100 sec without giving an answer, the experimenter announced, "Please move on to the next card." In cases where the subject gave a nonsense word, the experimenter said, "That's not a word. Please try again."

> All 20 anagrams were soluble and had the same letter sequence, that is, 3-4-2-1-5. The anagrams could be solved individually, but the simplest method was to learn the letter sequence. The anagrams were selected so that only one word could be arranged with each anagram. The specific letter sequence was taken from a list of five-letter anagrams judged to be of intermediate to high difficulty (Hiroto & Seligman, 1975; Tresselt & Mayzner,

1966). Examples of the anagrams were (1) I A R T D; (2) B I A H T; (3) G A U S R; (4) E R L C K.

Three measures of anagram performance were used as dependent variables: (1) trials to criterion for anagram solution, which was defined as solving three consecutive anagrams in less than 15 sec each[5]; (2) number of failures to solve the anagram within 100 sec; (3) mean response latency for the 20 anagrams. These variables were designed to measure interference with learning the anagrams task. They correspond to the indices used in the previous learned-helplessness study, just as the insolubility–solubility pretreatment was designed to parallel uncontrollable–controllable noise.

Results

Effectiveness of the solubility–insolubility manipulation. The procedures used during pretreatment appeared to be successful in inducing differential feelings of lack of control and helplessness. Three items from a postexperimental questionnaire provide the relevant information. Two of the items were worded to determine if subjects attributed uncontrollability to themselves or to the dimension tasks. The first asked, "To what extent did you believe that you couldn't solve the dimension problems?"; 7 represented "definitely believed I could solve them," and 1 represented "definitely believed I could not solve them." The mean ratings were 5.7 for Soluble subjects and 4.2 for Insoluble subjects, $F(1, 56) = 18.70$, $p < .002$. There was, in addition, a salience by solubility–insolubility interaction, $F(1, 56) = 2.83$, $p < .09$, and an A–B by solubility–insolubility interaction, $F(1, 56) = 4.12$, $p < .05$. The first of these terms reflects the greater effectiveness of the insolubility manipulation in the High Salience condition than in Low Salience. This manipulation is therefore discussed in the next section. The other term indicates that Bs reported greater control than did As in the Soluble condition ($Ms = 6.1, 5.1$; $p < .02$), whereas a nonsignificant reversal occurred in the Insoluble condition ($Ms = 3.8, 4.5$; $p > .15$).

The second item pertaining to the effectiveness of the insolubility manipulation asked, "To what extent did you believe the dimension problems were insoluble—that they couldn't be solved?"; 7 represented "definitely believed they were soluble," and 1 represented "definitely believed they were insoluble." Subjects in the Soluble conditions had a mean rating of 6.1, which was significantly greater than the mean rating of 4.5 for Insoluble subjects, $F(1, 56) = 17.64$, $p < .001$. There were no interactions among insolubility, salience, and the A–B variable on this item ($p s > .15$).

Self-ratings of helplessness were also made on a 7-point scale in the

---

[5] Reaching this criterion indicated that the subject had become aware of the principle of a fixed letter sequence.

postexperimental questionnaire. Subjects in the Insoluble conditions reported feeling more helpless during the study than those in the Soluble conditions [Ms = 4.4, 2.9; $F(1, 56)$ = 15.54, $p < .001$]. There were no other significant effects or interactions ($ps > .20$).

Effectiveness of the salience manipulation.   The procedures designed to induce differential salience appeared to be successful. Support for this conclusion comes from the two items reported in the previous section. Individual comparisons (using error terms from the analyses of variance) indicated that in the High Salience condition, Insoluble subjects believed that they lacked the ability to solve the dimension problems to a greater extent than did Soluble subjects (Ms = 3.9, 6.1, $p < .02$). A similar trend under Low Salience (Ms = 4.3, 5.3) did not reach statistical significance ($p > .10$). An almost identical set of contrasts was obtained with the item asking subjects if they believed that the dimension problems were actually insoluble. The difference between Soluble and Insoluble conditions under High Salience was again significant (Ms = 4.3, 6.4; $p < .02$), whereas a comparable difference under Low Salience failed to attain significance (Ms = 4.6, 5.6; $p > .10$).

In general, then, subjects exposed to the High Salience treatment tended to be affected by the solubility–insolubility manipulation to a greater extent than were subjects given the Low Salience treatment. There was no evidence, however, that Low Salience As denied lack of control in the Insoluble condition. This result would have been expected from our earlier theorizing about the tendency of As to engage in perceptual distortion. We indeed might have detected denial if more systematic efforts had been made to measure attributions designed to enhance a sense of task mastery. In any event, greater perceived control among As than Bs in the Low Salience–Insoluble condition is not a prerequisite for testing our main predictions concerning learned helplessness.

Test phase results.   Table 8.2 presents the results for one of the measures of learned helplessness, that is, mean response latency (in seconds) in solving the anagrams. A three-way analysis of variance revealed a solubility–insolubility main effect, $F(1, 56)$ = 4.27, $p < .05$, and the expected triple-order interaction, $F(1, 56)$ = 12.83, $p < .001$. Subsequent contrasts showed that the mean for Type As in the High Salience–Soluble condition was reliably lower than the mean for the comparable Insoluble condition ($p < .05$), whereas the difference between Soluble and Insoluble As under Low Salience failed to reach statistical significance ($p > .20$).

These results indicate that learned helplessness occurred in As only after uncontrollable pretreatment of high salience. Note, however, that the effect was as much attributable to short latencies in the Soluble treatment as to the relatively long latencies in the Insoluble treatment. Indeed, As in the High

TABLE 8.2
Mean Response Latency (in Seconds) for Solution of the
Anagrams[a]

Condition	Soluble	Insoluble
High Salience, Pattern A	19.7	43.6
High Salience, Pattern B	40.6	31.2
Low Salience, Pattern A	33.1	38.4
Low Salience, Pattern B	29.4	47.9

[a] Each cell mean is based on eight subjects. Comparisons between cell means were conducted using the error-mean-square from the three-way analysis of variance. These comparisons revealed a number of significant differences ($p < .05$ or better), including those between the following relevant cell means: (1) 43.6, 19.7; (2) 47.9, 29.4; (3) 40.6, 19.7. The differences between 43.6 and 38.4 and between 29.4 and 40.6 were not statistically significant ($ps > .20$). A trend toward significance appeared for the comparison between 47.9 and 31.2 ($p = .10$).

Salience—Soluble condition had significantly shorter latencies than did comparable Type B subjects ($p < .02$). Although this result was not specifically predicted, it does accord with the general notion that hard driving As exert greater efforts at control than less motivated Bs.

Further analysis of the data in Table 8.2 indicates that the mean for Type Bs in the Low Salience—Insoluble treatment was reliably greater than the comparable mean in the Low Salience—Soluble treatment ($p = .05$). By contrast, the difference between Soluble and Insoluble Bs under High Salience did not achieve an acceptable level of statistical significance ($p > .20$). Indeed, there is a curious and inexplicable reversal here, with Soluble Bs actually showing somewhat longer latencies than Insoluble Bs. We are inclined to attribute the reversal to random fluctuation, since the mean difference was clearly nonsignificant. The results for Type Bs, then, also replicate the findings of the previous learned-helplessness experiment.

The effects depicted in Table 8.2 were virtually duplicated with another of our response measures, namely, trials to criterion for anagram solution. This is perhaps not surprising, since the two measures are obviously not independent. Table 8.3 presents the group means for the trials-to-criterion variable. Again there is the unanticipated (though nonsignificant) reversal in High Salience, with Insoluble Bs taking fewer trials to reach criterion than Soluble Bs. Despite this peculiarity, however, the triple-order interaction was clearly significant, $F(1, 56) = 12.83$, $p = .001$. Subsequent contrasts showed that learned helplessness occurred for As in the High Salience treatment ($p < .05$) but not in Low Salience ($p > .20$). The difference between Soluble and Insoluble Bs

TABLE 8.3
Mean Trials to Criterion for Anagrams Solution[a]

Condition	Soluble	Insoluble
High Salience, Pattern A	7.8	14.9
High Salience, Pattern B	15.3	11.0
Low Salience, Pattern A	10.3	14.6
Low Salience, Pattern B	11.1	15.8

[a] Comparisons between cell means were conducted using the error-mean-square from the three-way analysis of variance. These comparisons revealed significant differences ($p < .05$ or better) between the following cell means: (1) 14.9, 7.8; (2) 15.3, 7.8. The differences between 15.8 and 11.0 and between 15.8 and 11.1 were near-significant at the .08 and .09 levels, respectively. The difference between 14.6 and 14.9 is obviously nonsignificant ($p > .20$), as is the contrast between 15.3 and 11.0 ($p > .15$).

in the Low Salience treatment approached statistical significance at the .08 level. The comparable comparison in High Salience was clearly nonsignificant ($p > .15$).

The third response variable, namely, number of failures to solve the anagrams within 100 sec, produced results that were virtually identical to those reported in Tables 8.2 and 8.3. There was a triple interaction, $F(1, 56) = 4.03$, $p < .05$, and a solubility–insolubility main effect, $F(1, 56) = 3.17$, $p < .08$. Individual contrasts indicated the presence of learned helplessness in High Salience As ($p = .02$) but not in Low Salience As ($p > .20$). By contrast, the helplessness effect appeared for Bs only in Low Salience, that is, Soluble Bs had reliably fewer failures than Insoluble Bs ($p < .05$).

Discussion

Cue salience was varied in this experiment by manipulating the subject's degree of awareness of his success or failure on a series of cognitive tasks. When cues were of high salience, Type As showed greater interference with subsequent learning after uncontrollable (Insoluble) than controllable (Soluble) pretreatment. When cues were of low salience, Type As performed at about the same level in the test phase, whether pretreatment was controllable or uncontrollable. The pattern of response was the opposite for Pattern B subjects, with learned helplessness tending to occur only after pretreatment with uncontrollability cues for low salience. Consideration of Pattern B effects is deferred to the next chapter, after presentation of data on A–B differences in initial responsivity to uncontrollable stimuli of high and low salience. The following discussion is, therefore, primarily concerned with the behavior of Type A individuals.

The overall set of results reported here correspond to those found in the helplessness experiment using noise. Indeed, comparisons of Tables 8.1, 8.2, and 8.3 reveal that the data in all three are quite similar; at least the principal contrasts are essentially the same. It would appear, therefore, that learned helplessness occurs in As after extended exposure to uncontrollable stress, only if some measure of salience is taken into account. This generalization must be regarded as tentative, however. An essential feature of our explanation is that Type A subjects are initially responsive to salient cues of uncontrollability. We have up to this point offered little evidence indicating that As are actually more responsive only under conditions of high salience. Similarly, we have not as yet shown that As are initially less responsive than Bs when uncontrollability cues are of low salience. Preliminary support for both propositions can be found in experiments reported in the next chapter.

Another difficulty with our interpretation of the helplessness data is the absence of evidence indicating that, compared to Bs, Type As experienced uncontrollable stimuli of low salience as less uncontrollable. While the first experiment produced self-ratings of control tending to support this notion of denial, the second study was unequivocal in its failure to replicate. However, we have already noted that denial of uncontrollability is not essential to the prediction of learned helplessness in As. Moreover, lack of control can be freely admitted on a questionnaire yet explained away by the subject in terms of attributions designed to enhance his sense of mastery; for example, "I didn't have control over the task because I was distracted or uninterested." We made little effort to collect such data, hence Low Salience As may well have engaged in perceptual distortions designed to increase their sense of mastery despite veridical perceptions of lack of control.

Of greater concern, perhaps, is the nature of the fit between our data and one of the statements we would obviously like to make, namely, learned helplessness occurs among As *only* after uncontrollable pretreatment of high salience. Examination of the relevant tables reveals that Pattern A subjects perform at about the same level under high and low salience in the uncontrollable condition—at least the observed differences are not statistically significant. This means that the difference between controllable and uncontrollable conditions for High Salience As is attributable to a high level of performance in the controllable condition. Looked at from this perspective, our data do not provide evidence of learned helplessness in As. An alternative hypothesis is that Pattern A behavior is stimulated by the challenge of social reinforcement, that As do best or work hardest for rewards when the experimenter makes clear mention of their success, or when he exposes them to loud noise and manipulanda which allow them to escape from unwanted sound.

This alternative, though seemingly plausible, overlooks an important fact.

Both manipulations (inescapable noise and noncontingent reinforcement) produced significant main effects which indicate that, on the average, subjects showed learned helplessness irrespective of their A–B classification. While Pattern B subjects in Low Salience conditions contributed substantially to this effect, nevertheless the other uncontrollable cells were certainly necessary for statistical significance. It is difficult to maintain, therefore, that we failed to demonstrate learned helplessness, although we freely admit that the demonstration was aided and abetted by the vigorous responses of As in High Salience–controllable conditions and the relative lack of response among Bs in Low Salience–uncontrollable conditions.

Another problem with a social-reinforcement interpretation is the fact that the means for Soluble (or Escapable) As in High and Low Salience (or Noise) conditions did not differ significantly from each other; Type As responded vigorously under both levels of salience. Thus, we find it difficult to understand how social reinforcement would account for the significant difference between Soluble (or Escape) and Insoluble (or No Escape) As in High Salience conditions. It would appear that the salience manipulation affected the performance of As in both conditions, albeit in different directions. The specific High–Low Salience comparison in the uncontrollable treatment may not be statistically significant, but the overall result indicates greater performance degradation after uncontrollable than controllable pretreatment in High Salience, and no difference between pretreatment conditions in Low Salience.

CONCLUSIONS

Several generalizations can be made at this time. First, we assume that, compared to Pattern B subjects, Pattern A subjects respond to salient threats to their sense of control with enhanced efforts to maintain control. Additional evidence for this assumption is presented in the next chapter. Second, extended exposure to uncontrollable stress eventually leads to the recognition of a noncontingency between responses and outcomes. Third, the certainty of this recognition is probably greater in As than Bs because of enhanced efforts by As to locate control-relevant cues. Fourth, initial controlling behavior of As is thus followed by a decrement in efforts at control; that is, the perception of uncontrollability transfers to subsequent task situations where it appears as learned helplessness. While the data base for some of these statements is less than unequivocal, nevertheless a consistent interpretation of all of the results seems to be one which emphasizes the notions of salience and uncontrollability.

9
Pattern A, Cue Salience, and Initial Exposure to Uncontrollable Stress

The salience–uncontrollability hypothesis outlined in the preceding chapter makes the assumption that As are more responsive than Bs after initial exposure to uncontrollability cues of high salience. When cues are of low salience, As do not effectively encode the threat of uncontrollability and are, therefore, less responsive than Bs. Stated in more specific terms, As react to salient signs of lack of control with greater efforts than Bs aimed at asserting control. In contrast, they exert less efforts when uncontrollability cues are low in salience. Although systematic evidence for this particular hypothesis has not as yet been presented, it is not unreasonable to interpret the studies in Chapter 7 as providing indirect support.

Consider the experiment which compared the acquisition performance of As and Bs on FR/5 and VR/5 training schedules. It will be recalled that the response unit dispensing reinforcement (that is, nickels) was illuminated by a high-intensity lamp in an otherwise darkened laboratory chamber. This procedure is, of course, consistent with a definition of cue salience in terms of physical properties of the stimulus. A brightly illuminated reinforcement apparatus might be expected to make lack of control on a VR/5 schedule more prominent than a dimly illuminated apparatus. The subject's attention is being directed toward contingency and noncontingency while other features of the situation are deliberately minimized. Admittedly, we did not have the appropriate control, namely, a dim illumination treatment, but an argument might still be made that the study was conducted under high salience conditions.

A similar view could be taken with respect to the two studies involving brief exposure to uncontrollable stress. The noise–RT experiment relied exclusively on 100-dB(A) sound in pretreatment. The noncontingent reinforcement–DRL experiment induced perceptions of contingency and noncontingency by having the experimenter emphasize his evaluations to the subject. Both of these procedures can be construed as instances of high salience. Indeed, we have treated each of them as inducing high salience in the learned-helplessness studies reported in Chapter 8.

The foregoing evidence for the initial hyperresponsiveness of As to uncontrollable stress, while suggestive, is clearly inadequate. The need for a systematic manipulation of the salience variable is palpably obvious. Two experiments have thus far been undertaken to test the hypothesis that level of salience and the A–B dimension interact to influence initial responding to uncontrollable stress. Both studies were conducted by James Pennebaker and the author. The first, though simple in conception, produced an equivocal set of results. Therefore, we describe it here in abbreviated form. The experiment was originally designed to examine the performance of As and Bs in the pretreatment phase of the learned-helplessness paradigm.

THE INESCAPABLE NOISE EXPERIMENT

The rationale for this experiment was as follows. In high salience pretreatment, Pattern A subjects will first exert greater efforts to escape from noise than will comparable Pattern B subjects. Enhanced activity to locate control-relevant cues will result in a stronger certainty that nothing can be done to terminate noise. Such a learned expectation might be expected to eventuate in extinction of escape attempts during the latter part of an extended pretreatment. In low salience pretreatment, by contrast, Type As will not effectively encode the noncontingency between responding and noise termination. Compared with the behavior of Bs, therefore, enhanced escape behavior and subsequent extinction will not be observed among Type A subjects. The preceding hypotheses were evaluated in what amounted to a replication of the pretreatment phase of the first learned-helplessness experiment in Chapter 8. However, the number of noise trials was increased from 35 to 45 in order to enhance the likelihood of detecting extinction.

Procedure

Subjects were exposed to 45 trials of inescapable 3000-Hz tones, delivered either at 105 dB(A) (High Salience condition) or 80 dB(A) (Low Salience condition[1]). Each noise burst lasted 8 sec and varied randomly from 15 to 25 sec in 5-sec steps.

[1] It might be appropriate to label the 80-decibel condition "Moderate Salience," in part because a 60-dB(A) treatment was added during the conduct of the study. The results from this latter treatment do not substantially alter our conclusions; hence, data are presented from only the 80-dB(A) condition, which is labeled "Low Salience."

The subject's response unit was a small box in which a spring-loaded push button was located. All subjects were told that there was something they could do to stop the noise and that it was up to them to figure this out. The taped instructions for the task were almost identical to those used in the previous noise-helplessness study. There was, however, no way in which any of the subjects in this experiment could have escaped from noise, because the push button was not connected to the sound-delivery system.

The number of button presses on each trial was automatically recorded throughout the experimental session. This measure constituted the principal dependent variable in the study.

Subjects

Twenty-two Type A and 21 Type B male undergraduates were selected from a larger pool of pretested students (see Appendix A). They were randomly assigned to the salience conditions.

Results

Checks on the effectiveness of the experimental manipulations. Analysis of postexperimental unpleasantness ratings of the noise (made on a 6-point scale) indicated that the mean for High Salience (3.9) was significantly higher than the mean for Low Salience (2.9) at less than the .001 level. There was no A–B main effect ($p > .20$) or interaction between this variable and noise level ($p > .20$).

Efforts to escape from noise. The number of button presses for each noise trial was subjected to a square root transformation, and the transformed scores were grouped into five blocks of nine noise trials each. The group means for these data are presented in Table 9.1 (next page).

A repeated-measures analysis of variance (A–B by High–Low Salience by Trial Blocks) produced a Trial Blocks effect ($p < .001$), and a nonsignificant A–B by Trial Blocks interaction at the .15 level. A separate analysis of data from the High Salience treatment indicated a Trial Blocks effect ($p = .02$), and the expected A–B by Trial Blocks interaction ($p = .02$). A comparable analysis on Low Salience data revealed the Trial Blocks effect ($p < .01$) and no interaction ($p > .01$) and no interaction ($p > .25$). Comparison of As and Bs on the first trial block failed to show reliable differences within either High or Low Salience conditions ($ps > .20$).

TABLE 9.1
Mean Number of Button Presses
(Transformed Data)[a]

| Experimental | Trial blocks | | | | |
group	1	2	3	4	5
High Salience, Pattern A	5.5	4.7	4.6	3.5	2.9
High Salience, Pattern B	4.2	3.9	3.8	3.8	4.2
Low Salience, Pattern A	4.6	3.3	2.9	2.2	2.2
Low Salience, Pattern B	5.8	4.8	4.8	4.2	4.0

[a] All cell means are based on 11 cases, except High Salience, Pattern B, which has only 10 subjects.

Discussion

Though the general pattern of results was in accord with predictions, statistical analyses failed to document the reliability of a number of important differences. It is true that initial responding was greater for As than for Bs in High Salience, whereas just the reverse occurred in Low Salience (see Table 9.1). However, individual contrasts for the first trial block did not demonstrate that the differences were statistically significant. On the other hand, High Salience As showed an eventual extinction effect, whereas Bs exhibited little evidence of extinction. Indeed, Bs increased their level of responding on the final block of 45 noise trials. The overall effect was reflected in the reliable interaction for the High Salience condition. Type Bs were also expected to extinguish in Low Salience, and the data tended to confirm this prediction. Contrary to expectations, however, Low Salience As also showed a decrement in responsivity over the course of the extended noise session.

In short, this experiment tends to confirm initial predictions, but because of a high degree of within-conditions variance, the results are often less than statistically reliable. We could speculate endlessly about the causes of this variability, but it is probably attributable to some inadequacy in the experimental procedure for controlling rate of responsivity. For this and related reasons, we decided to use a different set of empirical operations in order to provide a more unequivocal test of the hypothesized effects of salience on the initial hyperresponsiveness of As. The partial-reinforcement procedure described in Chapter 7 was selected as our experimental paradigm, since it had already produced strong A–B effects and in addition seemed readily amenable to incorporation of an explicit salience manipulation.

THE PARTIAL REINFORCEMENT-SALIENCE EXPERIMENT

Overview

Subjects depressed a switch in order to earn points which were defined as worth 1 cent apiece. Half of the cases were randomly assigned to an FR/5 training schedule (that is, a controllable condition), whereas the other half were allocated to a VR/5 schedule (an uncontrollable condition). Within each of these treatments, half of the subjects experienced the partial reinforcement procedure under High Salience conditions; that is, the response apparatus was illuminated in an otherwise darkened chamber, and a counter and bright signal light were activated whenever the subject earned a point. The remaining half of the cases in both VR/5 and FR/5 worked in a well-lit chamber, where there was no visible counter and the only indication of reinforcement was activation of a dim light whenever a point was earned. This was the so-called Low Salience treatment. Each cell in the basic design contained equal numbers of Type A and Type B subjects. The experimental session lasted 5 min, and the number of switch depressions within the total period constituted the major dependent variable.

Previous theorizing led to the following predictions: The response rate in High Salience–VR/5 was expected to be greater for As than for Bs, whereas in Low Salience–VR/5 As were expected to show a lower rate than Bs. No difference between As and Bs were predicted for FR/5, either under High or Low Salience conditions.

Subjects

Thirty-two males and 32 female undergraduates served as experimental subjects. The student JAS was administered to each subject after the experiment under the guise of a separate study. Irrespective of sex, subjects with scores above the median for the 64 cases were classified as Pattern A; those with scores below the median were designated Pattern B.

Apparatus

The subject's response unit in the High Salience condition was similar to the one used in the previous partial reinforcement study (see Chapter 7). Modifications were as follows: removal of the nickel chute, dispenser, and coin holder; addition of a 15-W light located above the counter; replacement of the response button with a response switch. The light flashed in conjunction with the counter whenever a point was earned by the subject. The laboratory chamber was darkened, and a high-intensity lamp was focused on the apparatus. In Low Salience, the display board containing the counter was hidden from the subject's view, and a covered 7.5-W bulb replaced the 15-W bulb. The chamber was fully illuminated and there was no light from the high-intensity lamp.

Procedure

Details of procedure were essentially the same as those used in the previous partial reinforcement study (see Chapter 7). Subjects were given the same introductory instructions, although the apparatus changes outlined above required some modification of task instructions. All subjects were thus told:

> By flipping this switch appropriately you will be rewarded with points that will register on a counter. The light will flash on at the same time. Each point you receive is worth one cent. In other words, the more efficiently you flip the switch, the more points you will get and, consequently, the more money you will have to take home.

The manipulation of cue salience was largely accomplished by means of differences in the response apparatus and physical conditions of the laboratory chamber, as described above. After giving the task instructions in High Salience, the experimenter turned off the overhead lights in the chamber and turned on the intensity lamp. The focused illumination of the response apparatus was presumed to make contingent and noncontingent reinforcement at the switch-pressing task highly salient. In addition, the subject's attention was directed toward the counter and signal light.

In Low Salience, the potency of contingent and noncontingent cues were reduced by covering the counter, minimizing the intensity of the signal light, and keeping on the overhead lights. There was no intensity light in this condition. The fully lit room allowed the subject to attend to stimuli other than the response apparatus, including wall posters. (These posters were present in High Salience but could not easily be seen in the dark room.)

Controllability was manipulated by exposing subjects either to a VR/5 or FR/5 schedule. As before, it was assumed that VR/5 would be experienced as more uncontrollable than FR/5, since the random nature of VR/5 made it difficult to discern a clear contingency between responding and reinforcement.

All subjects responded for points for 5 min. The number of responses and cumulative reinforcements were recorded continuously at 5-sec intervals throughout the session.

TABLE 9.2
Mean Number of Responses Per 5-Sec Interval
For a 5-Min Experimental Session[a]

| Experimental | Subject Classification | |
conditions	Pattern A	Pattern B
High Salience, VR/5	14.6	9.2
Low Salience, VR/5	6.7	12.8
High Salience, FR/5	13.0	11.4
Low Salience, FR/5	14.1	13.9

[a] There are eight cases in each cell.

Results

Table 9.2 presents group means for the average number of switch presses per 5-sec interval during the 5-min experimental session. These data were subjected to analysis of variance, which revealed the following relevant effects. There was a VR/5–FR/5 main effect, $F(1, 48) = 8.03$, $p < .01$, an interaction between this variable and salience, $F(1, 48) = 5.80$, $p < .02$, and a salience by A–B interaction, $F(1, 48) = 16.29$, $p < .001$.[2]

Of greater interest was the expected triple-order interaction between VR/5–FR/5, salience, and the A–B factor, $F(1, 48) = 9.91$, $p < .005$. A subsequent orthogonal-weighting analysis yielded a significant interaction in VR/5, $t(48) = 5.08$, $p < .001$, but not in FR/5, $t < 1$. Individual contrasts showed that High Salience As in VR/5 had a higher response rate than their Low Salience counterparts ($p < .001$). The reverse difference for Bs in VR/5 was also significant at the .02 level.

Perception of lack of control. Subjects in FR/5 reported having more control than those in VR/5, thereby confirming the effectiveness of the reinforcement manipulation in inducing differential perceptions of control. To the postexperimental question, "How much control did you have in earning points?" (1 represented "no control at all," and 7 represented "complete control"), the respective mean ratings were 6.3 and 3.8, $F(1, 56) = 59.89$, $p < .001$.

Analysis of responses to this item also revealed an A–B main effect, such that As reported more control than Bs [$Ms = 5.5$ and 4.5; $F(1, 56) = 8.42$, $p = .005$]. In addition there were interactions between the A–B factor and

[2] There was also evidence that males depressed the switch at a higher rate than females ($p < .001$), but there were no interactions involving the sex factor and other experimental variables ($ps > .20$). We have no particularly compelling explanation for this result, although it may reflect nothing more than a sex difference in strength. Depression of the switch did, after all, require considerable pressure.

VR/5–FR/5, $F(1, 56) = 6.33$, $p = .01$, and between A–B and Salience, $F(1, 56) = 8.42$, $p = .005$. These second-order interactions are explicable in terms of an obtained triple interaction, $F(1, 56) = 4.53$, $p < .05$. There were no differences in "control" ratings for the four cells in FR/5 ($Ms = 6.5, 6.1, 6.1,$ and 6.2); but in High Salience–VR/5, Type As showed an average rating of 5.9 compared to the mean ratings of 3.4 and 3.3 for Low Salience As and Bs, and 2.6 for High Salience Bs. It would appear that High Salience As in VR/5 not only showed a higher response rate than the other groups, but also reported feeling more control in the situation.

Discussion

The results of this experiment indicate that As are initially hyperresponsive only to uncontrollable stimuli of high salience. By contrast, there were no A–B differences in response to controllable stimulation, irrespective of its degree of salience. Taken together with the results on hyporesponsiveness reported in Chapter 8, we may now suggest the following: Compared to Bs, Type As respond to salient indications of uncontrollability with enhanced efforts to assert control. If a stressor stimulus is in fact uncontrollable, the more thorough search for control-relevant cues on the part of As eventually leads to greater certainty that a noncontingency exists between responses and outcomes. Extended experience with the uncontrollable stimulus thus results in expectations of no control (that is, learned helplessness), with As showing this effect to a greater extent than Bs.

A similar sequence of hyperresponsiveness followed by hyporesponsiveness appears to be characteristic of Pattern B individuals, providing the uncontrollable event has low rather than high salience. We observed that initial level of responding was greater among Low Salience Bs than Low Salience As in this study (see Table 9.2). It will also be recalled from Chapter 8 that prolonged exposure to uncontrollability tended to lead, though sometimes only marginally so, to learned helplessness in Bs under conditions of low salience. While we are somewhat at a loss to explain both sets of results, we might draw upon other data showing that Bs have a lower threshold than As for responding to aversive events. The Response Threshold Experiment (Chapter 4) provides some documentation for this assertion, since it indicated that Bs responded sooner than As to an unwanted sound stimulus. Assuming, then, that Type Bs have a lower general response threshold, we might explain their specific reaction to uncontrollability cues of low salience in terms of the fact that such cues exceed their threshold for response. It follows from this hypothesis that Bs should show greater learned helplessness after extended experience with non-prominent stimulation—presumably because they have more fully explored the possibility of a response-reinforcement contingency and concluded that they do not, in fact, have control over the situation.

The difficulty with this line of reasoning is that it leaves us without a satisfactory explanation for the low initial responsivity of Bs when the uncontrollable stimuli are of high salience. Since the threshold for Bs was presumably reached in low salience, the decrement in responsivity in high salience is indeed puzzling. Continued speculation about the reasons for this finding is not likely to prove useful at this time. Clearly, much empirical work is needed to clarify the psychological mechanisms underlying the reactions of Bs to uncontrollable events.

While the behavior of Type A subjects is more easily explicable in terms of our notion of cue salience, nevertheless there are at least two major difficulties with the interpretation. First, there is the interaction effect obtained with self-ratings of control in the VR/5 treatment. High Salience As in this condition reported themselves as having almost as much control as in FR/5. A similar effect was obtained in the previous partial reinforcement study (see Chapter 7). Moreover, we expected less felt control among As in High than Low Salience on the assumption that they would deny uncontrollability when its cues were relatively nonprominent. There was, however, little evidence for this prediction in prior experiments reported in this book, and now a reverse effect has been observed. We are inclined (as in Chapter 7) to attribute the overall interaction to the fact that As report more control than Bs because they actually exercise more control. The switch-pressing results showed that the rate of response in VR/5 was, in fact, greatest among High Salience As.

A second difficulty with our interpretation concerns the implicit assumption that VR/5–FR/5 schedules are experienced as stressful by the subjects. This issue was discussed in Chapter 7, where we suggested that nonreinforcement on a partial schedule is tantamount to failure on an achievement-related task. To the extent that such failure constitutes a threat to the individual's self-esteem, we may consider the partial reinforcement task as moderately stressful. In these terms, we may conclude that relative to Bs, As are initially hyperresponsive to uncontrollable stressor stimuli of high salience. This conclusion must, of course, be viewed with caution. Partial reinforcement procedures are not clear instances of stressful stimulation, hence A–B differences in the VR/5 condition could, for example, be interpreted as suggesting that As are more responsive than Bs to challenging tasks. Since our conclusions about the role of salience in Type A subjects' initial hyperresponsivity rest, in large part, on results obtained from the VR/5–FR/5 study, it is obvious that more definitive experimentation is needed with stimuli that are unequivocally stressful.

A final point concerning the results should be noted here. The observed hyperresponsiveness of As is probably a style of *response* rather than the result of *perceptual* effects. By and large, we have been unable to detect differences between As and Bs in the way they assess experimental situations. The only significant exceptions are the control-rating data reported in Chapter 7 and replicated in the present experiment, plus occasional differences between As and Bs in felt frustration. [Indeed, As in this study rated themselves as more "frustrated" than their Type B counterparts ($p < .02$) on a 7-point postexperimental scale.] It is, of course, possible that we have failed to sample a number of the more relevant perceptual dimensions. For example, we noted in an earlier chapter that Low Salience As might be denying lack of control through some unmeasured attributional process, and there may be still other differences in how experimental procedures were perceived by our subjects. However, in the absence of concrete evidence to the contrary, we tentatively conclude that the initial hyperresponsiveness of As is a characteristic style of response elicited by salient stressors that are perceived as threats to their sense of control.

GENERAL DISCUSSION AND CONCLUSIONS

An obvious question emerges from the research reported in this chapter: Why do As and Bs show differential responsivity to uncontrollability cues of high and low salience? One possibility is that Bs have lower expectations of control than As. Depressed expectations could produce a decrement in motivation to exercise control. There is, in fact, evidence that when lack of control (for example, failure) occurs in a context of expectations of control (success), performance suffers more than when the expectations of control are lower (e.g., Douglas & Anisman, 1975). Compared to As, then, the low control expectancies of Bs might lead them to exert minimal efforts when confronted by a stressor which threatens their sense of mastery. It is not immediately obvious, however, why expectations would have this effect only with cues of uncontrollability that are low in salience. There are, moreover, some difficulties with at least one of the basic assumptions underlying an expectational hypothesis.

It is assumed that (1) the incentive to assert control is related to expectations that one's controlling behavior will be successful; (2) Type As have higher expectations of control than Type Bs. The first proposition is probably correct. We cited research earlier that indicates a relationship between expectations and efforts at control. Still other studies suggest that the manipulation of control expectancies can both potentiate and alleviate performance degradations due to prolonged exposure to uncontrollable stressors (e.g., Dweck, 1975; Krantz, et al., 1974, Experiment II; Thornton & Powell, 1971). Moreover, at least one theoretical formulation emphasizes the role of expectations in determining reactions to uncontrollable events (Wortman & Brehm, 1975). This theory proposes that the greater one's expectations of control, the greater will be the motivation to assert control when confronted by evidence of uncontrollability. Not unlike our own formulation, the theory suggests that as uncontrollable stimulation continues, and the futility of responding is realized, expectations of control along with the motivation to control are lowered and learned helplessness ensues.

While the evidence seems clear that expectancies are related to efforts at control, there is little data to support the idea that As have higher expectations than Bs. The correlation between Pattern A and standard measures of control expectancies (e.g., Rotter's, 1966, I–E scale, or its variants) is of the order of .17 (see Appendix C). This coefficient is statistically significant because of the large number of cases on which it is based, but the magnitude of the relationship is obviously too small to warrant serious consideration.

Even more damaging to an expectational hypothesis are data from a recent study by Jack F. Hollis (1975) conducted for his doctoral dissertation at the University of Texas. Expectations of success or failure on a series of cognitive tasks (adapted from Roth & Kubal, 1975) were either raised, lowered, or left untreated by means of instructional manipulations. The tasks were deliberately insoluble, and an attempt was made to create conditions in which lack of control was highly salient to the subject. Rate of solution attempts over the course of the testing session was the principal measure of efforts to assert control. Expectations of task success were also assessed prior to actual performance.

While subjects in the High Expectation treatment had reliably greater expectancies of success than did those in the Low Expectation treatment, the results also showed that As in the No Expectation condition reported lower expectations than their Type B counterparts. Indeed, there was an A–B main effect, such that Bs in all three conditions anticipated more success than As. These results are indeed puzzling. They certainly cannot be construed as support for an expectational interpretation of the initial hyporesponsiveness of Bs in high salience. Other data from Hollis's study failed to give credence to the notion that generalized expectations of control mediate initial hyperresponsiveness of As in high salience. In short, there is little empirical support for the hypothesis that expectations play a significant role in the differential reactions of As and Bs to uncontrollable stressor stimuli.

The final word on this issue has not, of course, been said. The possibility still exists that control expectancies might interact with cue salience to determine both initial hyperresponsiveness and subsequent hyporesponsiveness to uncontrollable stress. The Hollis study had a number of unfortunate flaws in its design, including the fact that his measure of control had an equivocal interpretation. Future experimentation might, therefore, attempt more rigorous tests of the expectational hypothesis.

At present, we must be modest in our general conclusions. We may thus assert that, compared to Bs, Type As have an elevated threshold of responsivity for uncontrollability cues. For reasons discussed in this and the preceding chapter, we also conclude that enhanced efforts at control lead to greater vulnerability to helplessness after extended experience with uncontrollable stressors of high salience. Speculation beyond these two empirical assertions is probably unwarranted at this time.

We do not assume a completely atheoretical posture with respect to our findings, however. On the contrary, a behavioristic interpretation may be suggested in which Pattern A is treated as a response style for coping with perceived lack of control over environmental stress. In other words, the behavior pattern is a prepotent set of responses which are elicited by stressors that threaten the individual's sense of control. The overt reaction pattern is assumed to have developed through shaping practices of parents and/or parental modeling processes. We will have more to say about developmental factors in a later chapter. For now, it is sufficient to emphasize the initial hyperreactivity and later hyporeactivity of Type As to uncontrollable stressors of high salience. These conclusions are not unimportant, however. They serve to underscore the significance of the interplay between uncontrollable stimuli and cue salience in the elicitation of Pattern A behavior. The generalizability of this interaction to a nonlaboratory situation is explored in the next chapter.

10
Pattern A,
Uncontrollable Life Events,
and Clinical Coronary Heart Disease

Most of us have from time to time been confronted with salient events over which we have little or no control. Rejection by a loved one, a sudden financial setback, or a loss in occupational prestige, are all aspects of our lives that can only rarely be affected by our own actions. These losses often result in feelings of helplessness, depression, and a tendency to give up direct efforts to cope with the environment (e.g., Seligman, 1975). There are also indications that helplessness-inducing events which are prominent in an individual's life precede the onset of clinical CHD. In Chapter 2, we cited research showing that death of a close relative increases the likelihood of death in next of kin, usually due to some form of cardiovascular ailment (e.g., Parkes et al., 1969). In this connection, consideration was also given to the work of Engel (1968) and Greene (e.g., see Greene et al., 1972), which points to helplessness and depression as precursors of sudden death from coronary disease.

Of equal relevance to this relationship is the research of Holmes, Rahe, and Theorell concerning life change and the occurrence of cardiovascular pathology in a subsequent observation period (e.g., Theorell & Rahe, 1971; Rahe, Romo, Bennett, & Siltanen, 1974). For example, data from survivors of myocardial infarction show marked elevations in the total number of significant life changes during a 6-month period prior to infarction, compared to life changes in the same time interval 1 year earlier. Other studies indicate that the prodromal period in which change occurs is often as long as 1 year (e.g., Theorell & Rahe, 1975; Theorell et al., 1975). These studies generally use total life change scores derived from the Holmes and Rahe (e.g., 1967) Social Readjustment Scale (SRS) as their independent variable. These scores, it will be recalled, are based on a variety of life events which may be considered controllable or uncontrollable, and stressful or benign. While little effort is typically made to classify events into these or other categories, nevertheless

125

Theorell (e.g., see Theorell *et al.*, 1975) has conducted a number of studies showing that subsets of items from the SRS (for example, financial decline, or increased pressures at work) are related specifically to the occurrence of coronary heart disease. Other investigators have used item subsets in studies of the relationship between life events and psychic disease such as reactive depression (e.g., Paykel *et al.*, 1969; Paykel, 1974). One of the implications of this approach is that the prediction of disease may be improved by examining theoretically relevant subgroups of life event items rather than relying exclusively upon global life change scores (see Chapter 2).

In the case of coronary disease, for example, it might be argued that uncontrollable life events are more important than comparably unpleasant events that do not constitute unequivocal lack of control for the individual. This proposition derives from the work of Engel and Greene showing the importance of helplessness in sudden death. It is also based on our own laboratory research indicating an association between the coronary-prone behavior pattern, reactions to uncontrollable events, and learned helplessness. Indeed, we would suggest that, compared to a Pattern B individual, helplessness-inducing events in the life of a Pattern A individual increase the likelihood of his succumbing to a coronary incident.

PATTERN A, HELPLESSNESS, AND CORONARY DISEASE

Pattern A is a likely candidate for the predisposing condition that mediates a helplessness–coronary disease relationship. The Type A individual is motivated to maintain control in the face of its possible loss, at least where the loss involves a salient feature of his environment. However, our laboratory studies also indicate that extended experience with salient uncontrollable stimuli leads to the perception of unequivocal loss of control and thus to enhanced vulnerability to helplessness. Consider a comparable instance of loss of control in everyday life, such as being fired or demoted. If the Type A individual concludes that little can be done to rectify the situation, we may expect him to experience more intense feelings of helplessness than are experienced by a Type B in similar circumstances. This prediction derives from the assumption that Type As probably try harder than Type Bs to avoid losing their jobs when that possibility first becomes apparent. Having exerted greater initial efforts at control, Type As experience greater helplessness when they become convinced that nothing can be done about being fired.

The precise role of initial hyperresponsiveness and subsequent hyporesponsiveness (helplessness) in the development of cardiovascular pathology and clinical CHD remains unclear. We commented earlier on the possible influence of catecholamine production in this process, and we shall do so again in the final chapter of this book. Though obviously speculative, this line of thought suggests a fruitful approach to potential mechanisms mediating the impact of psychological variables on coronary disease. Before embarking on such an inquiry, however, we should first determine whether the interaction of Pattern A and helplessness is indeed prodromal to clinical CHD.

Under ideal circumstances, the appropriate study would be designed as a systematic prospective investigation. A variety of practical considerations made it impossible to conduct research of this type. While recognizing the biases in a retrospective design, we nevertheless decided to do a frankly exploratory study in which coronary patients and noncoronary controls were compared in terms of their A–B scores as well as their recall of life events during several time periods prior to disease onset.[1] Three general expectations guided our research: (1) coronary patients were expected to have higher Pattern A scores on the adult JAS than either noncoronary hospitalized subjects or nonhospitalized control subjects; (2) compared to nonhospitalized controls, more coronary and noncoronary patients should report helplessness-arousing life events during a 1–year period prior to hospitalization; (3) the occurrence of life events, irrespective of their helplessness-arousing character, should be the same in the coronary and noncoronary groups during the 1-year prodromal period.

THE HOUSTON STUDY

The Samples and Sampling Procedures

Three basic samples were used in the study: (1) a group of 45 patients on the coronary care (CC) unit of the VA Hospital in Houston, Texas; (2) 77 patients on the general medical service ward ($N = 22$) and psychiatric ward ($N = 55$) at the VA Hospital—the hospitalized control group; (3) 50 building maintenance employees of the University of Texas at Austin—the "healthy" nonhospitalized control group. (Approximately 90% of the latter group were veterans.)

Participation in the study was restricted to male subjects between the ages of 35 and 55. Other criteria included the following:

1. Subjects in the CC unit had to have a diagnosis of clinical CHD, that is,

[1] This study was a collaborative effort involving the following people: Dr. Kenneth F. Kopel, Staff Psychologist and Consultant to the Coronary Care Unit, Veterans Administration Hospital, Houston, Texas; Drs. Melvin L. Synder, David S. Krantz, and Jack F. Hollis of the author's laboratory in Austin; and Mr. James Cox and Ms. Carol Cohn, also of the laboratory. Dr. Alberto Montero, Chief Cardiologist of the Coronary Care Unit at the VA Hospital, Houston, collaborated in this research. We thank the medical and nursing staff of the VA Hospital, and especially Dr. Sidney E. Cleveland, Chief of Psychological Services, for their cooperation and assistance.

myocardial infarction, suspected myocardial infarction, or angina pectoris.

2. Coronary patients could not have a prior history of hospitalization for psychiatric problems.
3. Hospitalized controls could not have a history of cardiovascular disease or current coronary ailments.
4. Hospitalized controls from the psychiatric ward had to be given a specific diagnosis, providing it was not psychosis (for instance, schizophrenia), organic disorder, or drug addiction (other than alcoholism).
5. Hospitalized controls from the general-medical ward could not have a diagnosis of peptic or duodenal ulcers, since clinical evidence exists suggesting that ulcer patients may be Pattern A (e.g., Friedman, 1969).
6. Nonhospitalized controls could not have (a) current or previous cardiovascular disease (including clinical CHD and hypertension); (b) psychiatric problems; or (c) physical disorders of any kind requiring hospitalization within the last year.

The foregoing information was obtained primarily from the medical records of the hospitalized patients and from self-reports given on one of the study questionnaires by the nonhospitalized controls.

The two hospitalized samples consisted of those patients who agreed to participate when approached by one of the research staff. These requests were made almost weekly over an approximately 12-month period, from March 1973 through April 1974. Requests for participation were made, whenever possible, after the patients had been in hospital for about 1 week to 10 days. Approximately 40% of the CC patients approached declined to participate. Similar percentages of refusal occurred with patients approached on the other wards. Of the 214 cases who agreed to participate and satisfied age and diagnostic criteria, 50 subjects were subsequently dropped from the study because they were unable or unwilling to complete the questionnaires (described later).

Selection of the nonhospitalized controls was carried out during the months of June and July, 1973. The Director of Physical Plant on the Austin campus called for volunteers, in several age groups ranging from 35 to 55, to participate as the "normal comparison group in a study of male patients in a Houston hospital." Eighty-eight men out of a pool of about 125 agreed to participate. Ten of these cases were discarded because they admitted to cardiovascular disease or psychiatric problems. Of the 78 subjects tested, 18 were eliminated from data analysis because of substantial incompletions in their questionnaires.

Characteristics of the samples.   The descriptive characteristics of the subjects are presented in Table 10.1, where the figures represent percentages of each of the samples. It is immediately apparent that the mean age for each of

TABLE 10.1
Description of the Samples[a]

Characteristics	Coronary patients (N = 45)	Hospitalized controls (N = 77)	Nonhospitalized controls (N = 50)
Age			
35–39	2.2	10.4	16.0
40–49	46.7	57.1	50.0
50–55	51.1	32.5	34.0
Mean:	49.2	46.2	46.4
Race			
Black	11.1	14.0	2.0
White	80.0	67.5	68.0
Chicano	8.9	2.5	0.0
Unknown	0.0	16.0	30.0
Religion			
Protestant	75.6	80.5	78.0
Catholic	22.2	11.7	18.0
Jewish	2.2	0.0	0.0
Other	0.0	7.8	4.0
Hollingshead Index of Social Position			
I	2.2	5.1	0.0
II	8.9	11.7	0.0
III	22.2	28.6	24.0
IV	40.0	44.2	66.0
V	26.7	10.4	10.0

[a] Numbers represent percentages of each of the samples.

the control groups is lower (by about 3 years) than the mean age of the coronary sample. Most of the cases in each sample are white, but the percentage appears to be greater in the coronary group (80%) compared to the two other samples (67.5 and 68.0%). Moreover, there are distinctly fewer blacks in the nonhospitalized group (2%) than in the two hospitalized samples (11.1 and 14.0%). All three groups are similar in terms of religious affiliation (most are Protestant). Although the bulk of the cases are in Categories III, IV, and V on the social-class index, note the somewhat greater percentage in Category IV among the nonhospitalized controls (66%) compared to each of the hospitalized groups (40% and 44.2%). Taken together, these data do not permit the conclusion that the samples are clearly equivalent in terms of basic socioeconomic variables. On the other hand, we do not believe that the differences between groups are so large as to seriously bias the comparisons needed to test the hypotheses outlined earlier.

Diagnostic categories in the hospitalized groups. Twenty-three of the 45 coronary cases had definite myocardial infarction; another 7 had suspected myocardial infarction; and 15 were labeled as having angina pectoris or anginal symptoms. Of the 77 cases in the hospitalized control sample, 12 were diagnosed as depressive; 11 were anxiety state; 32 were alcoholics; 3 were diabetic; 2 had lung cancer; 2 were asthmatic; 5 had gastrointestinal or pancreatic ailments; 4 had lung problems such as emphysema or pneumonia; 2 had hernias; 1 had a liver ailment; 1 had arthritis; 1 had gout; and 1 had an ulcerated foot.

Testing Procedure

Potential coronary cases were approached in their ward by a member of the research team and asked to participate in a study of personality factors relevant to heart disease and its causes. A similar request was made in the psychiatric and general medical wards. Subjects who agreed to participate were left alone to complete the study questionnaires. In most cases, the researcher returned about 2 hrs later to collect the completed forms. Some effort was made at this time to determine if the subject had answered all questions. If not, the researcher assisted him in completing the questionnaire. In some instances, however, the patient was unwilling to work any further; in other instances the patient had to leave for a medical examination and was subsequently discharged before the researcher could contact him again to complete the questionnaire; and in still other cases the subject was unable to read and/or comprehend at a level necessary to answer the questions. As noted earlier, such problems resulted in elimination of 50 subjects from the two hospitalized samples.

Administration of the questionnaires to the nonhospitalized controls was carried out in a group testing session. Subjects were assured that their data would not be seen by their supervisors or the personnel department of the universtiy.

The Study Instruments

Two principal questionnaires were given to all subjects: the adult version of the JAS, and a modified version of the Schedule of Recent Experience (e.g., Hawkins *et al.,* 1957; Holmes & Masuda, 1970) called the Life Events Questionnaire (LEQ). The adult JAS was described in Chapter 3 and needs no further comment here.

The LEQ. The first 21 items in the LEQ asked for social and medical background data. Included were race, religion, education, occupation, smoking and drinking habits, and previous CHD and/or hypertension. The question on cardiovascular history and the one on hospitalization within the last year were used for purposes of screening nonhospitalized control subjects, as described earlier.

The remainder of the LEQ asked the respondent to indicate the number of times each of 47 life events[2] occurred during each of several time periods, for example, "during the 3 weeks before today"; "3 weeks to 3 months before today"; "3 months to 1 year before today"; and "1 year to 3 years before today." The number of occurrences listed by a subject for each time interval was coded into five categories: 0, 1, 2, 3, and 4 or more. For purposes of analysis and to avoid redundancy, the time periods were regrouped into the following categories: (a) 3 months before today; (b) 1 year before today; (c) 1 to 3 years before today.

The 47 life events in the questionnaire are summarized in Table 10.2. They are derived, in large part, from Holmes and Rahe (1967). However, there is some modification in the wording of a number of items, and we also added events that were not included in the original list.

Scoring the LEQ.   Three major scores were calculated from responses to the LEQ items. The first was a *life change score* based on whether one or more of the 47 events occurred during each of the three time periods.[3] The second score was called a *Loss Index,* since it was designed to reflect helplessness-inducing losses in the individual's life. It consisted of the percentage of cases in each sample who indicated the occurrence of one or more of 10 specific LEQ events described later. A Loss Index was computed for each time period. A third, closely related score, the *Negative Events Index,* consisted of the percentage of cases in each sample who endorsed one or more of seven LEQ events judged, a priori, to be unequivocally negative but not to involve a loss. A Negative Events Index was also computed for each time period.

---

[2] There were actually 51 events in the questionnaire, but one ("hospitalization for mental disorder") was used only to screen the nonhospitalized control subjects. The other item ("development of a close friendship") was included for reasons not relevant to the purposes of this study. The item was not used in the analyses reported here. Also not included in our analyses were the items "major personal injury" and "major personal illness." Coronary and/or hospitalized control cases had to endorse one or the other item during the 1-year or 3-month prodromal periods, which would have introduced bias into some of the LEQ scores described in the next section. Both items were included in the LEQ because they appeared on the original Holmes and Rahe (1967) list.

[3] We deliberately elected to use this relatively crude scoring procedure rather than the more sensitive weighting techniques of the Holmes and Rahe (1967). These procedures, it will be recalled, yield a *total* life change score (see Chapter 2). Our decision to rely on binary scoring was dictated by the fact that the weights used by Holmes and Rahe were derived from ratings made in the Seattle, Washington area over 15 years ago and may, therefore, be inappropriate for our samples.

TABLE 10.2
Life Events in the LEQ

Item number	Life event	Item number	Life event
1	Troubles with the boss	26	Changing to a different line of work
2	Moving to a new residence		
3	Marriage	27	Large decrease in number of arguments with spouse
4	Detention in jail	28	Large increase in number of arguments with spouse
5	Major change in sleeping or eating habits		
		29	Promotion
6	Death of a close family member	30	Wife beginning work
7	Death of a best friend	31	Wife stopping work
8	Foreclosure on a mortgage or loan	32	Major change in working hours or conditions
9	Revision of personal habits	33	Major change in usual type and/or amount of recreation
10	Minor violation of the law; court appearance		
		34	Taking on a mortgage greater than $10,000
11	Outstanding personal achievement	35	Taking on a mortgage less than $10,000
12	Pregnancy of wife		
13	Major change in the health or behavior of a family member	36	Business merger or reorganization
14	Sexual difficulties	37	Bankruptcy
15	In-law troubles	38	Large increase in social activities
16	Large decrease in number of family get-togethers	39	Large decrease in social activities
17	Large increase in number of family get-togethers		
		40	Deterioration of home or neighborhood
18	Large decline in financial status	41	Building a new home or remodeling
19	Large increase in financial status		
20	Gaining a new family member	42	Retirement from work
21	Your son or daughter leaving home	43	Vacation
		44	Changing to a new school
22	Marital separation	45	Beginning or ceasing schooling
23	Marital reconciliation	46	Laid off from work
24	Demotion or being fired	47	Quitting a job
25	Divorce		

Rationale for the LEQ indices.   The Loss Index was constructed to reflect stressful life events over which minimal control could be exerted compared to other stressful events in the LEQ. An attempt was made to design the Loss Index so that it would also include losses which previous research had implicated in the onset of clinical CHD. At the beginning of the study, three members of the research staff independently evaluated each of the LEQ items in the light of these general criteria. Disagreements regarding inclusion of a given item were resolved in the conservative direction by excluding it from the Loss Index. Selection of 10 items resulted from this procedure. They are Items 6, 7, 18, 21, 22, 24, 25, 37, 42, and 46 (see Table 10.2).

The rationale for selecting each of these items was as follows. The LEQ events "death of a close family member" (Item 6) and "death of a best friend" (Item 7) appear to be clear object losses which cannot easily be prevented and cannot often be predicted. Prior research, it will be recalled, has documented an association between these events and CHD (e.g., Parkes *et al.,* 1969). The items relating to job demotion, retirement, and being fired (Items 24, 42, 46) are also instances of loss to an individual that he can only rarely modify or avoid, and, moreover, such prodromal events appear to have an empirical linkage to the occurrence of clinical coronary disease (e.g., Engel, 1970). While divorce or separation (Items 22 and 25) are usually voluntary acts, nevertheless the partners often experience feelings of helplessness and depression immediately after they separate. The items "bankruptcy" (37) and "large decline in financial status" (18) were included because each is an instance of economic loss over which little control can usually be exerted. The last item, "son or daughter leaving home" (21), was selected for the Loss Index primarily because of reports linking the incident to prodromal helplessness and subsequent CHD (e.g., Greene *et al.,* 1972).

Other LEQ items could have been incorporated in the Loss Index. Likely candidates include "sexual difficulties" and "deterioration of home or neighborhood." For many individuals, such events constitute significant losses about which they feel considerable helplessness. Our criteria for inclusion and exclusion of items was deliberately intuitive. Reliance was placed upon unanimous agreement among the three judges as to the appropriateness of a given item for the Loss Index. While criticism can certainly be leveled at this procedure, as well as at the decisions resulting from it, nevertheless the most expeditious (and probably objective) approach seemed to be agreement among judges using essentially the same criteria.

The Negative Events Index was constructed by similar interjudge agreement procedures. Seven LEQ items which do not overlap with the Loss Index were agreed upon as reflecting life events that would be experienced by individuals as stressful but not necessarily as helplessness-inducing losses. Our purpose in constructing this index was to provide data against which to evaluate differences obtained with the Loss Index. We recognize, of course, that the seven negative events (listed in the next paragraph) may not be as aversive as some of those included in the Loss Index. This creates problems for interpreting the two indices in terms of a loss versus nonloss distinction, but given the nature of the LEQ there seemed to be no other viable alternative.

The items in the Negative Events Index are "troubles with the boss" (1); "detention in jail" (4); "foreclosure on a mortgage or loan" (8); "sexual difficulties" (14); "in-law troubles" (15); "large increase in number of arguments with spouse" (28); "deterioration of home or neighborhood" (40). While a few other LEQ items might conceivably have been added to this list (like "major change in working hours or conditions"), the foregoing events were the only ones about which there was interjudge unanimity regarding their inclusion in the Negative Events Index.

Results

In evaluating the results of this study, only significance tests that attain or exceed .01 will be considered statistically reliable. A stringent alpha level seems indicated in view of the sizeable number of cases in the study, the high refusal rate, and the self-selection biases probably operative in the study. Moreover, unlike laboratory experiments reported in previous chapters, random assignment of subjects to experimental groups was obviously an impossibility. Small differences might, therefore, be due to chance factors which increase the likelihood of Type I errors. With these considerations in mind, let us turn to the first set of data, namely, the JAS scores.

The JAS scores.   The mean JAS score for the coronary group was $+5.4$, where 0 is the mean of the distribution, and positive scores indicate Pattern A while negative scores indicate Pattern B (see Chapter 3 and Appendix A). The means for the hospitalized and nonhospitalized controls were $+0.8$ and -5.6, respectively. A one-way analysis of variance followed by individual contrasts revealed that each group was significantly different from the others at better than the .01 level. The reliable differences between the coronary group and each of the controls confirms initial predictions. The difference between the two control groups was unexpected. However, closer examination of the hospitalized sample indicates that its positive JAS score was attributable, in large part, to the alcoholic patients. By eliminating this group, the mean score became -1.67, which does not differ from that of the nonhospitalized controls, $t(137) = 1.89, p > .05$. We will have more to say about the alcoholic sample later in this chapter. Suffice it to note here that the alcoholic patients appear to be a special subgroup of noncoronary patients.

The Loss Index. Sixty-four percent of the coronary subjects reported at least one loss in the 1-year period prior to hospitalization, whereas only 36% of the nonhospitalized controls experienced an event of this type during the same period. The two distributions were independent as evaluated by χ^2 ("Yes–No" by coronary patients versus nonhospitalized controls). The significance level was .01. Eighty percent of the hospitalized controls reported at least one loss, which is clearly greater than the percentage for the nonhospitalized controls ($p < .001$). The χ^2 test comparing the noncoronary and coronary patients failed to achieve our criterion level of statistical significance ($p = .08$). Initial expectations have thus been confirmed. A reliably higher percentage of each patient group experienced a loss compared to the healthy controls.

The next question is whether a similar effect appears in other time intervals. The relevant Loss Index percentages for the period "3 months prior to today" were 40% for the coronaries, 54% for the hospitalized controls, and 30% for the nonhospitalized group. Only the χ^2 involving the two control groups was statistically significant ($p = .01$). A similar pattern of results was obtained for the period 1–3 years before today." The percentages were 60, 70, and 56 for the coronaries, hospitalized controls, and nonhospitalized controls, respectively. None of the χ^2 tests achieved acceptable levels of significance ($ps \geqslant .10$).

The preceding analyses indicate that the relationship between hospitalization and helplessness-inducing life events was limited to a specific time period, namely, 1 year before hospitalization. The only exception to this generalization occurred in the 3-month period, with more hospitalized controls reporting losses than healthy controls. Given that a sizeable number of statistical tests were performed, this difference can probably be attributed to chance fluctuation. It is unclear, however, that the greater likelihood of life events among hospitalized individuals is restricted to losses. Perhaps life change in general is more characteristic of such samples. It is also possible that negative events, even if they are not judged to be helplessness-inducing, distinguish sick from healthy subjects. Both possibilities were examined with data from the other LEQ indices.

Other LEQ indices. The life change scores (namely, percentages of cases reporting one or more of the 47 LEQ events during each time period) were virtually the same for the three samples. During the 1-year period, the relevant percentages were 87 for the coronaries, 94 for the hospitalized controls, and 92 for the healthy controls. None of the comparisons achieved statistical significance ($ps > .20$). Similar sets of percentages values were obtained for the other two prodromal periods, and, with one exception, all of the relevant χ^2 values failed to attain statistical significance ($ps > .20$). The exception was for the 3-month period, where 90% of the hospitalized controls reported at least one LEQ event compared to 67% of the coronary group ($p < .01$).

The foregoing results indicate that coronary and noncoronary patients do not differ from healthy controls in terms of life change. It would appear that the differences obtained for the Loss Index cannot be attributed to the greater likelihood of life events among hospitalized patients, irrespective of whether those events constitute a loss. While this conclusion is consistent with initial expectations, nevertheless it is somewhat surprising that the patient samples did not differ from the nonhospitalized control group in reported life change. After all, Holmes and Rahe (e.g., see Rahe, 1968) have shown that individuals who experience events that yield higher total life change scores are more likely than individuals with lower scores to become ill during a subsequent observation period.

A possible explanation for the null effect obtained in this study is our relatively crude measure of life change. Recall that a more sensitive procedure for computing such change involves summation of all weighted LEQ items which a subject has endorsed (see Chapter 2). For reasons given earlier (see footnote 3 in this chapter), this procedure for computing total life change seemed inappropriate for use with our data. Nevertheless, we explored the efficacy of the Holmes–Rahe approach by calculating a total life change score using a modification of their scale weights to take account of the LEQ items we added to their original list. For the 1-year period, hospitalized controls showed a higher average amount of life change than the nonhospitalized controls (Ms = 449.6 and 149.7; $p < .001$ by t test), whereas the mean for the coronaries (194.9) still did not differ from that of the healthy subjects ($p > .20$ by t test). An almost identical pattern of results appeared in the other two time periods. These findings suggest that a total life change score might indeed be suitable for detecting differences between sick and healthy cases. The life change procedure could thus be used in future research of the type reported here, albeit with revised and updated item weights.

Turning to the Negative Events Index, approximately the same percentage of coronary and nonhospitalized-control cases reported one or more negative events during the 1-year prodromal period (49% and 46%, respectively). Although 57% of the hospitalized controls reported at least one negative event, this percentage value was not reliably different from those obtained with the other two samples ($ps > .10$). A similar set of percentages was obtained for the 3-month time period, that is, approximately the same proportion of cases in each sample reported at least one negative event. For the 1–3-year period, however, more hospitalized controls (60%) reported negative events than did either the coronary or healthy samples (22% and 42%, respectively). The two χ^2 comparisons were statistically significant ($ps < .01$).

In general, then, comparable proportions of coronary patients, hospitalized controls, and nonhospitalized controls experienced negative events that were not classified as losses. On the other hand, a greater percentage of hospitalized controls reported negative events during the specific time period of 1–3 years prior to hospitalization. We are frankly at a loss to explain this exceptionally high Negative Events score of the hospitalized control group. However, while not explicable at this time, the result does not seriously compromise the major conclusions given below.

Summary and Conclusions

Since a greater proportion of both coronary and noncoronary patients reported losses than did the healthy controls, but since the patients did not differ from these controls on the Negative Events Index (at least during the critical 1-year period), we may conclude that helplessness-inducing life events are more likely to have occurred in individuals with illness compared to those without physical or psychic disease. This conclusion must, however, be viewed with caution. As we noted earlier, it is difficult to compare the Loss and Negative Events indices in terms of a loss–nonloss, or controllability–uncontrollability, distinction. The observed differences obtained with the two types of scores could be attributable to the more stressful nature of the events in the Loss Index, as well as to their presumed greater uncontrollability. While the interjudge agreement procedure attempted to select LEQ items for the Negative Events Index that, at once, were stressful and relatively nonhelplessness-inducing, nevertheless many of the items might not be considered as aversive as those incorporated in the Loss Index. Despite this problem, the overall findings at least suggest that compared to nonhospitalized controls, coronary patients are Type As who experience losses during a 1-year prodromal period, whereas noncoronary patients are Type Bs who experience such events during the same time frame. This conclusion is, of course, consistent with the original expectations guiding our research.

The Alcoholic Subsample

Alcholic patients among the hospitalized controls[4] had a mean JAS score that did not differ significantly from the coronary patients [$Ms = +5.4$ and $+2.8$; $t(74) = 1.31, p = .20$]. Both groups might thus be characterized as Pattern A.

There is also evidence indicating that more alcoholics than healthy controls report losses in each of the three time periods. During the 1-year interval, for example, the percentages were 81 and 36, which by χ^2 reflects a significant difference at the .01 level. On the other hand, there was no reliable difference between the percentages of coronaries and alcoholics, indicating one or more losses during this same prodromal period (64% and 81%, respectively;

---

[4] The criteria used to diagnose alcoholism at the Houston VA Hospital were as follows: excessive drinking which leads to improper social or physical functioning; trouble on the job or at home; and/or delirium tremens. This information is customarily obtained from the patient's family, police authorities, or in some cases from the patient himself.

$p > .15$). Similar sets of results were obtained with the Negative Events Index, and with reports of life change in general, although in both instances the relevant comparisons did not achieve criterion levels of significance.

Taken together, the foregoing results suggest that alcoholics are Type As and that, in addition, a greater proportion of these cases than healthy controls tend to give "yes" answers to various items in the LEQ. Other research indicates that alcoholics endorse significantly more symptoms on a health questionnaire than nonalcoholic controls (Hagnell & Tunving, 1972), and Dudley, Roszell, Mules, and Hague (1974) find that high total life change scores are associated with alcoholism. On the other hand, the latter study observed that alcoholics consistently underperceive the significance of life change compared to nonalcoholic normative samples. Thus, alcoholics gave lower rankings to over half of the life events in the original Holmes–Rahe (1967) list. This finding means that alcoholics believed less adjustment was required for the various events than did nonalcoholic subjects. It seems that the alcohol addict does not appreciate the importance of the "psychosocial turmoil" surrounding him.

There is no unitary personality basis for alcoholism, but a characteristic pattern of psychic dynamics is often found in the alcoholic patient. The pattern includes depressive trends; passive-dependent longings; poor impulse control; and, perhaps more important, a tendency to deny inadequacies in his personality—a refusal to admit them (Zwerling & Rosenbaum, 1959). While the alcoholic typically does not act upon his "feelings of omnipotence" and thus does not exhibit hard driving tendencies toward success (he is, after all, a dependent individual), nevertheless his refusal to accept the idea of personal limitation is not wholly unlike the extreme Type A person who is convinced of his ability to overcome all obstacles. It is likely, too, that if the alcoholic will not accept inadequacy, he will tend to externalize his problems. Such externalization might be reflected in the experience of a large number of stressful life events, the significance of which is underperceived or denied. In short, we are suggesting that alcoholics respond to threats to their sense of control by readily acknowledging their existence, locating them outside of themselves, and then denying their significance.

This coping strategy is in many ways what we would expect from a Type A individual. Although Type As react to uncontrollability with enhanced initial efforts at control, extended exposure results in greater helplessness. Though obviously speculative, it may be that a particular class of Type As avoids the helplessness inherent in certain life events by denying their importance and finding more passive ways of handling these difficulties. One of these ways is abusive drinking.

There seems to be some basis for the notion that alcoholism and cardiovascular pathology are alternative outcomes of the way in which Type As cope with helplessness-inducing life events. Medical research suggests that cirrhosis of the liver and alcoholism may have a protective effect against coronary disease

(Friedberg, 1966). For example, in one postmortem study of over 800 cases, coronary occlusion was present in only 4.3% of the males with cirrhosis versus 19.7% of controls; and myocardial infarction occurred in 5.8% of cases with cirrhosis versus 25.4% of controls (Hirst, Hadley, & Gore, 1965). Assuming that the heart victims and alcoholics were Type As, we might suggest that the two diseases are alternative consequences of Pattern A behavior.

Further support for this notion comes from data indicating that, compared to heatlhy controls, more teetotalers were present in the coronary sample of our study. The first part of the LEQ contained an item asking, *"On the average, how many shots, mixed drinks, beers, and glasses of wine do you consume in the course of a week?"* There were five response categories: "none"; "1–3"; "4–7"; "8–14"; and "15 or more." The results indicated that 33% of the nonhospitalized controls never drank alcohol, whereas 53% of the coronary cases were teetotalers. While not achieving our criterion significance level of .01, the relevant χ^2 (coronary patients versus nonhospitalized controls by "None" versus "One or more drinks") was not inconsiderable at 3.96, $p < .05$.

There is still other evidence that alcoholism and clinical CHD may be alternative outcomes of Pattern A behavior. Appels (1973) found a positive relationship of the order of .50 between CHD mortality rates for 1925 and 1950 and McClelland's (1961) projective measure of national achievement motivation in 22 different countries during the same two time periods. If we consider the achievement motivation index as reflecting a Pattern A society, that is, one which emphasizes competitiveness, success, and aggressiveness, the positive correlation reported by Appels suggests a direct relationship between the behavior pattern and mortality due to CHD.

A related analysis on alcoholism was conducted in our own laboratory. Alcohol consumption was tabulated as gallons of alcohol consumed per person of legal drinking age during the year 1965. Figures were available for 19 of the 22 countries (Maxwell, 1966). Also included in the tabulation were mortality rates due to cirrhosis of the liver in each of the 19 countries for the year 1956 (World Health Organization, 1960). The rank-order correlation between gallons of alcohol consumed and CHD mortality rates across nations was – .47. The comparable ρ coefficient between cirrhosis and CHD was – .55. Whereas substantial correlations between alcoholism and the achievement motivation index failed to emerge in our analysis ($\rho = .02$), nevertheless the inverse relationship observed between the diseases themselves suggests that alcoholism and CHD might be construed as alternative consequences of Pattern A.

GENERAL CONCLUSIONS

The major findings reported in this chapter indicate that (1) coronary patients have higher average JAS scores than do either the hospitalized or nonhospitalized control group; (2) in contrast to healthy controls, a greater proportion of hospitalized patients (both coronaries and noncoronaries) experience stressful losses in their lives during a 1-year prodromal period. We may suggest, therefore, that CHD is more likely to be found among Type As than among Type Bs, providing an excess of life events occur which are interpretable as losses of environmental control. This conclusion and the results on which it is based provide external validity for our laboratory-based notions about Pattern A as a style of coping with uncontrollability. It appears that the coronary-prone behavior pattern and real-life analogs of helplessness-inducing stressful events characterize patients with CHD relative to noncoronary subjects.

The findings of this study must be treated with caution, however. There are a number of factors which constrain easy generalization. First, the way in which subjects were selected leaves much to be desired. As we noted earlier, self-selection biases were probably operative in our samples. Approximately 40% of each of the hospitalized groups approached by our staff declined to participate. Other cases were excluded from analysis, it will be recalled, because they failed to complete all of the questionnaires. Second, several unsubstantiated assumptions were made concerning the life events labeled losses. While these events are likely to have induced feelings of helplessness, independent verification that they were so perceived by our subjects is lacking. We have also assumed that the uncontrollable events were salient, but again there was no independent evidence for this contention. A third obstacle to generalization has to do with the fact that the Loss Index was constructed, de novo, as a measure of uncontrollable life events, and the interjudge agreement procedures used to select the 10 LEQ items were based on admittedly intuitive criteria. While specific conclusions regarding the Loss Index results are strengthened by the null effects obtained with the Negative Events Index (presumably a measure of *controllable* stressful events), nevertheless cross-validation in subsequent research is clearly indicated before unequivocal conclusions may be drawn.

The retrospective nature of the Houston study is, perhaps, an even more serious defect in the design of our research. We commented on this point in the introduction to the chapter, but it warrants reiteration here. The LEQ responses (and even the JAS scores) may reflect the fact that patient samples were hospitalized and this experience colored their perceptions and self-reports. The only reasonable way to deal with this problem is, of course, to conduct a prospective investigation. Until such research is carried out, the results described in this chapter can only be viewed as providing tentative support for our hypotheses. Notwithstanding these limitations, this study emphasizes the importance of Pattern A and helplessness coronary disease. The study has, moreover, indicated a number of lines of future inquiry, including the possibility that alcoholism and CHD are alternative consequences of a particular mode of adapting to uncontrollable life events.

11
Development of Behavior Pattern A

This monograph has been concerned with the interplay of the coronary-prone behavior pattern and stressful conditions in the physical and social environment. Our methods of study have emphasized the operation of these variables in a contemporaneous context. With the exception of the retrospective Houston study (Chapter 10), virtually no attention has been given to the significance of past events in affecting current behavior. Yet the conditions that foster Type A behavior during the first and second decades of life may create a basis for coronary disease in the fourth and fifth decades. Unfortunately, there is little in the way of systematic data on the psychosocial conditions in an individual's life history that may lead to the emergence of Pattern A, and there is certainly a death of data bearing the role of biological (that is, genetic) factors in Pattern A development. Indeed, virtually no information exists with respect to the age level at which Pattern A behavior can first be observed.

Fundamental to this last problem is the question of how to decide when a youngster is Type A or Type B. What criteria can be used for making this classification? How reliable is the assessment, particularly at age levels below 8 or 9 years when personality characteristics show considerable variability? A number of investigators have, in fact, distinguished stable individual differences in the cognitive styles of children that are reminiscent of the A–B classification. For example, Kagan and his associates (Kagan, Moss, & Sigel, 1963; Kagan, Rosman, Day, Albert, & Phillips, 1964) discuss the difference between "reflective" children, who inhibit their initial impulses, and "impulsive" children, who respond with shorter latencies and higher frequencies of errors on cognitive tasks. Positive correlations between self-reports of activity level and Pattern A in adults are discussed in Appendixes B and C. These results suggest that judgments of the vigor and tempo of a child's responses might be used, in part, for diagnosing his or her position on the A–B continuum. Still another approach to the measurement of Pattern A in children comes from the work of Bortner (see Bortner & Rosenman, 1967; Bortner, Rosenman, & Friedman, 1970), who uses a battery of cognitive and psychomotor tests that, in adults, yield a Pattern A classification having a modest 66% agreement with diagnoses made on the basis of the standardized stress interview (see Chapter 3). However, since Bortner's tests are relatively simple, they have the virtue of being easily adapted for use with young children.

Each of these approaches to the detection of Pattern A at young ages (and there are probably still other suitable techniques that could be developed), requires evaluation in predictive validation studies, where the criterion is the development of coronary artery disease. This entails a long-term commitment, in which the behavior pattern is examined in terms of how it might be conditioned by sociopsychological factors present in early childhood. Of equal importance in the evaluation of measurement techniques are construct-validity experiments. If, for example, children classified as A and B respond like their older counterparts to standard laboratory procedures, we have presumptive evidence that our A–B index for children reflects the dimension observed in adult subjects. Clearly, one experiment would not, in itself, be adequate. The development of construct-validity data requires a variety of experimental paradigms and substantial replication. However, as a first step toward validation of a potential measure of Pattern A in children, we conducted an experiment using 9-year-old boys and the learned helplessness paradigm described in earlier chapters. Karen Matthews and the author were responsible for this study.

LEARNED HELPLESSNESS IN CHILDREN

The major purpose of this experiment was to determine whether Pattern A is evident in children as young as 9 years of age and, if so, to assess whether youngsters so classified would respond to a learned-helplessness induction in much the same way as their adult counterparts. Our design was a partial replication of Learned-Helplessness Experiment I with moderate levels of noise stimulation (see Chapter 8). It was predicted that Type A children would show significantly less learned helplessness than would those classified as Type B—precisely the effect obtained with adult subjects under moderate levels of uncontrollable stress (see, for example, Table 8.1).

Overview of the Design

Subjects were exposed to two series of 2200-Hz noise bursts delivered at 90 dB(A).[1] Half of the subjects were presented with two successive tasks which did not enable them to escape from the noise (No Escape condition), whereas the other half could terminate the sounds by manipulating a sequence of buttons on the first task, or two rotary knobs on the second task (Escape condition). Within each of the two conditions, subjects were divided into As and Bs based on their scores on the diagnostic test battery (to be described later). After pretreatment, subjects were again exposed to the noise level they had received in the first part of the experiment.[2] All subjects in this test phase could escape by making appropriate responses on still another task. The effects of learned helplessness were measured in this phase of the study. The principal dependent variable was latency of escape responses.

Subjects

Subjects were 88 fourth- and fifth-grade boys ranging in age from 9 to 11. All subjects had scores of 90 to 120 on the Stanford–Binet or WISC, and there were no measurable hearing deficits in the group. They were randomly assigned to experimental conditions with two stipulations: (1) average IQ should be about equal in all conditions; (2) equal numbers of fourth- and fifth-graders should be represented in each condition.

Measurement of Pattern A

All subjects were classified as Pattern A or Pattern B on the basis of their scores on the battery of tests developed by Bortner. The tests were administered 1 month after the subject's participation in the study by a second experimenter who was unaware of the subject's experimental data. A set of 11 scores are generated from the test battery administered to our subjects. These

---

[1] Although a noise intensity of 90 dB(A) delivered at 2200 Hz is different from 78 dB(A) at 3000 Hz used in the learned-helplessness study reported in Chapter 8, nevertheless subjective ratings of annoyance appear to be about the same for the two types of noise (Kryter, 1970, p. 474). Both sets of ratings are, in addition, lower than those customarily given to comparable 107 dB(A) sounds.

[2] A set of helplessness-alleviation procedures actually intervened between pretreatment and test phases of the study. However, since these procedures were ineffective and in no way altered the major results, we do not describe them in this chapter.

scores can be grouped into three categories corresponding to various aspects of Pattern A, including time urgency and achievement striving.

Time urgency was measured by the Writing Speed task. The subject is asked to write the words *United States of America* at his regular writing speed, very rapidly, slowly, and very slowly. Since Type As have difficulty in slowing down, three scores are computed to reflect speed and impatience: (1) Slow minus Regular Writing Speed; (2) Regular minus Fast; (3) Very Slow divided by Regular.

Achievement-striving tendencies were measured by three scores from the Arrow Dot test (Dombrose & Slobin, 1958). In this test the subject is required to draw a line from the point of an arrow to a dot without crossing a series of heavy lines. There are 23 such problems. Failure to follow instructions is considered a form of impulsive behavior that is incompatible with successful performance. Type As are expected to obtain Low Impulse (I) scores, that is, relatively few forbidden crossings of heavy lines. On the other hand, Type As are expected to give solutions that follow instructions not to cross the heavy lines, that is, high Ego (E) scores. Each problem also contains dotted lines, although these are not mentioned in the instructions. Subjects who treat these lines as uncrossable are given what is called Superego (S) scores.

The seventh score in the battery also measures achievement striving. It is the amount of time the subject spends on each of the problems of the Arrow Dot test divided by the time he devotes to each item on another test in the battery—the Embedded Figures test (discussed next). The Arrow Dot test has no explicit deadline, although subjects know that they are being timed. Instructions for Embedded Figures state that the subject has 2½ min to complete the items. Since As work at maximum capacity irrespective of the presence or absence of a deadline (see Chapter 4), they should obtain higher scores on the time-ratio measure than Type Bs; that is, As are expected to work about equally fast on both tests, whereas Bs should work faster on the explicitly timed Embedded Figures test.

Though not a principal component of Pattern A, exaggerated mental alertness is thought to characterize Type A compared to Type B individuals (see Friedman, 1969). Accordingly, two measures of this trait are included in the test battery, namely, performance (number of items attempted) on the Thurstone (1944) Embedded Figures test and a flicker–fusion (FF) task. The FF task is administered as follows. A subject is shown how a stroboscopic light can be made to flicker or fuse into a steady light. He is then asked to indicate transition from apparent flicker to fusion and from fusion to flicker for five ascending and five descending trials. Transition points are read from the control dial of a flicker–fusion apparatus in cycles per second. Alertness is measured by two scores: (1) the flicker–fusion threshold averaged over the 10 test trials; (2) the range of flicker–fusion thresholds, as indicated by the difference between the highest and lowest thresholds obtained on the 10 trials.

The eleventh item in the test battery is a more general measure of Pattern A called Behavioral Signs. These signs include fist clenching, restless motor behavior, sighs, and anticipation of instructions. These behaviors are systematically recorded during administration of the other tests. The score is the total number of signs that occur at least once during the testing session. Type As are expected to show more behavioral signs than Type Bs, just as they do in the stress interview (see Chapter 3).

The eleven test scores were converted to standard-score units based on all of the cases used in this study. The first index used to classify subjects consisted of the nine standardized scores originally reported by Bortner (see Bortner *et al.*, 1970). They are (1) the difference between regular and fast writing speed; (2) the ratio—very slow writing speed divided by regular writing speed; (3) flicker–fusion threshold; (4) flicker–fusion range; (5) number of I, E, and S responses on the Arrow Dot test; (6) time per item on the Arrow Dot test divided by time per item on the Embedded Figures test; (7) number of behavioral signs. These scores were unit weighted and algebraically added to form a Pattern A index. Each test score was assigned a positive and negative sign following data reported by Bortner in his regression analysis of the original pool of test scores (see Bortner *et al.*, 1970). Subjects scoring above the sample median for the distribution of the nine-item index were classified as Type A; those scoring below the median were designated Type B. For ease of exposition, we will hereafter refer to the nine-item index as *Bortner's A–B Index*.

The second Pattern A index was based on an examination of the relationship between each of the 11 test scores and one of the dependent measures used in this study. This preliminary analysis revealed that 7 of the 11 scores predicted the trials-to-criterion measure of the test-phase task. The scores were as follows: (1) the difference between regular and fast writing speed; (2) the ratio—very slow writing speed divided by regular writing speed; (3) the difference between slow and regular writing speed; (4) number of I responses on the Arrow Dot test; (5) flicker–fusion threshold; (6) behavioral signs; (7) number of attempted items on the Embedded Figures test. These scores were combined in the same way as the items contributing Bortner's A–B Index, thereby forming what we shall call the *Texas A–B Index*.

Apparatus

In pretreatment, the subject's first task was a wooden box containing two rows of three buttons. Each button could be depressed individually, but when all six were depressed in any order the noise bursts were instantaneously terminated.

The second task used in pretreatment was a box with two spring-loaded knobs which could be turned in one direction only. Noise terminated if the right knob and then the left knob were successively rotated in clockwise direction.

In the test phase, the task was a box containing spring-loaded handles mounted on separate sliding blocks embedded in two channels. One channel was horizontal, and the other vertical. Moving the handles in appropriate directions deactivated hidden relays terminating all circuits delivering noise. Automatic timers recorded response latencies to the nearest .01 sec.

A solid state programmer delivered the 2200-Hz tone generated by an audiooscillator set for 90 dB(A). The sound was presented over earphones and decibel level was measured at these phones. The oscillator output used with each Escape subject was recorded on tape for later delivery to a yoked subject assigned to a comparable No Escape condition. This procedure equated each set of Escape and No Escape treatments in terms of duration and intermittency of noise.

Procedure

The experimenter explained to each subject that she was interested in learning how children solve problems and the subject was being asked to assist her in this project. The pretreatment instructions were as follows: "In a moment, you will put on these headphones and hear noises come on from time to time. When a noise burst comes on, there is something you can do to stop it." After placing the headphones over the subject's ears, the first series of noise trials was initiated.

Subjects in Escape conditions listened to 25 bursts of noise. The maximum possible duration of each burst was 10.8 sec, with intertrial intervals varying randomly from 10 to 30 sec. A correct response on the first task, that is, depressing all six buttons, terminated the noise almost immediately. Subjects in the yoked No Escape conditions were unable to terminate noise. The switches were unconnected to the stimulus circuitry, hence button pressing had no effect on noise duration.

After 25 trials, the experimenter removed the headphones and gave the following instructions: "Now we are going to do another task. You will again hear those noises come on. There is something you can do to stop them. However, this time I want you to use only one hand. . . ." The headphones were replaced and a second series of 25 noise bursts were delivered. All aspects of procedure were identical to those used with the first task, except the correct response for Escape subjects was turning two knobs. Rotation of the knobs by yoked No Escape subjects again had no effect on the noise.

Test phase. The test phase of the study followed pretreatment almost immediately. It also consisted of 25 90-db(A) noise trials. Subjects were again told that they could terminate the noise. The correct response was to slide the horizontal handle to the left and the vertical handle toward the bottom of the box, in that order. If the correct response was not made within 10.8 sec, the noise terminated automatically and an escape latency of 10.8 was recorded for that trial. All subjects could escape during this phase of the study.

Results

Effectiveness of the inescapability manipulation.   The Escape–No Escape manipulation was successful in inducing differential perceptions of control over noise termination. Support for this conclusion comes from an item in a postexperimental questionnaire: "In general, I had control over the length of noises." The question was "How often?" (6 represented "Always," and 1 signified "Never"). Analysis of variance of responses to the item revealed a significant Escape–No Escape main effect [$F(1, 76) = 3.91, p < .05$]. There were no other reliable effects or interactions ($ps > .20$).

Learned helplessness.   The response latencies for each of the 25 test-phase trials were grouped into five equal blocks. These data were treated in a repeated-measures analysis of variance, which showed an Escape–No Escape main effect, $F(1, 76) = 31.94, p < .001$), such that Escape subjects had shorter latencies than No Escape subjects ($Ms = 3.0, 5.8$ sec). There was also a Trial Blocks effect, $F(4, 304) = 86.15, p < .001$, and a Trial Blocks by Escape–No Escape interaction, $F(4, 304) = 3.38, p < .01$. These terms indicate that although all subjects responded more quickly over the course of the test phase, the incremental effect was somewhat greater in the No Escape condition.

The helplessness-induced interference effects reported for response latency were virtually duplicated with two other dependent variables derived from the same data. Thus, average number of escapes was greater for Escape than for No Escape subjects [$Ms = 24.6, 19.6; F(1, 76) = 18.23, p < .001$], and mean number of trials to a criterion of four consecutive escapes was lower in Escape than No Escape [$Ms = 4.4, 9.8; F(1, 76) = 15.82, p < .001$].

Pattern A and learned helplessness.   The analysis of variance of response latencies, just reported, also yielded an interaction involving Escape–No Escape, Bortner's A–B Index, and Trial Blocks, $F(4, 304) = 2.46, p < .05$. Table 11.1 on the next page presents the relevant data. Type As in No Escape showed less learned helplessness (that is, a greater decline in latencies of response) than did their Type B counterparts. In the Escape treatment, the trend of the data was reversed, with Bs showing a some-what greater decrease in latencies over the course of the test phase.

Analysis of the other two response variables (discussed earlier) failed to reveal a similar pattern of results. Bortner's A–B Index was not involved in any

TABLE 11.1
Mean Response Latency (in Seconds) by Bortner's A–B Index

Subject	Trial blocks				
classification	1	2	3	4	5
Escape, Pattern A (N = 23)	4.7	3.2	2.6	2.4	2.3
Escape, Pattern B (N = 21)	5.2	2.9	2.6	2.1	2.2
No Escape, Pattern A (N = 16)	7.9	6.4	5.0	4.6	4.3
No Escape, Pattern B (N = 28)	7.3	6.7	5.8	5.1	4.7

of the significant terms ($ps > .20$). However, correlational analysis revealed that the higher the A–B score, the greater the number of escapes ($r = +.25$, $p < .007$), and the fewer the trials to criterion ($r = -.23$, $p < .01$). Taken together with the response latency data, these findings suggest that learned helplessness may indeed be greater among Type Bs than Type As on all three measures used in the study.

The Texas A–B Index. Table 11.2 presents group means for test-phase response latencies, where the A–B classification is based on the seven-item Texas A–B Index described earlier. A repeated-measures analysis of variance of these data revealed an Escape–No Escape main effect, $F(1, 76) = 35.80$, $p < .001$; a Trial Blocks effect, $F(4, 304) = 86.70$, $p < .001$; and an interaction between the two variables, $F(4, 304) = 3.13$, $p < .02$. These results obviously duplicate what was obtained in the previous analysis using Bortner's A–B Index. The present analysis also revealed the same type of triple interaction observed before, $F(4, 304) = 3.35$, $p = .01$. This time, of course, the interaction involves the Texas A–B Index. It is clear from examining Table 11.2 that No Escape Bs showed greater learned helplessness than did comparable Type As, whereas differences in response latency were minimal in the Escape treatment.

Almost identical results were obtained with number of escapes. The relevant interaction indicated that Bs had fewer escapes than As in No Escape, whereas

TABLE 11.2
Mean Response Latency (in Seconds) by the Texas A–B Index

Subject	Trial blocks				
classification	1	2	3	4	5
Escape, Pattern A (N = 25)	4.7	3.2	2.6	2.4	2.3
Escape, Pattern B (N = 19)	4.9	2.7	2.5	2.0	2.1
No Escape, Pattern A (N = 18)	7.3	6.0	4.6	3.8	3.6
No Escape, Pattern B (N = 26)	7.7	6.9	6.2	5.9	5.5

no difference occurred between the two types of subjects in Escape, $F(1, 76) = 4.78$, $p < .03$. A reliable interaction also appeared, not surprisingly, in the analysis of the trials-to-criterion variable, $F(1,76) = 5.18$, $p < .03$; that is, As took fewer trials than Bs in No Escape.

Discussion

This experiment has demonstrated that learned helplessness can occur in children as young as 9 years of age. The finding supplements previous research by Dweck and Repucci (1973), which showed that children who attribute failure to their own lack of ability exhibit a decrement of motivation in subsequent achievement situations. A learned-helplessness interpretation was given to these earlier data. It now appears that depressed task performance in children can result from prior exposure to uncontrollable stressors such as noise, as well as from experience with failure on cognitive tasks.

Of greater significance for our purposes, however, are data indicating that Type B youngsters behave like Type B college students, insofar as both showed greater learned helplessness than their Type A counterparts when aversive noise stimulation is of moderate intensity (see Tables 8.1 and 10.2 for the relevant comparisons). The similarity was unequivocal with the Texas A–B Index; and though less clear-cut, similar effects appeared with Bortner's A–B Index. The latter result constitutes a cross-validation of Bortner's approach to the measurement of Pattern A and, hence, supports the idea that the test battery might be used to identify Type As and Type Bs in young children. Now that potential diagnostic utility has been indicated, much work is needed to establish the reliability and limits of validity of the test battery as an index of Pattern A.

GENETIC AND ENVIRONMENTAL ANTECEDENTS OF PATTERN A

Assuming, for a moment, that Pattern A can be identified in preadolescents, an obvious next question concerns its possible origins and antecedents. How is it that certain individuals develop a mode of response to uncontrollable stress which we have identified with the coronary-prone behavior pattern? What is it in their biological background and/or previous psychosocial condition that leads to the emergence of the Type A coping style? It has been suggested that genetic factors may play a part in the genesis of the behavior pattern. Let us consider the evidence for this hypothesis.

Genetic Factors

One set of relevant data comes from studies showing an association between Pattern A and self-reports of activity level on such temperament inventories as the Thurstone Temperament Schedule (TTS) and the Buss-Plomin (1975) EASI Temperament Survey (see Appendixes B and C). Moderately high heritability has been indicated for the vigor and tempo of behavior as measured by these tests, as well as by other clinical techniques (Wilson, 1975; Cantwell, 1972).

More systematic evidence for a genetic hypothesis comes from a study of 93 monozygotic (MZ) and 97 dizygotic (DZ) sets of twins, whose mean ages were 48 years (Rosenman, Rahe, Borhani, & Feinlieb, 1974). Appendix B reports the positive correlations obtained in this study between Pattern A and the Active, Impulsive, Dominant, and Sociable scales of the TTS. Since there is a significant heritability coefficient for each of these scales ($ps < .01$), support exists for the notion that at least some correlates of the behavior pattern are partially transmitted through genetic processes. On the other hand, the Type A behavior pattern itself did not show a significant heritability estimate. This latter finding is indeed puzzling, although it does underscore the possibility that while the behavior pattern is not inherited per se certain aspects of it (say, activity level) may have a strong genetic component. Perhaps people do learn to be Type As, but the process of shaping is potentiated in susceptible individuals—those who begin life with high energy output.

It can, of course, be argued that the Rosenman *et al.* (1974) study was flawed in relying on a binary classification of subjects as Type A or Type B. Such a classification may not provide sufficient individual variation to detect genetic influences. Accordingly, Karen Matthews and David Krantz conducted a study of the resemblance of college-age twin pairs and their parents on the JAS, which, it will be recalled, provides a continuous distribution of A–B scores.[3]

The Twin Study

The twin method for studying inheritance of personality dispositions in humans relies on the fact that MZ twins are identical genetically, whereas DZ twins have, on the average, only half of their genes in common—as do siblings born at different times. If MZ twins are significantly more alike than DZ twins, and provided that relevant environmental experiences do not differ for the two types of twins, it follows that the characteristic has an inherited component. The Rosenman research used this general approach, and the study reported here employed a similar procedure.

[3] An expanded report of this study has been done by Matthews and Krantz (1976).

Method. The names and permanent addresses of approximately 100 sets of same-sex twins (all of whom were current or former Texas students) and their parents were obtained from the records of the University of Texas at Austin. Each parent completed the adult JAS. Each twin completed the JAS, the TTS, and a zygosity questionnaire. Of the 100 families contacted, complete data were obtained from 56 sets of twins, 48 of the mothers, and 45 of the fathers. The average age of the twins was 21.2 years and the range was 19–25 years. The average educational level of the twins was 15.5 years, that is about 3½ years of college. Parents had a mean age of 52.4 years and an educational level of 14.7 years. MZ twins did not differ from DZ twins in either age or educational attainment.

Measurement of twin zygosity. Zygosity of twins was determined by a questionnaire modified from Nichols and Bilbro (1966). The original questionnaire yielded 93% accuracy of diagnosis when compared to serological techniques. This procedure classified 35 pairs as monozygotic and 21 pairs as dizygotic. Of the monozygotic twins, 16 pairs were female and 19 were male. Thirteen sets of dizygotic pairs were female and eight were male.

Results. Intraclass correlations were computed for male and female MZ and DZ twins on the A–B score derived from the JAS. Table 11.3 reports these results. The correlation for all MZ twins is significant ($p < .05$), whereas the comparable coefficient for DZ twins is 0. An examination of the separate correlation coefficients for female MZ and DZ twins reveals a comparable pattern of results. By contrast, the coefficient for male MZ twins failed to

TABLE 11.3
Intraclass Correlations on the JAS for Male and Female
MZ and DZ Twin Pairs

Twin type	Correlation
All MZ (N = 35 pairs)	.41*
Female MZ (N = 16 pairs)	.58**
Male MZ (N = 19 pairs)	.16
All DZ (N = 21 pairs)	.00
Female DZ (N = 13 pairs)	.00
Male DZ (N = 8 pairs)	.00

*$p < .05.$ **$p < .01.$

reach statistical significance ($p > .20$). The significance of difference between the correlations of all MZ and DZ twins did not reach an acceptable level of significance ($p > .10$).

Correlation coefficients were computed between the A–B score and the seven scales of the TTS. The following scales yielded significant correlations: (1) Active ($r = .52, p < .01$); (2) Impulsive ($r = .31, p < .01$); (3) Dominant ($r = .33, p < .01$); (4) Reflective ($r = .43, p < .01$). Similar coefficients are reported for these variables in the studies described in Appendixes B and C.

Product–moment correlations were calculated for the average JAS score of each set of twins and the corresponding scores of their parents. This technique is one of the accepted methods for describing the relationship between parents and children (Falconer, 1960). Recall that data were available only for a subset of the parents. Table 11.4 presents the relevant correlations. It is immediately apparent that the scores of female twins are closer to the JAS scores of the mother than of the father. Among male twins, the JAS scores of father and son tend to be closer than those between mother and son.

TABLE 11.4
Correlations between JAS Scores of Parents and Their
Children[a]

Child	Parent	Correlation
Daughter	Mother (N = 24)	.45*
	Father (N = 23)	.19
Son	Mother (N = 24)	−.09
	Father (N = 22)	.33

[a]Since the average score of each pair of twins was correlated with the corresponding parent's score, N is equal to the number of parents.
*$p < .05$.

Discussion.   The difference between MZ and DZ correlations was not statistically reliable, hence the previously reported absence of support for the heritability of Pattern A (Rosenman *et al.*, 1974) received replication in this study. It would appear that more refined measurement of the A–B continuum does not alter the conclusion that Pattern A does not per se have a genetic component.

Rosenman *et al.* (1974) reported that four personality correlates of Pattern A had relatively high heritability coefficients. Since three of these correlates—the Active, Impulsive, and Dominant scales of the TTS—were also related to

Pattern A in this study, our results appear to resemble those obtained in the earlier research with a larger sample of twins.

We tentatively conclude, therefore, that while the coronary-prone behavior pattern does not appear to be inherited, correlates of Type A do show some degree of heritability. As we noted earlier, Pattern A behavior may be shaped by environmental conditions, but the process seems to be facilitated in susceptible individuals who have inherited certain temperamental characteristics. This notion is obviously speculative and must be treated with caution. However, it does suggest an interesting line of inquiry which might be pursued in future research on the antecedents of Pattern A.

Environmental Factors

The results of the preceding research do not rule out the possible influence of environmental factors in the emergence of Pattern A. At the minimum, such factors act as eliciting stimuli. As we have seen, the behavior pattern appears when the milieu presents suitable threats to the individual's sense of control. Of somewhat greater significance for an environmental hypothesis are data reported in Table 11.4 showing mother–daughter and father–son similarities in JAS scores. Although genetic factors might conceivably be at work here, the results are also consistent with the notion that modeling processes and/or child-rearing practices may contribute to the development of Pattern A. That the acquisition of internal values and overt behavior are determined by parental role models is readily documented by examining the developmental literature of the past decade (cf. Parke, 1972). There is also evidence indicating that different child-rearing practices are used by mothers of sons with high and low need for achievement—one of the components of the behavior pattern (e.g., Rosen & D'Andrade, 1959; C. P. Smith, 1969; Winterbottom, 1958).

The Rosen–D'Andrade (1959) study is an especially good illustration. Male children classified as high or low in need for achievement worked jointly with their parents on a series of psychomotor tasks. Mothers of high achievement sons gave less autonomy and set higher goals on such tasks as ring toss and block stacking. It has been concluded from this and similar studies that the setting of high standards of excellence is more closely related to the child's achievement motivation than is independence training. The important point to emphasize here, however, is that data exist indicating that child-rearing practices influence one of the descriptive components of Pattern A. It is not untenable to assume, therefore, that such practices may be important in the development of other aspects of the behavior pattern.

This chapter will conclude with the presentation of a study on child rearing practices conducted by Karen Matthews, Marsha Richins, and the author. Systematic observations were made of Type A and Type B mothers and their

Type A and Type B sons working together on a series of achievement related tasks. Such data were expected to indicate some of the ways in which parents shape Pattern A behavior in their children, for example, by emphasizing the values of success, speed, and persistence.

The Mother–Son Observation Study

Though admittedly exploratory, several general hunches guided this research. It was expected that achievement-oriented mothers of Type As would have higher aspirations for their child's performance than the mothers of Type Bs. It was also expected that mothers of Type As would show less satisfaction with their son's performance than the mothers of Type Bs, presumably because Type A parents are determined that their offspring strive to master more and more aspects of their environment. Closely related to this prediction was the idea that Type A parents not only want their children to succeed, but want this done as quickly and efficiently as possible. It was predicted therefore that, compared to mothers of Type Bs, mothers of Type As would make more "hurrying comments" while their children worked on various experimental tasks.

We also expected that the mother of a Type A child would reward him for behaviors leading to success (approval, encouragement, and the like), whereas support would be withdrawn following failure. A similar pattern of reward and nonreward was not expected to the same degree from mothers of Type B children. This prediction was based on the notion that striving for success is shaped according to the basic law of effect in learning; that is, reward increases the probability of a response, whereas nonreward results in its extinction.

Overview of the study.   Four- to ten-year-old male children, classified as Pattern A or Pattern B, worked on three psychomotor and perceptual tasks. The mother of each child assisted the experimenter in administering the experimental tasks. Data were recorded by an observer who was present during the session. At the conclusion of the experiment, the mother was given the stress interview assessing her behavior pattern, and a measure of her attitudes toward child rearing.

Measurement of Pattern A in children.   This study relied upon a new technique for classification of children into As and Bs, in an effort to develop an instrument that could be used more easily with large numbers of children. In retrospect, it would have been wiser to employ Bortner's test battery, since this would have added to the cross-validation of a measure of proven utility. By developing an entirely new method of A–B classification, our results must be viewed as tentative until replications have been carried with the new measure. Given this caveat, let us turn to the actual procedures of A–B classification.

The Children's Activity Scale (CAS) was developed to measure the three descriptive characteristics of the Type A behavior pattern—time urgency, competitive achievement-striving, and hostility. The CAS consists of nine 5-point rating scales, which are made by the child's classroom teacher. A total score is based on the sum of the nine ratings. Illustrative CAS items include the following:

1. "When this child has to wait for others before beginning a task, does he become impatient?"
2. "Does this child work very hard on his school work?"
3. "Does this child like to argue or debate?"

The 5-point scale used with all items is as follows: "almost always," "usually," "sometimes," "occasionally," and "nearly never."

Interrater reliability for the total CAS score was computed in a pilot study of two samples of nursery school children. The correlation coefficient between two teacher-raters was .60 for a sample of 72 boys. In the second sample of 110 male and female children, the correlation between raters was .58. When data from the second sample were analyzed by age, increasing interrater reliability was observed. For the 34 three-year-olds, the reliability was .57; for the 46 four-year-olds, it was .59; for the 30 five-year-olds, it was .71.

Test–retest reliability was computed on the scores of some 90 third- and fourth-grade public-school boys. Each child was rated twice by the same teacher, with ratings done 2 months apart. The correlation computed between total CAS scores for the first and second administration was .85.

Subjects.   Ninety-one Austin elementary-school children, for whom CAS scores were available, constituted our potential pool of subjects. Those scoring in approximately the bottom third of the distribution of CAS scores, that is, 21 and below, were considered Type A; children scoring 27 and above (the upper third) were considered Type B. The final set of 58 subjects were drawn from these two extremes.

There were 19 Type A children and Type A mothers, 10 pairs from an older age group (8–10 years old) and 9 pairs from a younger age group (4 to 6 years old); 11 Type A children and Type B mothers, 6 pairs from the older group and 5 pairs from the younger group; 18 Type B children and Type A mothers, 7 pairs from the older group and 11 pairs from the younger group; and 10 Type B children and Type B mothers, 7 pairs from the older group and 3 pairs from the younger group.

Procedure.   A female experimenter greeted the mother and child and explained that the child would be working on three tasks designed to measure "personality characteristics which may influence whether people have heart attacks later in life." The mother was told that she would assist in the administration of the tests. A female observer, present to record mother–child interactions, was introduced as an assistant who would be making informal notes about the child's behavior. Both experimenter and observer were blind to the A–B classification of child and mother.

The first task was introduced as a measure of ability to work with abstract figures, but it was actually designed to determine the mother's level of aspiration for her child (see Rosen & D'Andrade, 1959). While blindfolded and having one arm behind his back, the child was required to stack wooden blocks, one on top of the other. A trial was complete when he either stacked all of the blocks successfully or more than one block fell off the stack. Prior to each trial, the mother was asked to estimate the number of blocks she believed her son would be able to stack. Mothers of older children were told that the average child her son's age could stack nine blocks; mothers of younger children were told that the average child her son's age could stack four blocks.

The second task was designed to observe the mother's verbal and nonverbal reactions to the success and failure of her son. The child was given a series of geometric designs to duplicate with a set of nine blocks. He was allowed a maximum of 60 sec to complete each design. The mother was told to time the child on this task and call out at the end of 30 sec that half of his allotted time for the trial remained.

The designs and blocks were identical to the Block Design subtest of the Wechsler Intelligence Scale for Adults and Children. Young children tire easily on the task; hence, younger subjects were given 8 designs to copy, whereas older subjects were given 10 designs. Approximately half of the designs were sufficiently difficult for the child's age level to cause him to fail. The other designs were extremely easy.

The final task was designed to collect further information on how mothers interact with their children on achievement-related tasks. The child was instructed to throw 15 bean bags into a wicker basket. He could choose to throw them from any one of 12 lines marked (and numbered) on the floor, but he was told he would not be given extra points for greater distances from the basket. The mother was asked to record the number of the marker where her son stood when he threw the bean bags, and whether or not he succeeded in getting the bags into the basket.

Observation categories for mother–son interactions.   The dependent measures used in this study were based on recorded observations of the interactions between mother and son during the experimental session. The observation categories were adapted from a set used by Rosen and D'Andrade (1959) in their study of parents of children with high and low need for achievement. Other categories were added to test specific hypotheses, including the following: *hurry up comments* (like "Hurry, you only have a little time remaining"); *positive pushing statements* (like "Keep trying"); *negative pushing statements* ("You can do a whole lot better than that"); *approval comments*

("That's a good boy"); and *disapproval comments* ("You're being silly"). The frequency of behaviors that could be classified in one of the 19 observation categories was coded separately for each trial of each task. The first task had 3 trials; the second had 10 trials for older children and 8 trials for younger children; the third task had 15 trials.

Results. There were no reliable age differences on the principal dependent measures; hence, the two age groups are combined for purposes of presentation in this chapter. Analyses are reported here only for those observation categories that relate to our original predictions. Data from the other categories were also examined, but the results failed to reveal consistent and interpretable effects.

1. *Aspirations of the mothers.* Estimates of the child's performance on each of the trials of the block stacking task were used to examine the possibility that mothers of Type As would have higher aspirations for their children than mothers of Type Bs. Because the mothers of older and younger children were given different performance norms (discussed earlier), each of the estimates was converted to a standard score. Analysis of the means of these three standardized estimates revealed a marginally significant interaction between the child's and mother's behavior pattern, $F(1, 54) = 2.78$, $p < .10$. The other terms in the analysis were not significant ($Fs < 1$). It would appear that Type A mothers of Type A children and Type B mothers of Type B children have lower aspirations than A mothers of B children and B mothers of A children.

2. *Satisfaction with the child's performance.* Since the mother of a Type A child was expected to be less satisfied with her son's performance than the mother of a Type B child, we examined the ratio of positive to negative evaluations of the child's task performance (for example, "You are doing very well" versus "You're doing it wrong"). Difference scores were computed between total number of positive evaluations and total number of negative evaluations observed during the entire testing session. The results indicated that Type A children received fewer positive evaluations than their Type B counterparts [$Ms = 2.6$, 9.4; $F(1, 54) = 5.86$, $p < .02$].

Separate analyses of positive evaluations and negative evaluations revealed that the main effect for the difference scores was due to the greater number of remarks positively evaluating the B child's task performance, $F(1, 54) = 3.72$, $p < .06$. Type B children were given an average of 16.5 positive evaluations, whereas Type A children received only 11.1 reinforcements. Analysis of the negative evaluations revealed that all effects were nonsignificant ($ps > .30$).

3. *Hurrying comments by the mother.* To test the notion that mothers of Type As accelerate the pace of their children's performance, hurry up comments were summed across all tasks. There was a significant interaction between behavior patterns of mother and child, $F(1, 54) = 3.92$, $p < .05$, and a near-significant main effect for the mother's behavior pattern, $F(1, 54) = 3.50$, $p < .07$. Subsequent contrasts indicated that Type A mothers attempted to hurry their Type B children more than their Type A children

(Ms = 4.2 and 1.9; $p <$ .05). Also, the Type B child was hurried by the Type A mother more than by the Type B mother (Ms = 4.2 and 0.6; $p <$ .01). The most frequently hurried subject was the Type B child of a Type A mother.

4. *Parental support and nonsupport.* The notion that mothers of Type A children are supportive during success trials and withdraw support during failure trials was tested by examining the amount of encouragement given during each type of trial on the Block Design test. These data were selected for analysis because they reflected the only instance in which success and failure was deliberately manipulated in the study.

Two so-called *support* indices were constructed as follows: (1) the sum of (a) positive evaluations of task performance, (b) positive pushing statements, and (c) approval comments, divided by the number of success trials; (2) the sum of (a) positive evaluations, (b) positive pushing statements, and (c) approval comments, divided by the number of failure trials.[4] Mean scores were then calculated for the difference between the amount of support given during success and failure trials. A positive score indicates more support during success trials, whereas a negative score indicates more during failure trials.

The results showed that Type A mothers provided more support during failure relative to success than did Type B mothers [Ms = -0.7, $+0.1$; F(1, 54) = 7.20, $p <$ .01]. A separate analysis of the support index for success trials failed to reveal reliable differences (Fs < 1). During failure trials, however, Type A mothers gave more support than B mothers [Ms = $+1.4$, $+0.5$; F(1, 54) = 7.08, $p <$ .01].

Rejection indices were also computed for success and failure trials of the Block Design test. The sum of (a) negative evaluations of task performance, (b) negative pushing statements, and (c) disapproval comments, divided by the number of success trials, was the rejection index during each success trial. The sum of (a) negative evaluations, (b) negative pushing statements, and (c) disapproval comments, divided by the number of failure trials, was the rejection index during each failure trial. Mean difference scores between these indices were calculated: the higher the negative score, the more the rejection during failure trials; the higher the positive score, the more the rejection during success trials.

Type A mothers gave more rejection during failure relative to success than did Type B mothers [Ms = -1.0, -0.5; F(1, 54) = 3.69, $p <$ .06]. This effect can be attributed to the fact that while no differences appeared during failure (ps > .15), Type A children tended to receive more rejection during success than did Type B children [Ms = $+0.3$ and $+0.1$; F(1, 54) = 3.20, $p <$ .08].

---

[4] Children varied in the number of block designs successfully completed. For this reason, the number of supportive comments given by the mother were divided by the number of success and failure trials for each child. Data on actual number of successes and failures on block design are presented in a later section.

To sum up, Type A mothers gave more support *and* more rejection during failure than success. Type B mothers gave equal amounts of support on the two types of trials, but more rejection during failure than success. Type A children received more support and rejection during success trials than did Type B children.

5. *Task performance of the children.*   Pattern A and Pattern B children performed similarly on the number of blocks stacked on the first task, the number of bean bags successfully placed in the basket, and the distances from the basket where they chose to stand ($ps > .20$). However, Pattern A children copied significantly more block designs than Pattern B children [$Ms = 5.6$, 4.3; $F(1, 54) = 12.60; p < .001$]. A possible explanation for this difference is the behavior of the mothers during success trials on the Block Design task. Recall that Type A children were told to try harder and were given more rejection than were Type Bs. Assuming these parental behaviors increased motivation to succeed, Type A children would be expected to complete more designs than Type B children.

6. *Attitudes toward child-rearing practices.*   All mothers completed the Maryland Parent Attitude Survey (e.g., Pumroy, 1966) at the completion of the experimental session. This measure, hereafter called the MPAS, consists of 95 pairs of attitude statements about child rearing. The test items are grouped into four categories: Disciplinarian, Rejecting, Protective, and Indulgent. The Disciplinarian scale signifies the belief that parents need and expect strict obedience from their children. The Rejecting scale contains items which indicate that parents are openly hostile toward their children. Protective parents report that they are watchful of their child and always alert to possible dangers for him. The Indulgent scale reflects a child-centered set of attitudes; the child is allowed to have his way in all matters.

Analysis of the mother's responses to the MPAS revealed that only the Disciplinarian and Protective scales yielded reliable differences between experimental groups. Table 11.5 presents the group means. In each case, there

TABLE 11.5
Mean Scores on Two Scales from the
Maryland Parental Attitude Survey (MPAS)

Children's behavior pattern	Mother's behavior pattern	N^a	MPAS scale	
			Disciplinarian	Protective
A	A	15	21.67	27.40
A	B	9	27.33	23.44
B	A	16	25.88	25.13
B	B	9	21.11	28.00

[a] Nine mothers failed to complete the MPAS, thereby reducing the size of each group as indicated in the table.

was a significant interaction between behavior-pattern assessments of mother and son (ps < .02). There were no other main effects or interactions (ps > .20). These results indicate that Pattern A mothers of A children and Pattern B mothers of B children have high protective and low disciplinarian attitudes toward raising their offspring. By contrast, A mothers of Type Bs and B mothers of Type As have high disciplinarian and low protective attitudes.

Discussion.   The results of this study can be summarized in terms of three main categories: (1) those associated with the behavior pattern of the mother; (2) those associated with the behavior pattern of the child; (3) those reflecting an interaction between the two patterns. Note that the second category of results is probably of greatest interest here, for it relates directly to our original predictions concerning the behavior of mothers of Type A and Type B children.

The behavior pattern of the mother was related to two of our dependent measures: (1) in contrast to Type Bs, Type A mothers gave more support as well as more rejection when their children experienced failure; (2) Type A mothers tended to hurry task performance to a greater degree than did Type Bs. While neither of these findings was specifically predicted at the outset of the study, they are at least consistent with what we know of Type A individuals and, indeed, might almost be considered obvious. Type A mothers seem more concerned about their children's achievement efforts than Type B mothers. They respond to their sons' failures by telling them to continue trying, support their efforts, and reject unsuccessful performances. It is not unreasonable to conclude that the child of a Type A mother will perceive her as determined that he overcome failure and achieve success.

The study documented the following relationships involving the child's behavior pattern:

1. The mother of an A child gave fewer positive relative to negative evaluations than the mother of a B child.
2. While her child was succeeding, the mother of a Type A encouraged him to try harder compared to the mother of a Type B.
3. While her child was succeeding, the mother of a Type A also gave more rejection than the mother of a Type B.

In short, the mother of a Type A tends to be critical of his performance, repeatedly trying to motivate him to do better.

One component of Pattern A is the quest for increasingly greater amounts of success. The foregoing results reflect child-rearing practices that might be expected to lead to this type of achievement striving. The Pattern A child, learning that his performance is not quite acceptable and being told to try harder, might seek higher and higher goals in an effort to please his mother. On the other hand, the parent of a B child provides fewer extrinsic incentives aimed at increasing efforts to succeed. She treats her son's successful performance as acceptable and does not suggest that aspirations should be increased. Differences in achievement training of this kind might well potentiate the formation of the two behavior patterns.

The following interactive effects were observed in this study:

1. Type A mothers of A children and Type B mothers of B children showed less of a tendency to accelerate their children's performance than the A mothers of B children and the B mothers of A children;

2. Type A mothers of A children and Type B mothers of B children indicated lower aspirations for their children's performances than A mothers of B children and B mothers of A children;

3. Type A mothers of A children and Type B mothers of B children were more protective and less disciplinarian in their attitudes toward raising children.

These results suggest that Type A mothers of Type As and Type B mothers of Type Bs are less demanding of their children than the other two types of parent–child dyads. They avoid hurrying their children; they do not demand high levels of aspiration; and they are less likely to use direct disciplinary action. We are indeed puzzled by these data, for they are not fully in accord with effects reported for the behavior pattern of the child (discussed earlier), nor are they consistent with what might be expected from Pattern A parents. However, part of our perplexity may be unwarranted in view of the following observations.

Bell (1968) has pointed out that parental child-rearing practices are often influenced by the child's personality characteristics. For example, an aggressive youngster may elicit deliberate counteraggressive training practices from his mother. Similarly, the mother of a competitive and success-oriented boy may structure his environment so as to reduce his need to be better than his peers. At minimum, she will avoid creating high aspirations for her son, and we would certainly not expect efforts to accelerate his task performance. This line of interpretation appears consistent with our observational data. The ways in which mothers in our study interacted with their sons were seemingly influenced by the son's behavior pattern. However, it was also affected by the mother's pattern, and for this result we have no reasonable explanation at this time.

Conclusions.   This study does not provide support for a coherent theory of Pattern A development. There was evidence suggesting that mothers of Type A sons engage in achievement training that might eventuate in certain Type A characteristics. There were also indications that the child-rearing practices of Type A mothers may encourage Pattern A behavior in their children, but this was more evident when the child was a Type B. It is possible that Pattern A will emerge in these children later in life. It is also possible that Pattern A is more directly influenced by the practices of the father. Indeed, research suggests that prior to the age of 5, a boy models the behavior of his mother, but after that age he begins to imitate his father (Biller, 1971). There are closer and more frequent contacts between mother and child during the early years of childhood. When male children grow older and identify with the father, their behavior pattern and that of the father may become increasingly similar. Unfortunately, data from fathers were not uniformly available in this study; hence, a systematic test of these speculations must await future research. As a first step in the area, however, the findings we did obtain in this study indicate the feasibility of more systematic work on the development of Pattern A.

12
Summary, Conclusions, and Implications

Having investigated the interplay of Pattern A and eliciting environmental conditions, let us summarize our principal findings and attempt to fit them into a more general formulation of the etiology of coronary heart disease. The best combination of traditional risk factors (for example, cigarette smoking, serum cholesterol level, and hypertension) does not identify most new cases of CHD. Some set of unrecognized variables is missing from the predictive equation. On the basis of psychobiological and epidemiological research over the past decade, there is good reason to believe that stress and the coronary-prone behavior pattern are among the unrecognized variables. Evidence for this statement was presented in Chapters 2 and 3, where it was suggested that cardiovascular dysfunction and clinical CHD are influenced by uncontrollable aversive stimuli. It was also shown that Pattern A is directly related to coronary disease variables, even when simultaneous adjustment is made for combinations of traditional risk factors for the disease. It was thus concluded that behavior pattern A and stress make significant contributions to the pathogenesis of CHD.

BEHAVIORAL STUDIES OF STRESS AND PATTERN A: SUMMARY

An analysis of the relationship between these two predictive variables was the primary purpose of the research reported in this book. Our aim was to elucidate a possible psychological dimension underlying the descriptive components of Pattern A, that is, competitive achievement striving, time urgency, and hostility-aggressiveness. It was believed that this dimension could best be specified by examining the interaction between the behavior pattern and uncontrollable stress, for our general hypothesis was that Type A behavior constitutes a style of responding to uncontrollable life stresses. However, before embarking on tests of this line of thought, systematic documentation was first made of the presumed characteristics of Pattern A.

We demonstrated that Type As are in fact hard driving individuals who are motivated by the desire for success. In both laboratory and field settings, Type As were shown to be achievement-oriented people who work at near-maximum capacity relative to Type Bs. Evidence was also presented indicating that, compared to Bs, Type As suppress feelings of fatigue that might interfere with successful task performance. Even as they do this, Type As were observed to approach their maximal capacities.

Other research documented the time-urgency component of Pattern A. It was found that As become impatient with delay and report that a specific time interval elapses sooner than do Type Bs. The arousal of impatience had behavioral consequences as well, for As did more poorly than Bs on tasks requiring a delayed response. In addition, Type As exhibited greater annoyance and irritation at having the pace of their activities slowed down by another individual. This finding suggests that As may indeed harbor more hostile feelings than do their Type B counterparts. The presence of greater hostility and aggressiveness in As received further support in another experiment showing that aroused As delivered seemingly more intense electric shock to a confederate than did comparably aroused Type Bs.

It was an interpretive analysis of the foregoing results, as well as a priori theorizing, that led to our conceptualization of Pattern A as a style of responding to environmental stress which is appraised as a threat to the individual's sense of control. It was suggested that Type As try harder than Bs to assert and maintain control over such stressors. After extended experience with the uncontrollable stimulus, however, Type As realize the futility of their efforts at mastery and, in consequence, manifest behavioral signs of helplessness.

The initial hyperresponsiveness part of our hypothesis received support in a series of laboratory experiments using, for the most part, the student JAS to classify subjects as Pattern A or Pattern B. In a two-phase experimental paradigm not unlike that customarily used in learned-helplessness research (cf. Seligman, 1975), subjects were briefly exposed to an escapable or inescapable stressor (pretreatment) and then tested on a psychomotor task in a nonstressful phase of the study. It was assumed that exposure to a few trials of uncontrollable stimulation (for instance, 12 inescapable noise bursts) would constitute a threat to the subject's feelings of control. Compared to Type Bs, Type As were expected to react to this threat with enhanced motivation to master a subsequent task, presumably in order to reestablish their sense of control. Two experiments were conducted with this paradigm. Both yielded almost identical curves showing the expected interaction between the A–B variable and the escape–no escape manipulation (see Chapter 7). The dependent measure in each study was performance on a timing task (choice RT or DRL) on which Bs normally do better than As. Pretreatment with an inescapable stressor potentiated the performance of As (and depressed the performance of Bs), such that As were faster than Bs on the RT task, but slower on DRL where delayed responding was the appropriate response. These data may be interpreted as suggesting that As react to stressors that threaten their feelings of control with enhanced efforts to assert and maintain control.

Subsequent experimentation reported in Chapter 9 placed a qualification on this conclusion, however. It appears that As are initially hyperresponsive only when the uncontrollable stimulus is high in salience. An uncontrollability cue may be considered salient or prominent when it compels or attracts the attention of the subject, for example, loud rather than soft noise. Under conditions of high salience, Type As do indeed display greater efforts at control than do Type Bs. When control cues are low in salience, Type As show depressed control efforts compared to Type Bs. These generalizations emerged from experiments using either differential levels of inescapable noise or a variable-ratio (that is, uncontrollable) training schedule administered under conditions where task failure was made a prominent versus a nonprominent event.

The salience–uncontrollability hypothesis was given further support in a pair of studies on the hyporesponsiveness of As following *extended exposure* to uncontrollable stressful stimulation (see Chapter 8). Using an explicit learned-helplessness paradigm, Type As exhibitied greater evidence of giving up (relative to Type Bs) when they become convinced that a salient stressor was in fact uncontrollable. The amount of exposure to uncontrollability (for example, 12 versus 35 inescapable noise bursts) appears to determine whether facilitation or helplessness responses will occur in the test phase of the paradigm. While the first reaction of Pattern A individuals is to assert control, extended experience with lack of control leads to passive behavior. However, just as As have an elevated initial threshold for responding to uncontrollability, it was also found that As show greater helplessness only when uncontrollability cues are salient. It was suggested that this stems from the fact that As exert enhanced efforts to locate control-relevant cues in high-salience pretreatment. This activity is presumed to lead to greater certainty of the noncontingency between responses and reinforcement, hence to an eventual decrement of escape efforts. The resultant hyporesponsivity is thought to transfer to the test phase of the study, where it is recorded as the learned-helplessness phenomenon.

The differential responsiveness of As and Bs to short- and long-term salient uncontrollable stress was treated as a style of *response* rather than the result of *perceptual* effects. This conclusion was reached after repeatedly failing to detect differences in the way Type As and Type Bs perceived various experimental situations. Aside from occasional differences in felt frustration, all subjects tended to describe the procedures in much the same way irrespective of their position on the A–B continuum. We concluded, therefore, that Pattern A is a style of response which is designed to assist the individual in adapting to stressful life events which threaten his sense of environmental control. The case for this view was strengthened by the range of conditions under which predicted effects were observed, including different subject populations; different experimenters who were blind to the subject's A–B classification; and a variety of experimental procedures designed to induce perceived lack of control.

An attempt was made to test the applicability of this line of thought to the actual occurrence of CHD in the retrospective Houston Study. The results showed that, compared to noncoronary controls, CHD patients had higher JAS scores, as well as higher Loss Index scores (a measure of helplessness) during a 1-year prodromal period. It was tentatively concluded that helplessness-inducing life events in conjunction with Pattern A may well be implicated in the onset of coronary disease. At minimum, CHD is more likely to be found among individuals who exhibit Pattern A and who also report an excess of stressful life events leading them to give up efforts to control their environment.

We are not proposing that helplessness and Pattern A are both necessary and sufficient for the occurrence of CHD. Conditions are optimal for cardiac pathology when there are (1) biological predispositions, including genetic factors and the presence of traditional risk factors such as elevated serum cholesterol and smoking; (2) a stressful life event that is perceived as threatening to one's sense of control; (3) eventual recognition that there is no way to cope with the stressor; (4) a mode of coping which has been described as the Type A coronary-prone behavior pattern. But, even the simultaneous presence of these conditions does not invariably result in CHD. For, it will be recalled, alcoholics were Type As and also reported an excess of helplessness-inducing life events. It would appear that the Pattern A mode of adaptive response may be generally costly to the individual (see Glass & Singer, 1972)—sometimes in the form of atherosclerosis and eventual clinical CHD, and sometimes in the form of another disorder. It is interesting to note, in this connection, that the occurrence of CHD and alcoholism are inversely related, thereby suggesting that they may be alternative outcomes of a particular mode of coping with stresses and strains in the environment. It is, of course, possible that still other negative outcomes have yet to be detected. Indeed, there is already a suggestion that peptic ulcers may be associated with Pattern A (Friedman, 1969).

Experimentation reported in Chapter 11 constitutes a digression from the main theme of our research. We were able to establish that while Pattern A per se has no discernible heritability coefficient, at least one major correlate of the behavior pattern—self-reported activity level—does reflect a genetic component. This finding gives rise to the following line of speculation. The coronary-prone behavior pattern is considered to be a continuum, ranging from the fully developed A_1 through the less fully developed A_2 and B_3 to the fully developed B_4 (see Chapter 3). The notion of a normally distributed A–B continuum is also consistent with assumptions underlying the questionnaire approach to the measurement of the behavior pattern. From this it follows that some Type As and some Type Bs are more extreme than others, and it may be precisely these individuals whose Type A behavior is determined largely by genetic factors.

It is also possible, perhaps likely, that most As are predisposed to the behavior pattern by virtue of their inheritance of a high level of activity. Whether or not they develop Pattern A characteristics, however, depends on a concatenation of events, including parental shaping, sociocultural values transmitted by societal institutions such as the school, peer pressure, and related factors. In other words, Pattern A may be a learned mode of coping with uncontrollable life stress, but it emerges only in individuals whose genetic makeup renders them susceptible to the relevant shaping processes. This line of thought is obviously speculative and can only be treated as hypothetical until further empirical work is completed. It is noteworthy, nevertheless, that we have been able to locate the origins of Pattern A early in life and, in addition, point to the feasibility of its measurement in young children.

The results reported in this book form, by and large, a coherent picture of the interplay between Pattern A and uncontrollable stressful events. We have suggested that Pattern A is a response style for coping with perceived threats to the individual's sense of environmental control. We have also proposed that the behavior pattern is a prepotent set of responses in the individual's response hierarchy that are elicited by stressful stimuli signifying lack of control. In other words, an explanation for the hyperreactivity and hyporeactivity of Type As need not rely upon such perceptual–cognitive factors as greater expectations of control or perceptions of greater lack of control.

By proposing a behavioristic hypothesis, we do not impugn the viability of a cognitive approach. On the contrary, we suggested earlier that an expectational interpretation might well account for the reactions of Pattern A subjects to uncontrollable stress (see Chapter 9). While the one experimental effort designed to test this hypothesis proved inconclusive, nevertheless we are not now prepared to dismiss the idea that As have higher expectations of environmental control than do Type Bs. Until further research adjudicates this issue, however, we are inclined to interpret the specific reactions of Type A individuals to uncontrollable stressors in terms of a learned pattern of response to a particular set of eliciting circumstances.

A number of unresolved issues inject somewhat discordant notes into our attempt at summary and integration. We have noted most of these issues at various places throughout the monograph. Among the more significant is the notion of cue salience. This variable was shown to affect the way in which As and Bs respond to brief as well as extended uncontrollable stressful stimulation. However, future research must determine why As have an elevated threshold for responding to initial signs of uncontrollability, and why Bs are more responsive than As to uncontrollability cues of low salience (see Chapters 8 and 9). Of equal importance is the need for additional experimentation with explicitly stressful stimuli in order to provide more unequivocal documentation for generalizations about salience and initial hyperresponsivity. We also need to formulate a more precise conceptualization of the salience variable itself, along with reliable techniques for its measurement. As it now stands, we are hard pressed to give an a priori specification of the salience of uncontrollability, although we have been indeed fortunate in producing manipulations that, by and large, influence behavior according to intended purposes.

On the methodological side of our research, we can certainly find fault with the way in which evidence was obtained for the hyperreactivity and hyporeactivity of Type As. Support for hyperresponsiveness came primarily from comparisons of the performance of As and Bs after brief pretreatment with uncontrollable aversive stimuli. Evidence for hyporeactivity was derived almost exclusively from performance comparisons after extended pretreatment with aversive stimuli. What is clearly needed now is measurement of hyperreactivity and hyporeactivity within the same design; that is, pretreatment *and* test-phase responses should be examined in the same study.

More important, perhaps, than any of the preceding problems is the possibility of interpreting our behavioral results not in terms of uncontrollability and salience but on the basis of an assumption that As are more aroused than Bs. Such an interpretation was dismissed earlier in this book because we were unable to detect A–B differences in autonomic arousal in several of our experiments (see Chapter 8). As we noted previously, however, it is possible that the specific autonomic measurements used in our research were insensitive to A–B effects. Moreover, activation or arousal is not a unitary concept, and states of behavioral, autonomic, electrocortical, and biochemical arousal are often dissociated from one another (see Lacey, 1967). Indeed, there are data available which suggest that As may be more aroused than Bs, as measured by some of these other indices. For example, Friedman *et al.* (1975) report that, compared with Type Bs, Type As have greater norepinephrine responses to stressful stimulation. Our own research has shown that Pattern A correlates positively with self-reports of activity level (see, for example, Chapter 11), and that As appear more agitated and hyperactive than Bs (see, for example, the DRL experiment reported in Chapter 5).

Making the assumption, then, that As may be more aroused than Bs, how might we use this notion to explain the various results of our research? A simple arousal concept can probably account for a good deal of the data showing that As work near maximum capacity, deny subjective feelings of fatigue, and exhibit exaggerated striving toward success. Elevated levels of arousal in As can also explain the aggression data, providing that we think of activation as potentiating the impact of aggressive cues (cf. Berkowitz, 1962). Some of the time-urgency experiments are explicable on the assumption that more aroused Type As deviate from the optimal level of activation necessary for efficient task performance. Given a relatively complex RT task, for example, aroused subjects may be expected to do more poorly than less aroused subjects (cf. Easterbrook, 1959; Kahneman, 1973).

The general notion of activation–arousal has greater difficulty in accounting for the hyperreactivity and hyporeactivity of As relative to Bs after brief and extended exposure to uncontrollable stressors. The test-phase tasks used in our research (for example, choice RT or anagrams) were relatively complex, and therefore we might expect that more aroused Inescapable As would do poorly compared to their less aroused Type B counterparts (Easterbrook, 1959). Such an effect did, in fact, occur after extended uncontrollable pretreatment, where the level of stressful stimulation was high (see Chapter 8). In contrast, Type As showed less test-phase task degradation when extended pretreatment stimulation was of moderate intensity, or when pretreatment was brief and stimulation was of high intensity. Indeed, the RT and DRL performance of Type As under the latter condition was faciliated relative to that of the Type Bs (see Chapter 7).

An obvious problem for an arousal interpretation of these results is our inability to determine how uncontrollable stimulation, whether high or moderate, affected the level of arousal of Type A and Type B subjects. It would thus appear that activation does not provide a coherent and parsimonious explanation for the range of effects observed in our research. However, we do not gainsay the possibility that a more sophisticated analysis of the arousal concept—one which permits specification of the subject's location on the arousal continuum—may yet prove to be an accurate interpretation of Pattern A behavior. Such a conclusion must await theoretical and empirical work. For the time being, we are inclined to interpret our findings in the general terms given earlier, namely, Pattern A is a style of response aimed at coping with stressors that constitute threats to the individual's sense of control. Initial hyperreactivity and subsequent hyporeactivity to such threats are the characteristics of this response style.

A PROPOSED BIOBEHAVIORAL MODEL

Our program of research has been limited primarily to the investigation of Pattern A and uncontrollable stressful stimulation. However, the long-range goal is to show how the interplay of these two variables influences the pathogenesis of coronary disease. The pursuit of this goal necessarily involves systematic examination of physiological and biochemical processes. For, in the final analysis, it is such processes that mediate the impact of behavioral factors on coronary disease. While the Houston Study suggested a linkage between Pattern A, helplessness, and clinical CHD, it had little to say about mediating physiological mechanisms. How does the experience of helplessness, for example, precipitate myocardial infarction in Type As? What kind of hormonal imbalance, or autonomic nervous system discharge, might be produced by a loss in the life of a Type A individual, thereby accelerating the formation of lethal thrombi? These and related issues remain unanswered by our studies.

Even more basic is the relationship between Pattern A behavior, uncontrollable life stress, and the development of CAD. Atherosclerosis occurs, after all, long before any visible signs of clinical CHD. Aside from findings of an association between the behavior pattern and certain biochemical states (like elevated serum cholesterol), our studies shed little direct light upon the behavioral variables involved in atheromatic disease. We can, of course, make a number of inferences about mechanism from the behavioral data. For example, it is not unreasonable to suggest that the Type A style of coping will lead to disturbances of physiological regulatory processes that may constitute predisposing factors for the development of atherosclerosis. Alternatively, it might be suggested that CAD is accelerated by a failure of internal homeostasis induced by repeated behavioral responses of As to uncontrollable stressors.

The obvious difficulty with such hypotheses is that they lack specificity. In order to speak meaningfully about physiological mechanisms mediating a disease–behavior relationship, care must be taken to state what is meant, for example, by a disease of homoestasis. A preliminary effort in this direction was adumbrated in some of the earlier chapters. The catecholamines and related neural structures may be important components of the mechanisms involved in the pathogenesis of CAD. Since these physiological variables are affected by behavioral factors (see Chapters 2 and 3), they may also account for the observed associations among coronary disease, Pattern A, and uncontrollable stress. It is, therefore, incumbent upon us to consider the role of the catecholamines in the coronary process.

The catecholaminic neurotransmitters, particularly epinephrine and norepinephrine, are thought to potentiate the pathogenesis of CAD via such hemodynamic effects as increased cardiac rate and blood pressure, and the elevation of blood lipids like free fatty acids (cf. Carlson, Levi, & Orö, 1972; Friedman, 1969; Netter, 1969; Theorell, 1974). The catecholamines can also accelerate the rate of development of damage to the intima (inner layer) of the coronary arteries over time and, indeed, induce myocardial lesions (e.g., Raab, Stark, MacMillan, & Gigee, 1961; Raab, Chaplin, & Bajusz, 1964). Epinephrine and norepinephrine are also believed to facilitate the aggregation of blood platelets, and the release of platelet contents are considered important factors in atherogenesis as well as in the genesis of thrombosis (Duguid, 1946; Ardlie, Glew, & Schwartz, 1966, Theorell, 1974). From this it follows that any agent which increases circulating catecholamines may be a potential pathogen for cardiovascular function. Since epinephrine and norepinephrine are intimately involved in autonomic nervous system discharge, it is not surprising that stress has been found to influence their concentration levels in blood and urine.

Evidence for this latter assertion was presented in Chapters 2 and 3, along with results documenting an association between Pattern A and catecholamines. We shall now attempt to summarize this discussion and relate the biochemical facts to our behavioral results. It is generally agreed that environmental stress produces elevations in catecholamines relative to resting level values (Mason, 1972). It is also recognized that active coping with a stressor leads to an increased specific discharge of norepinephrine, whereas epinephrine levels remain relatively unchanged (e.g., Elmadjian, 1963; Funkenstein et al., 1957; Weiss et al., 1970). There are other data indicating that while epinephrine levels may rise initially in response to stressful stimulation, they decrease successively as the individual increases his felt ability to master the disturbing stimuli (Frankenhaeuser, 1971).

Much recent research has concentrated specifically on norepinephrine responses to uncontrollable stressors. It is believed in some quarters that severe depletion of this catecholamine (and a concomitant rise in cholinergic activity) is associated with depression and helplessness. Indeed, Weiss, Glazer, and Pohorecky (1977) maintain that the "learned helplessness phenomenon" is a misnomer; that subjects show a depression of response initiation in the test phase of the paradigm not because they learned it was futile to try, but because they were so lacking in norepinephrine, owing to a transitory decline induced by lack of control, that they could not organize themselves to react. Seligman (e.g., 1975) disagrees with this view, but a possible reconciliation is to accept the notion that subjects learn to give up and treat norepinephrine depletion as a biochemical correlate of this process. Without digressing further into what for us is a tangential issue, suffice it to note that both Weiss and Seligman seem to agree that helplessness has behavioral as well as biochemical consequences.

Let us now consider a preliminary integration of the behavioral and biochemical data. Once an individual perceives a threat to his sense of environmental control, he struggles, albeit with differential vigor, to reestablish and maintain control. During this period, we may expect active coping efforts and concomitant elevations in circulating norepinephrine. Epinephrine levels should remain unchanged or perhaps even show a decline. When the realization comes that control has been lost, the individual will become passive and give up. During this period, norepinephrine levels are likely to decline and central cholinergic dominance may prevail (cf. Anisman, 1975). Although these generalizations do not have uncontested support (e.g., see Frankenhaeuser & Rissler, 1970), there is sufficient evidence to warrant at least entertaining them as serious hypotheses at this time.

The alternation of control efforts followed by giving up is undoubtedly repeated over and over again during the life of an individual. It is not unreasonable to suggest that the more frequently this cycle occurs, the more the coronary arteries are likely to be affected by atherosclerotic disease. This extrapolation derives, in part, from results cited earlier suggesting that excessive elevations of catecholamines over time may serve as an intermediary process whereby reactions to stressful events induce biochemical and pathogenetic phenomena leading to coronary disease (see, for example, Raab *et al.*, 1964; Rosenman and Friedman, 1974). It also derives from more speculative notions implicating the rise and fall of catecholamines and rapid shifts between sympathetic and parasympathetic activity in the etiology of CHD and sudden death (Engel, 1970; Richter, 1957; see, also, Seligman, 1975, pp. 166–188).

Although no one has verified this line of thought, let us accept it as a working hypothesis in order to see how Pattern A might fit into the overall picture. We noted earlier that relative to Type Bs, Type As seem to show enhanced platelet aggregation in response to norepinephrine (Simpson, Olewine, Jenkins, Ramsey, Zyzanski, Thomas, & Hames, 1974). Moreover, Type As have faster blood-clotting times than Type Bs (Friedman and Rosenman, 1974), and at least three studies report that As display elevated norepinephrine reactions to stressful stimulation, whereas Bs fail to show this type of responsiveness (Friedman, St. George, Byers and Rosenman, 1960; Friedman *et al.*, 1975; Simpson *et al.*, 1974). Given these findings, it might be argued that the atherogenetic processes described above for individuals in general apply, *a fortiori*, to Type A individuals. In other words, Pattern A subjects experience the alternation of active coping and giving up more frequently and intensely than Pattern B subjects. This assumption seems reasonable if we recall that while As vigorously engage in efforts to master their environment, nevertheless many of these struggles end in failure and helplessness. To the extent that coronary disease is influenced by a cycle of hyperreactivity and hypo-reactivity, the greater likelihood of the disease in As might be explained in terms of the cumulative effects of the excessive rise and fall of catecholamines released by the repetitive interplay of Pattern A and uncontrollable stress.

We are well aware of the fact that the foregoing speculations do not tell the whole story, or even a significant portion of it. A general explanation has been offered only as a heuristic guide to future thinking and research in the area. We have speculated that uncontrollable stressors and Pattern A affect cardiovascular functioning via adrenal medullary and autonomic nervous system activity. Since we have emphasized the role of loss of control in developing this formulation, central nervous system (CNS) structures should also be involved in the sequence of events leading to coronary disease. A more detailed analysis of these and related complexities are beyond the scope of this book. Our research was designed to document the importance of behavioral factors in cardiovascular pathology. In so doing, we have added experimental support to the growing body of epidemiological data that emphasize the role of stress and behavior patterns in the etiology of coronary disease.

The major contribution of our research has probably been to formulate behavioral issues in a new way. The underlying assumption in our thinking is that coronary disease is a long-term risk involved in repeated adaptive efforts. Although individuals are capable of adjusting to threats to their sense of environmental control, such adjustments have aftereffects which render them less able to cope with subsequent demands and less resistant to later stress and strain. These aftereffects may occur as psychic diseases (Seligman, 1975), as impairments of performance efficiency (Glass & Singer, 1972), as psychophysiological disturbances (Frankenhaeuser, 1975), or as somatic diseases such as cardiovascular pathology. This is, admittedly, an oversimplified interpretation. We recognize that CAD has a multifaceted etiology. Many of the traditional risk factors, and, perhaps, enzymes related to cardiac pathology as well, must eventually be incorporated in any complete analysis of its pathogenesis. Still, it may be useful at this time to note briefly some of the preventive and ameliorative implications of our studies. It is to this topic that the final section is devoted.

IMPLICATIONS FOR APPLICATION

The general aim in the treatment and prevention of coronary disease is, in addition to altering dietary and smoking habits, to correct the seemingly pathogenic life style characteristic of Pattern A. Since elimination of uncontrollable aversive events or protection from them is probably an unattainable goal, the important consideration is how the individual attempts to cope with threats to his sense of control. The Pattern A style of response may be adaptive for initial confrontations, since good adjustment requires efficient mechanisms for rapidly mobilizing biopsychological resources. In the long run, however, Pattern A behavior is probably maladaptive and entails considerable risk to health. A major change in coping style would thus seem indicated. Whether such change is feasible is another matter, although there is some evidence indicating that clinical and psychopharmocological techniques might prove effecitve in depressing hard driving and time-urgent behavior.

Sigg (1974), for example, suggests that the therapeutic process can be assisted by the administration of psychotropic drugs of the sedative type. Pharmocologically such drugs reduce emotional and muscular tension, which is likely to characterize Pattern A patients. Sigg also suggests that β-adrenergic blocking agents (like propranolol) may be useful in any program designed to alter the ways in which coronary-prone individuals cope with psychosocial stressors. Since catecholaminic effects on the cardiovascular system (particularly the heart) are predominantly mediated by β receptors, and since the catecholamines appear to figure in the Type A response to uncontrollable stressors, a specific blockade of β receptors by propranolol-type drugs would seem appropriate.

That so-called sedative drugs and blocking agents are effective in altering Pattern A responses receives indirect support from human and animal studies showing that biochemical and behavioral responses to psychosocial strain were depressed by diazepam and barbiturates (see Sigg (1974) for citations of some of this research). Experiments have also established that the partial reinforcement acquisition-extinction effect (PRAE) is blocked by amylobarbitone (e.g., Gray, 1969), and Drewnowski and Gray (1975) report a similar effect for a liquid form of marihuana. The blockage of the PRAE may have special relevance for alteration of Pattern A behavior since, it will be recalled, Type As showed faster acquistion times than Type Bs on variable-ratio reinforcement schedules compared to fixed-ratio schedules (see Chapters 7 and 9).

Despite evidence suggesting the value of drug therapy, many cardiologists remain properly skeptical of the effectiveness of sedatives in ameliorating Pattern A behavior (e.g. Friedman & Rosenman, 1974). A number of nondrug clinical techniques have thus been proposed. Benson (e.g., see Benson, Marzetta, & Rosner, 1974), for example, has been engaged in research on the efficacy of a secularized version of transcendental meditation (TM). While the regular practice of TM appears to reduce blood pressure and heart rate, there is no empirical evidence to show that it alters Pattern A. On the other hand, it is not unreasonable to suggest that relaxation exercises can improve a person's ability to cope with environmental stressors in a less compulsively hard-driving manner. However, relaxation can probably be induced not only by TM procedures, but also by a variety of other muscular and psychic techniques.

General relaxation therapies are but one instance of the use of clinical procedures in altering the coronary-prone behavior pattern. There are more sophisticated, though not necessarily more effective, techniques for teaching individuals to cope differently with life stresses. The use of biofeedback in reducing blood pressure and related cardiovascular symptoms is well known (e.g., Shapiro, Schwartz, & Benson, 1974). While the principal purpose of biofeedback conditioning techniques is to control symptons in stress-related disorders, the technique could be extended to the regulation of stress itself. In conjunction with other methods, biofeedback might be used to teach the individual to approach stressful events in an adaptive manner which does not entail the long-term risks inherent in Pattern A.

There has been growing interest in the last few years in the feasibility of applying behavior modification and group therapy techniques to the alteration of Pattern A. Illustrative of the first approach is the work of Richard Suinn (e.g., 1974a,b; 1975). This investigator has developed what is called a Cardiac Stress Management Program (CSMP) designed to aid the Type A patient. Two assumptions are made regarding this patient: (1) the Pattern A individual, by his life style, subjects himself to situations which produce stress reactions; (2) he is unable to alter the behavior pattern by himself. Suinn's CSMP first trains the individual in self-control of his stress reactions. To this extent, it is not unlike simple relaxation therapies. Next, the Type A individual is taught to develop alternate behaviors as a substitute for Type A characteristics. The goal is "to encourage . . . different life style actions which retain productivity . . . but without the risks to health" (Suinn, 1975, p. 14).

In one evaluation study (Suinn, Brock, & Edie, 1975), 10 postcoronary patients were treated with CSMP and compared with a control sample of 10 untreated patients. A second set of CHD patients was also given CSMP treatment. The initial experimental group showed pretest serum cholesterol and triglyceride levels comparable to that of the control sample. However, posttest improvements were more substantial for CSMP patients than for the nontreated patients. The mean decline in cholesterol, for example, was 15.0 mg per 100 ml for the former group and only 2.6 mg per 100 ml for the controls. The second treated group also showed large decrements in serum lipid levels.

While these biochemical data are certainly encouraging, only anecdotal reports have been published indicating that the technique actually modifies the behavior pattern. It is not all that surprising that relaxation produces an acute decline in serum lipids. Until evidence is presented showing systematic changes in behavior as well, we can only acknowledge the existence of a promising technique.

The use of group therapy for modifying Pattern A has been recommended in a number of quarters (cf. Friedman & Rosenman, 1974). Rahe (see Rahe, 1975b; Rahe, O'Neil, & Arthur, 1975; Rahe, Tuffli, Suchor, & Arthur, 1973) has recently reported research designed to evaluate the effectiveness of brief group therapy in the management of patients recovering from myocardial infarction. Sixty patients were followed for up to 18 months after their infarction. Forty randomly selected cases completed a series of 4–6 group therapy sessions during the early rehabilitation phase, whereas the other 20 cases received no group therapy. Subjects were less than 60 years of age, and all were patients at the U.S. Naval Hospital in San Diego. One of the key features of the therapy program was discussion of a booklet, previously distributed to the treated patients, which summarized data concerning the nature of a heart attack, its emergency treatment, and optimal rehabilitation procedures. Subjects answered a CHD Training Evaluation Form composed of objective questions concerning these issues, as well as those relating to psychological factors important in patients with CHD. The form was usually completed by the therapy patients after their last session, and by control cases via the mail.

The results indicated that group therapy patients experienced reliably fewer rehospitalizations than similar controls. On the CHD Training Form, therapy patients demonstrated significantly greater knowledge of their disease and its rehabilitation than did control subjects.

These findings must be viewed with caution, however. First, the sizes of the samples were small. Second, in the course of the study, control patients learned of the educational materials being given to the therapy group and, as Rahe correctly points out, it is difficult to argue that the therapy patients were not inadvertently given a more encouraging outlook than the controls. Third, while the results of the CHD Training Form document clinical impressions that group therapy imparted critical knowledge to the patients, such a finding has only tangential relevance for actual behavior change. While Rahe *et al.* (1975) report that therapy patients seemed to modify their "previous habits of overwork, rushing against time deadlines, lack of enjoyment of life, and so forth" (pp. 10–11), these data were also based on impressions formed by the investigators from what subjects said in the group discussions.

To sum up, it would appear that a number of promising techniques exist for Pattern A modification, but none of them—behavioral or pharmacological— has yet received systematic evaluation using controlled designs. For the present, we may only conclude that it is probably feasible to alter some forms of Type A behavior, but unequivocal support for this assertion must await future research.

A major theme underlying this book has been the relationship between behavior and disease, hence the present section was largely concerned with the modification of behavioral variables. However, the treatment and prevention of coronary disease is, like its etiology, a multifaceted matter. Since advances in the medical treatment of disease often occur without full understanding of the disease itself, we can probably expect to see a variety of pragmatic techniques developed in the next few years that will effectively reduce the likelihood of clinical CHD. Indeed, there is already evidence which suggests that a drug like cholestyramine may be valuable not only in lowering cholesterol levels in the blood, but in producing marked reductions in existing atheromatic plaques (see *The New York Times*, November 18, 1975). The emergence of such methods does not mean that modification of the coronary-prone behavior pattern is unnecessary in the reduction and abolition of heart disease. We can only guess at this time, but in the end the prevention and treatment of cardiovascular pathology will probably rely upon behavioral and pharmacological alterations of Pattern A, along with biomedical therapies aimed a rducing the effects of other risk factors for the disease.

Measurement and Classification of Pattern A

This appendix presents psychometric data on the techniques used to measure and classify Pattern A, including the interview, adult JAS, and student JAS. We have arranged these details into a series of subsections corresponding to the references first made to them in Chapter 3.

Reliability of the Stress Interview

Jenkins, Rosenman, and Friedman (1968) report that two trained judges rated the behavior-pattern interviews the same way in 84% of 75 cases drawn from a larger sample of over 3000 men. The judgment was dichotomous, that is, either A or B. In a study of 1433 American Benedictine and Trappist monks, Caffrey (1968) obtained a moderate degree of agreement between all possible pairs of three interviewers. The range was 75% to 77.4%. Studies by Keith, Lown, and Stare (1965), and by E. H. Friedman *et al.* (1968) report similar degrees of agreement among trained interviewers in classifying subjects as Type A or Type B. Note, however, that the judgment of the behavior pattern from the stress interview has a reliability comparable to many accepted medical diagnostic procedures (Jenkins *et al.*, 1968).

As for test–retest reliability, Jenkins *et al.* (1968) have shown that of 1064 adult male subjects, 80% were placed in the same A–B category on the basis of interviews conducted 12–20 months apart.

Test–Retest Reliability of the Adult JAS

The test–retest reliability of the JAS A–B scale, based on a separation interval of 1 year, was .66 (Jenkins *et al.*, 1971). Indeed, 90% of over 2000 persons who took the JAS in 1965 and again in 1969 had less than 10 points difference in their A–B scores (Jenkins *et al.*, 1974).

Agreement between Adult JAS and Interview Assessments of Pattern A

The JAS agrees about 73% of the time with Pattern A and Pattern B judgments made from the stress interview (e.g., Jenkins *et al.*, 1971). Extreme JAS scores agree with interview judgments 88–91% of the time. These agreement values, particularly the overall figure of 73%, are less than one would like to see with standardized instruments. Indeed, Jenkins admits that the JAS in its present form still misclassifies too many subjects to allow its use in clinical settings (see Jenkins *et al.*, 1974). Perhaps the difficulty stems from the fact that speech stylistics, given such emphasis in the interview, cannot be assessed with a paper-and-pencil inventory. The JAS must rely on content exclusively.

Despite marginal agreement with the interview, we decided to use a modification of the JAS as our principal index of Pattern A (discussed next). The decision was made because (1) the questionnaire is an objective way of measuring Pattern A, and (2) it is relatively easy to administer to large groups of subjects. In making our choice of instrument, we could only hope that the JAS would prove to be a reliable and valid procedure for classifying subjects in our various studies. The experimental results reported in the substantive chapters of this book appear to have vindicated our decision.

Student Version of the JAS

Items in the original JAS referring to income, job involvement, and job responsibility were either eliminated from or modified for the student version of the questionnaire. Almost all of these items came from the Factor J scale (see Chapter 3). Five items on the A–B scale of the JAS required minor modification. For example, "Do you ever set deadlines or quotas for yourself at work or at home?" was changed by substituting the words *in courses or other things* for *at work or at home*. Similarly, for "How often are there deadlines *on your job?*" the italicized words were changed to *in your courses*. Alterations on the other three items were equally trivial and need no comment here. One additional A–B item was, however, completely eliminated and a substitute inserted in its place. The original item read: "In the past three years have you ever taken less than your allotted number of vacation days?"; here "Yes" and "My type of job does not provide regular vacations" are Pattern A responses, and "No" is a B response. The student version eliminated this item and substitued the following: "Do you maintain a regular study schedule during vacations such as Thanksgiving, Christmas, and Easter?''; here ''Yes'' is a Pattern A answer, and ''No'' and ''Sometimes'' are B answers.

Scoring the student JAS.   The student JAS is scored by unit-weighting procedures; that is, for each of the 21 items on the A–B scale, the A responses receive a score of 1, and the B responses receive a score of 0. The median A–B score for college-age males, at least in Texas where most of our research was conducted, typically falls between 7 and 8, where 0 is the maximal Pattern B score and 21 is the maximal Pattern A score. The characteristic range of scores is between 0 and 18. Female college students show a similar range, but the median often occurs between 6 and 7.

Classification of subjects based on the student JAS.   The typical procedure in most of our research was to administer the student JAS to a large number of potential subjects (namely, introductory psychology students at the University of Texas at Austin) several weeks to months prior to a given study. The median A–B score was then computed, and subjects scoring above this median (say, 8 or higher) were designated Pattern A. Those scoring below the median (say, 7 or less) were classified as Pattern B. It should be noted that in virtually all of our studies, the experimenter was unaware of the subject's A–B classification.

In some experiments, we deliberately selected extreme scorers on the JAS (like the upper and lower fifths, or upper and lower thirds, of a pretested pool of cases). These exceptions were noted when we presented the relevant studies in the text of this monograph.

In some semesters, we were unable to pretest a potential pool of subjects. Experiments conducted during these times administered the JAS at the conclusion of the experimental session. A different room was used and the test was presented as a ''separate study being conducted by the Psychology Department.'' Subjects who completed the JAS in this way were classified as A or B depending upon whether they scored above or below the median JAS score for the experimental sample. We also noted these exceptions when presenting the relevant studies (see, for example, the Deadline Experiment in Chapter 4).

Reliability of the student JAS.   Minimal effort was made to collect systematic data on the test–retest reliability of the student JAS. The differences between student and adult versions of the test are, as we indicated above, quite small. However, we did record some nonsystematic data on the stability of student A–B scores. Recall that the JAS was usually administered to potential subjects several months prior to an experiment. In a number of instances, the JAS had to be given again after a given experiment. This procedure was necessitated by the fact that not all of our experimental subjects completed the JAS at the time of original testing.

the fact that not all of our experimental subjects completed the JAS at the time of original testing.

We thus had two A–B scale scores for approximately half of the subjects in some of the experiments reported in this book; namely, the DRL and Interruption experiments in Chapter 5, and Learned-Helplessness Experiment II in Chapter 8. In all three studies, only about 9% of the 83 cases with two JAS scores changed from a Pattern A to a Pattern B classification, or vice versa. Intervals between the two testings ranged from 2 weeks to 4 months.

Factor analysis of the student JAS. In addition to the a priori A–B score, the student version of the JAS yields H and S factor scores. A factor score corresponding to J in the adult version is, of course, impossible since most job-related items were eliminated in modifying the JAS. The items making up each of the two factor scores were derived from a factor analysis of the student JAS responses of 459 male college students. We followed essentially the same procedures used in factor analyses of the adult version of the JAS (e.g., Zyzanski & Jenkins, 1970), including a principal axes solution and varimax rotation.

Two factors emerged which closely resemble the H and S dimensions extracted with adult samples. Tables A.1 and A. 2 present the primary defining items from the student JAS and their factor loadings. [The relevant comparison data for adult samples can be found in Tables 3 and 5 of Zyzanski and Jenkins (1970).] Seven of the 10 defining items for Factor H in the adult samples appear on Factor H in the student sample. Three of the six defining items for Factor S overlap in the two samples.

It is important to note here that a separate factor defined by hostility items from the JAS failed to emerge in our analysis. Items such as ''becomes irritated easily,'' ''has a fiery temper,'' and ''becomes annoyed when interrupted'' showed low to moderate loadings (.20 to .31) on our S and H factors. A similar phenomenon occurred in the factor analyses conducted by Jenkins and his colleagues. Hostility is presumably one of the major aspects of Pattern A, yet it does not appear as a separate dimension in statistical analyses. We are still inclined to treat hostility as a principal, though perhaps not orthogonal, component of Pattern A. This inclination is based upon extensive clinical observation (e.g., Friedman, 1969), as well as on experimentation presented in this book (see, for example, the aggression study reported in Chapter 6).

TABLE A.1

Primary Defining Items from the Student
Version of the JAS for Factor H and Their
Loadings on This Varimax Factor[a]

JAS item (abridged)	Loading
Rated definitely hard driving and competitive by wife and friends	.55
Rates self definitely hard driving and competitive	.51
Considers himself more responsible than the average student	.49
Gives much more effort than the average student	.46
Is stirred into action by college	.46
Considers himself more precise than the average student	.45
Approaches life much more seriously than the average student	.41
Rated probably relaxed and easy going by most people	−.41
Rates self as definitely not having less energy than most people	.36
Frequently sets deadlines for himself	.36
Maintains a regular study schedule during vacations	.35

[a] This factor is defined by items with loadings greater than .35.

TABLE A.2

Primary Defining Items from the Student
Version of the JAS for Factor S and Their
Loadings on This Varimax Factor[a]

JAS item (abridged)	Loading
Often hurries even when there is plenty of time	.43
Often told of eating too fast	.40
Eats more rapidly than most people	.39
Frequently hurries a speaker to the point	.38
Rated by most people as probably not doing most things in a hurry	−.38
Hurries much less than the average student	−.37

[a] The factor is defined by items with loadings greater than .35.

Pattern A and Personality Traits: I

Here we shall summarize studies showing correlations between the coronary-prone behavior pattern, as measured by the interview or adult JAS, and other selected personality traits.

Rosenman *et al.* (1974) have conducted an extensive investigation of male MZ and DZ twins, with an average age of 48 years (see Chapter 11). These subjects were given the stress interview for Pattern A, along with the following battery of psychological tests: the Thurstone (1949) Temperament Schedule (TTS); the Gough (1952) 300 Adjective Check List (ACL); the California (Gough, 1957) Psychological Inventory (CPI); the MMPI (Hathaway & McKinley, 1951); and the Cattell 16-PF Questionnaire (Cattell, Saunders, & Stice, 1950).

The results showed that four of the seven TTS scales correlated significantly ($ps < .05$) with Pattern A: Active ("likes to be on the go"); Impulsive ("likes to take chances and make decisions quickly"); Dominant ("takes initiative and assumes responsibility"); Sociable ("enjoys the company of others"). Of the four, Active and Impulsive showed the highest correlations—approximately .37 and .32. As for the ACL, 10 adjective scales showed reliable correlations with the behavior pattern. Only six of these exceeded a product-moment coefficient of .20, including Aggression (.28), Exhibition (.27), Self-Confidence (.24), Change (.21), Dominance (.20), Self-Control ($-.25$), and Counseling Readiness ($-.27$). Achievement also correlated with Pattern A, but the coefficient was only .16 ($p = .05$). None of the CPI scales, only one of the MMPI scales (Worried Breadwinner), and only two of the 16-PF scales (Imaginative and Relaxed–Tense) showed significant relations to the behavior pattern. The correlations ranged from .28 down to .20.

An earlier study by Caffrey (1968) showed no important associations between Pattern A (as assessed by a modified stress interview) and neurotic anxiety, introversion, or level of responsibility (as measured by the 16-PF and ad hoc self-rating scales). The subjects were 1433 Benedictine and Trappist monks. Low correlations (for example, .22 and below) were obtained between Pattern A and several other scales of the 16-PF, but factor analysis indicated that behavior-pattern items loaded a single dimension on which none of the 16-PF scales appeared.

An attempt to relate the adult JAS to objective psychological tests was conducted in our own laboratory as part of another experiment, reported in Chapter 7. All 69 cases (including pilots) were males ranging in age from 40 to 50 years. Sixty-three completed the JAS, the EASI Temperament Survey (Buss & Plomin, 1975; Plomin, 1974), and the ACL. The EASI data are reported in Appendix C in connection with a discussion of the student JAS and activity level. Suffice it to note here that the EASI yields Activity and Impulsivity scores which relate to the adult JAS in much the same way as the comparable TTS scales relate to the interview. The ACL showed 12 reliable correlations with the JAS. Only eight of these exceeded a product-moment coefficient of .25, including Aggression (.37), Exhibition (.25), Self-Confidence (.30), Self-Control (−.26), Achievement (.45), Dominance (.31), Change (.31), and Counseling Readiness (−.28). The eight are obviously identical to those ennumerated for the interview, although the magnitudes of the coefficients are clearly higher with the JAS.

The correlational findings reported here suggest that standard psychological tests are, by and large, unlikely to be useful measures of Pattern A. On the other hand, the behavior pattern does show modest relationships with a number of dimensions that have been used to describe the coronary-prone behavior pattern, for example, activity level, impulsivity, self-confidence, achievement, and aggression. These associations attest to the psychological meaningfulness of the A–B dimension, and thus provide additional evidence for the validity of the notion of a coronary-prone behavior pattern.

Pattern A and Personality Traits: II

Here we shall report the results of several studies designed to examine the relationship between the student JAS and various objective measures of personality. During the academic year 1973–1974, and again in 1974–1975, we administered the JAS and a battery of personality and ability tests to two samples of male undergraduates on the Austin campus. Testing was conducted in groups ranging from 10 to 35.

The tests administered to the first sample of 275 subjects were as follows: (1) Rotter's (1966) Internal–External Control (I—E) Scale; (2) Taylor's (1953) Manifest Anxiety Scale; (3) the K and L scales of the MMPI; (4) the need achievement subscale of the Edwards (1957) Personal Preference Schedule (EPPS); (5) Lykken's (1957) ''thrill-seeking'' scale, which measures the extent to which an individual seeks out anxiety-arousing situations rather than equally unpleasant but distasteful situations; (6) a test of self-image called the TSBI, that is, the Texas Social Behavior Inventory (Helmreich, Stapp, & Ervin, 1973). In addition to a total-self-esteem score, the TSBI yields four factor scores which measure (a) self-confidence; (b) feelings of social effectiveness and competence; (c) the belief that one is forceful, influential, and dominant in interpersonal situations; (d) feelings of social withdrawal, including insecurity and awkwardness in social encounters.

Recent work (Gurin, Gurin, Lao, & Beattie, 1969; Mirels, 1970) with the I–E Scale indicates that a Personal Control factor should be scored separately from the total I–E scale. The Personal Control score presumably reflects beliefs about mastery over one's life as distinct from beliefs concerning the extent to which individual citizens can influence political institutions. Accordingly, we computed two Personal Control scores, along with the total I–E score: one based on the factor analysis of Mirels (1970), and the other on the work of Gurin et al. (1969). Thirteen test scores were thus available for each of the 275 cases. Moreover, the admissions office at the University of Texas provided us with the Scholastic Achievement Test (SAT) scores of about 80% of our sample.

The specific tests used in this study were selected for a variety of ad hoc reasons. The I–E Scale was included because of notions about Pattern A as response style for coping with uncontrollable events. The TSBI was used because we expected Pattern A subjects to have higher levels of self-esteem and feelings of dominance than Pattern B subjects. Need for achievement was included in our test battery because achievement striving is a major component of the behavior pattern; and manifest anxiety was used because Pattern A is supposed to be unrelated to *trait* measures of anxiety (Caffrey, 1968; Friedman, 1969). The L and K scales were included because of reports in the literature that coronary-prone subjects are often defensive in their transactions with the environment (e.g., Hackett & Cassem, 1969). Finally, we secured the SAT scores in order to have a crude measure of intellective ability.

Sixteen scores were correlated with the A–B scale score of the student JAS. The results are given in Table C.1. There are only three product-moment

TABLE C.1
Product-Moment Correlations between the
Student JAS and Selected Personality Tests
(Group I)

Tests	r with A–B ($N = 275$)
I–E Control Scale (Rotter)	$-.17**$
Personal Control Scale 1 (Mirels)	$-.17**$
Personal Control Scale 2 (Gurin)	$-.19**$
Texas Social Behavior Inventory (TSBI)	$.30***$
Self-Confidence Factor (TSBI)	$.24***$
Social Competence Factor (TSBI)	$.17**$
Dominance Factor (TSBI)	$.40***$
Social Withdrawal Factor (TSBI)	$-.15*$
Manifest Anxiety Scale	$.07$
Defensiveness Scale (K)	$-.04$
Lie Scale (L)	$-.01$
"Thrill-Seeking" Scale	$-.03$
Need Achievement (EPPS)	$.15*$
SAT—Verbal	$.03$
SAT—Quantitative	$.10$
SAT—Total	$.06$

$*p < .05.$ $**p < .01.$ $***p < .001.$

coefficients of sizeable magnitude. Pattern A is positively related to self-esteem (.30), particularly to feelings of interpersonal dominance (.40), and self-confidence (.24). The JAS is also directly related to the I–E scale and to the two Personal Control scales (the scoring is reversed on these scales). While these latter results suggest that As may have higher expectations of environmental control than Bs, nevertheless the magnitudes of the coefficients are much too small to warrant a firm conclusion.

Equally low is the correlation between need for achievement and the JAS (.15), but it should be noted that the validity of the EPPS achievement scale is less than well established. It has not been consistently associated with other objective and projective measures of need for achievement (see, for example, Stricker, 1970). It is conceivable, therefore, that the true relationship between Pattern A and achievement might be somewhat higher than the correlation reported here. Recall, in this connection, that the *adult* JAS correlated .45 with the Gough ACL achievement measure (see Appendix B).

Trait anxiety was unrelated to the student JAS, and a similar absence of relationship occurred with the K and L scales. The L scale is considered a measure of denial and defensiveness; the K scale is treated as an index of social desirability. Null associations have also been obtained between L and K and Pattern A as assessed by the interview. We were able to secure all three of these scores on 90 adult male subjects tested by Rosenman *et al.* (1974). The coefficient for Pattern A and the L scale was − .04; for the K scale, the relationship was − .14 ($p = .07$). The negative sign means As were somewhat less concerned than Bs with presenting a socially desirable image.

As a final check on the possibility of an association between the student JAS and defensiveness, Byrne's (1961) Repression–Sensitization (R–S) scale was administered to 189 male students enrolled in introductory psychology at the University of Texas during the summer session of 1974. The JAS was given to these subjects at the same time. The product-moment coefficient between the two scores was 0.00.

After completing the first study, we became aware of the relationship between Pattern A and activity level, as described in Appendix B. It thus seemed desirable to administer a test of activity level to a group of subjects who had also completed the student JAS. The EASI Temperament Survey, Form III (Buss & Plomin, 1975; Plomin, 1974) was chosen for various practical reasons. It yields four scores, including Activity, Emotionality, Sociability, and Impulsivity. Along with this test, subjects were given (1) the need achievement scale of the EPPS; (2) the TAQ, or Test Anxiety Questionnaire (Mandler & Sarason, 1952), which measures fear of failure; (3) the Otis (1954) Quick-Scoring Mental Ability Tests, Gamma Test: Form AM.

Table C.2 presents the correlations between each of the test scores and the JAS. It is immediately apparent that Pattern A correlates substantially with

TABLE C.2
Product-Moment Correlations between the
Student JAS and Selected Personality Tests
(Group II)

Tests	r with A–B ($N = 294$)
Need Achievement (EPPS)	.17**
Fear of Failure (TAQ)	−.02
IQ (Otis)	.03
Emotionality (EASI III)	.11
Activity (EASI III)	.52***
Sociability (EASI III)	.17**
Impulsivity (EASI III)	.13*

*$p < .05$.   **$p < .01$.   ***$p < .001$.

Activity.[1] The coefficient of .52 is actually higher than that reported in Appendix B for the interview and the Active scale of the TTS (.37).[2] On the other hand, the coefficient for Impulsivity (.13), while significant, is considerably lower than that reported in Appendix B for adults (.32). Sociability correlates modestly with the student JAS at .17. The TTS version of sociability had a similar coefficient (.16) with the interview (see Rosenman *et al.*, 1974).

The only other significant correlation in Table C.2 is between need achievement and the JAS. The coefficient of .17 is virtually identical to that obtained in the first study, and about at the level reported in Appendix B for the interview. There was no association between fear of failure and the JAS.

The findings reported in this section are comparable to those obtained with the interview assessment of Pattern A. The modest associations of the A–B scale with external control, self-esteem, and need for achievement attest to the concurrent validity of the student JAS. We would expect these factors to be present in Type A individuals. The more substantial correlation of Dominance with the JAS (.40) is also what would be expected, since Pattern A individuals are alleged to be hard driving, self-centered, and forceful in interpersonal relationships.

Of even greater interest is the sizeable correlation (.52) between Activity and the JAS, for this suggests that the vigor and tempo of behavior are major components of Pattern A. Such a relationship is perhaps not surprising in view

[1] Typical Activity items on the EASI include "I usually seem to be in a hurry"; "I often feel as if I'm bursting with energy"; "When I do things, I do them vigorously."
[2] Active responses on the TTS consist of affirmative answers to such items as "Are you often in a hurry?"; "Do you ordinarily work quickly and energetically?"; "Do you usually work fast?"

of the fact that some JAS items are remarkably similar to those on the Activity scales (see footnotes 1 and 2 in this appendix). Recall, however, that Active scores also show substantial correlations with Pattern A as measured by the standardized interview. Since the interview does not contain questions that can be construed as the same as those in the Active scales, it is not likely that a coefficient of .50 reflects substantial artifactual inflation.

Traditional Risk Factors and Pattern A in College Students

In Chapter 4, we described a study designed to provide information on past and present achievements of 22 Type A and 24 Type B college students. This study also collected measures of some of the traditional risk factors for CHD, including blood pressure, serum cholesterol, and smoking. Here we shall present these additional data, which are relevant to the construct validity of the student JAS.

Medical History Data

All 46 subjects in the study were free of cardiovascular and related ailments at the time of testing; at least they uniformly responded "No" to questions asking whether they had diabetes mellitus, heart trouble, and high or low blood pressure. There was also little evidence of these disorders among the parents of the subjects: certainly there were no differences between As and Bs in the frequency with which they reported that their parents had cardiovascular disease.

Anthropometric Data

The mean height and weight of As were 70.0 in. and 165.2 lb (1.8 m and 75.0 kg); for Bs, 71.2 in. and 168.8 lb (1.9 m and 76.7 kg). The percentage of weight deviation from norms of the Metropolitan Life Insurance Company (1959) was calculated separately for each subject. The means of these indices of obesity were + 10.7% for As and + 10.6% for Bs. There were also no differences between As and Bs in triceps skinfold thickness, as determined by measurements made with Lange Skinfold Calipers. The median of three such measurements was averaged over each of the two types of subjects, giving mean values of 10.2 mm for As and 8.9 for Bs.

Physical Exercise

Subjects were also asked, "How often do you get physical exercise (other than walks) during the week?" (1 signified "never"; 2, "less than once a week"; 3, "once or twice a week"; 4, "several times a week"; 5, "every day"). The mean responses for As was 3.95; for Bs, 3.67 [$t(44) = 1.14, p > .20$]. These data indicate that both types of subjects indulged in some kind of physical exercise more than twice a week.

Blood Pressure

Systolic and diastolic blood pressure readings were taken manually with a blood pressure gauge and stethoscope. The medians for each of two sets of three blood pressure values (taken 40 min apart) were averaged for each subject. The resulting mean systolic pressure for As was 124; for Bs, 126 ($t < 1$). The average diastolic readings were 70 and 70.

Serum Lipids

The case for an association of Pattern A with traditional risk factors is somewhat more impressive when we turn to an examination of serum cholesterol. (Determinations were made by the direct method of Hycel, Inc.). While our Pattern A and Pattern B college students had relatively low cholesterol levels by clinical standards ($Ms = 183$ and 168 mg per 100 ml), the mean value for As exceeded that of Bs at less than the .04 level, $t(44) = 2.16$. Our results did not reveal a similar A–B effect for 12-hr fasting serum triglycerides ($p > .20$). (The method of determination was the Dade Tri-25 Triglyceride Method.)

Diet and serum cholesterol. From the outset of this study, we were aware of the possible influence of diet upon serum lipid values. We were also aware of the possible unreliability of a dietary survey that depends upon the recall abilities of subjects, but for various logistical reasons it was impossible to do more than take a recall diet history. Karen Brewton of St. David's Hospital (Austin, Texas) served as consultant dietitian in collection, analysis, and interpretation of the nutrient intake data.

The subject was asked how many times over the last week he had eaten each of 53 types of food, including 4 oz of hamburger; 1 oz of cheese; one egg; 2 cookies; a 12-oz soft drink; 1 tablespoon of jelly or jam; and so forth. To assist in recall, food models were shown to the subject as he was questioned (for example, a foam rubber model of a 4-oz hamburger pattie, or a similar model of a 1-oz piece of cheese). To facilitate subsequent calculations of fat, cholesterol, and carbohydrate intake, subjects were also asked questions concerning the usual method of preparation of their meat (for instance, fried, broiled, baked, or stewed); type of milk used; type of ''spread'' used; and types of cheese customarily eaten.

A collection sheet was compiled from the recall data for each subject. This sheet gave the number of servings of each food item, which was then multiplied by factors given in a nutrient composition table. This procedure yielded weekly totals of saturated fatty acid, linoleic acid, cholesterol, and simple carbohydrates consumed. The results indicated no differences between the As and Bs in terms of average weekly totals of dietary cholesterol, simple carbohydrates, and a ratio of polyunsaturated to saturated fats ($ps > .15$). Analyses of covariance were conducted to determine whether cholesterol levels in As and Bs might nevertheless be affected by the subject's diet. There was no evidence of an interaction between the A–B variable and any of the three dietary factors with regard to serum cholesterol level ($ps > .50$).

We tentatively conclude that elevations of serum cholesterol in Pattern A college students compared to their Pattern B counterparts are not attributable to differences in the dietary intake of these two groups of subjects. These results take on added significance when viewed in the light of studies by Sloane and his colleagues (Sloane, Davidson, Holland, & Payne, 1962; Sloane, Habib, Eveson, & Payne, 1961). These investigators describe a pattern of behavior (aggressiveness, competitiveness, and impatience) which they found associated with small but significant elevations in serum cholesterol in college students. Sloane and his colleagues' description of the ''high cholesterol type'' is similar to the characteristics of the Type A behavior pattern. Moreover, while our Type A and Type B groups had relatively low cholesterol levels (183 and 168 mg per 100 ml), the values are in the same range as those reported by Sloane (163 and 134 mg per 100 ml). It would appear that even at relatively young ages, Pattern A individuals exhibit higher serum lipid concentrations than Pattern B individuals, albeit at levels below what may be considered pathological.

Cigarette Smoking

Smoking behavior was the final risk factor examined in this study. The results were as follows. Less than 15% of the 46 cases reported that they currently smoked cigarettes. Another 13% said they "used to smoke" but have not done so for more than a year. About 72% never smoked cigarettes. This latter figure is somewhat higher than that reported by the Monthly Vital Statistics Report of the U.S. National Center for Health Statistics (June 1972), which places the figure of "never smoked" at slightly under 50% for the 17- through 24-year-old age category.

There was no evidence of more As in the "smoking" than "nonsmoking" categories. The percentages were as follows: 10% of the As were in the "smoking" group; 70% were in the "never smoked" group. For Bs, the comparable percentages were 10 and 75. A similar pattern of results has been obtained with adult samples (e.g., Jenkins, Rosenman, & Zyzanski, 1968). However, of those who smoked cigarettes, older As were somewhat heavier smokers than older Bs. A similar analysis was performed on our student data. Subjects who said they currently smoked cigarettes were asked, "How many do you smoke?" Type Bs reported an average of 7.6 cigarettes per day, whereas Type As gave a mean of 5.0 per day ($t < 1$).

It seems clear that unlike adult subjects (aged 35 or more), college-student subjects not only smoke less, but among those who smoke, Type As are not likely to be overrepresented relative to Bs. We could speculate endlessly on the significance of these findings, but it may reflect a change in style of life among young American adults—at least those studied in Texas.

Summary

Like the adult samples (e.g., Rosenman *et al.*, 1964), college-student As and Bs show essentially the same parental CHD history; indulge in about the same amount of physical exercise; are about the same height and weight; and do not show differential degrees of obesity. There are, in addition, no A–B differences in reported diabetes, hypertension, and other cardiovascular-related diseases. Unlike the adults, however, our college-student As were not heavier smokers than their Type B counterparts. On the other hand, college students with Pattern A characteristics had higher serum cholesterol concentrations than did their peers with Pattern B characteristics, and these differences could not be attributed to systematic variations in quality of diet. These latter results are consistent with those reported for older samples of subjects.

References

Abrahams, J. P., & Birren, J. E. Reaction time as a function of age and behavioral predisposition to coronary heart disease. *Journal of Gerontology*, 1973, *28*, 471–478.

Amsel, A., & Roussel, J. Motivational properties of frustration: I. Effect of a running response on the addition of frustration to the motivational complex. *Journal of Experimental Psychology*, 1952, *43*, 363–368.

Anderson, T. Mortality from ischemic heart disease: Changes in middle-aged men since 1900. *Journal of the American Medical Association*, 1973, *224*, 336–338.

Anisman, H. Time-dependent variations in aversively motivated behaviors: Nonassociative effects of cholinergic and catecholaminergic activity. *Psychological Review*, 1975, *82*, 359–385.

Appels, A. Coronary heart disease as a cultural disease. *Psychotherapy and Psychosomatics*, 1973, *22*, 320–324.

Appley, M. H., & Trumbull, R. *Psychological stress*. New York: Appleton-Century Crofts, 1967.

Ardlie, N. G., Glew, G., & Schwartz, C. J. Influence of catecholamines on nucleotide-induced platelet aggregation. *Nature*, 1966, *212*, 415–417.

Atkinson, J. W. Motivational determinants of risk-taking behavior. *Psychological Review*, 1957, *64*, 359–372.

Ax, A. F. The physiological differentiation between fear and anger in humans. *Psychosomatic Medicine*, 1953, *15*, 433–442.

Balke, B. Optimale koerperliche leistungsfaehigkeit, ihre Messung und Veraenderung infolge Arbeitsermuedung. *Arbeitsphysiologie*, 1954, *15*, 311–323.

Balke, B., Grillo, G. P., Konecci, E. B., & Luft, U. C. Work capacity after blood donation. *Journal of Applied Physiology*, 1954, *7*, 231–238.

Bell, R. Q. A reinterpretation of the direction of effects in studies of socialization. *Psychological Review*, 1968, *75*, 81–95.

Benson, H., Marzetta, B. R., & Rosner, B. A. Decreased blood pressure associated with the regular elicitation of relaxation response: A study of hypertensive subjects. In R. S. Eliot (Ed.), *Stress and the heart*. Mount Kisco, New York: Futura, 1974.

Berkowitz, L. *Aggression*. New York: McGraw-Hill, 1962.

Biller, H. B. *Father, child and sex-role*. Lexington, Massachusetts: Heath, 1971.

Birren, J. E. Personality stress takes its toll. *Medical World News Review*, 1974, *1*, 42–43.

Blumenthal, J. A., Williams, R. B., Jr., Kong, Y., Thompson, L. W., Jenkins, C. D., &

Rosenman, R. H. Coronary-prone behavior and angiographically documented coronary disease. Paper presented at the Annual Meeting of the 'American Psychosomatic Society, New Orleans, Louisiana, March 21, 1975.

Borhani, N. O. Magnitude of the problem of cardiovascular–renal diseases. In A. M. Lilienfeld & A. J. Gifford (Eds.), *Chronic diseases and public health,* Baltimore: Johns Hopkins Press, 1966.

Bortner, R. W., & Rosenman, R. H. The measurement of Pattern A behavior. *Journal of Chronic Diseases,* 1967, *20,* 525–533.

Bortner, R. W., Rosenman, R. H., & Friedman, M. Familial similarity in Pattern A behavior. *Journal of Chronic Diseases,* 1970, *23,* 39–43.

Bowers, K. S. Situationism in psychology: An analysis and a critique. *Psychological Review,* 1973, *80,* 307–336.

Brand, R. J., Rosenman, R. H., Sholtz, R. I., & Friedman, M. Multivariate prediction of coronary heart disease in the Western collaborative group study compared to the findings of the Framingham study. *Circulation,* 1976, *53,* 348–355.

Brenner, M. H. Economic changes and heart disease mortality. *American Journal of Public Health,* 1971, *61,* 606–611.

Brest, A. N., & Moyer, J. H. *Atherosclerotic vascular disease.* New York: Appleton-Century-Crofts, 1967.

Brooks, G. W., & Mueller, E. F. Serum urate concentrations among university professors. *Journal of the American Medical Association,* 1966, *195,* 415—418.

Brown, G. M., Schalch, D. S., & Reichlin, S. Patterns of growth hormone and cortisol responses to psychological stress in the squirrel monkey. *Endocrinology,* 1971, *88,* 956–963.

Bruhn, J. G., McGrady, K. E., & duPlessis, A. Evidence of "emotional drain" preceding death from myocardial infarction. *Psychiatric Diagnosis,* 1968, *29,* 34–40.

Bruhn, J. G., Paredes, A., Adsett, C. A., & Wolf, S. Psychological predictors of sudden death in myocardial infarction: *Journal of Psychosomatic Research,* 1974, *18,* 187–191.

Burnam, M. A., Pennebaker, J. W., & Glass, D. C. Time consciousness, achievement striving, and the Type A coronary-prone behavior pattern. *Journal of Abnormal Psychology,* 1973, *84,* 76–79.

Buss, A. H. *The psychology of aggression.* New York: Wiley, 1961.

Buss, A. H., & Plomin, R. J. *A temperament theory of personality development.* New York: Wiley, 1975.

Byrne, D. The repression-sensitization scale: Rationale, reliability and validity. *Journal of Personality,* 1961, *29,* 334–349.

Caffrey, B. Reliability and validity of personality and behavioral measures in a study of coronary heart disease. *Journal of Chronic Diseases,* 1968, *21,* 191–204.

Caffrey, B. Behavior patterns and personality characteristics related to prevalence rates of coronary heart disease. *Journal of Chronic Diseases,* 1969, *22,* 93–103.

Cantwell, D. P. Psychiatric illness in the families of hyperactive children. *Archives of General Psychiatry,* 1972, *27,* 414–417.

Carlson, L. A., Levi, L., & Orö, L. Stressor-induced changes in plasma lipids and urinary excretion of catecholamines and their modification by nicotinic acid. In L. Levi (Ed.), *Stress and distress in response to psychosocial stimuli.* New York: Pergamon, 1972.

Carver, C. S., Coleman, A. E., & Glass, D. C. The coronary-prone behavior pattern and the suppression of fatigue on a treadmill test. *Journal of Personality and Social Psychology,* 1976, *33,* 460–466.

Cattell, R. B., Saunders, D. R., & Stice, G. *The Sixteen Personality Factor Questionnaire: Handbook.* Champaign, Illinois: Institute of Personality and Ability Testing, 1950.

Cofer, C. N., & Appley, M. H. *Motivation: Theory and research.* New York: Wiley, 1964.

Cohen, S. I., Rothbart, M., & Phillips, S. Locus of control and the generality of learned helplessness in humans. *Journal of Personality and Social Psychology,* 1976, *34,* 1049–1056.

Costill, D. L., & Fox, E. L. Energetics of marathon running. *Medicine and Science in Sports,* 1969, *1,* 81–86.

Davis, K. E., & Jones, E. E. Changes in interpersonal perception as a means of reducing cognitive dissonance. *Journal of Abnormal and Social Psychology,* 1960, *61,* 402–410.

Dawber, T. R., & Kannel, W. B. Susceptibility to coronary heart disease. *Modern Concepts in Cardiovascular Disease,* 1961, *30,* 671–676.

Dombrose, L. A., & Slobin, M. S. The IES test. *Perceptual and Motor Skills,* 1958, *8,* 347–378.

Douglas, D., & Anisman, H. Helplessness or expectation incongruence: Effect of aversive stimulation on subsequent performance. *Journal of Experimental Psychology,* 1975, *1,* 411–417.

Drewnowski, A., & Gray, J. A. Influence of Δ^9-tetrahydrocannabinol on partial reinforcement effects. *Psychopharmacologia,* 1975, *43,* 233–237.

Dreyfuss, F., & Czazckes, J. W. Blood cholesterol and uric acid of healthy medical students under the stress of an examination. *Archives of Internal Medicine,* 1959, *103,* 708–711.

Dreyfuss, F., Shanan, J., & Sharon, M. Some personality characteristics of middle-aged men with coronary artery disease. *Psychotherapy and Psychosomatics,* 1966, *14,* 1–16.

Dudley, D. L., Roszell, D. K., Mules, J. E., & Hague, W. H. Heroin vs. alcohol addiction— Quantifiable psychosocial similarities and differences. *Journal of Psychosomatic Research,* 1974, *18,* 327–335.

Duguid, J. B. Thrombosis as a factor in the pathogenesis of coronary atherosclerosis. *Journal of Pathology and Bacteriology,* 1946, *58,* 207–212.

Dweck, C. S. The role of expectations and attributions in the alleviation of learned helplessness. *Journal of Personality and Social Psychology,* 1975, *31,* 674–685.

Dweck, C. S., & Repucci, N. D. Learned helplessness and reinforcement responsibility in children. *Journal of Personality and Social Psychology,* 1973, *25,* 109–116.

Easterbrook, J. A. The effect of emotion on cue utilization and organization of behavior. *Psychological Review,* 1959, *66,* 183–201.

Edwards, A. L. *Manual for the Edwards Personal Preference Schedule* (rev. ed.). New York: Psychological Corporation, 1957.

Elmadjian, F. Excretion and metabolism of epinephrine and norepinephrine in various emotional states. *Proceedings of the 5th Pan American Congress of Endocrinology. Lima, Peru,* November 1963. Pp. 341–370.

Elmadjian, F., Hope J. M., & Larson, C. T. Excretion of epinephrine and norepinephrine under stress. *Recent Progress in Hormone Research,* 1958, *14,* 513–553.

Engel, G. L. A life setting conducive to illness: The giving-up–given-up complex. *Annals of Internal Medicine,* 1968, *69,* 293–300.

Engel, G. L. Sudden death and the ''medical model'' in psychiatry. *Canadian Psychiatric Association Journal,* 1970, *15,* 527–538.

Falconer, D. S. *Introduction to quantitative genetics.* New York: Ronald Press, 1960.

Fenigstein, A., & Buss, A. H. Association and affect as determinants of displaced aggression. *Journal of Research in Personality,* 1974, *7,* 306–313.

Fiske, D. W., & Maddi, S. R. *Functions of varied experience.* Homewood, Illinois: Dorsey, 1961.

Fraisse, P. *The psychology of time.* New York: Harper & Row, 1963.

Frankel, E. Coronary disease and personality. *British Medical Journal,* 1969, *1,* 382–383.

Frankenhaeuser, M. *Estimation of time: An experimental study.* Stockholm: Almqvist & Wiksell, 1959.

Frankenhaeuser, M. Behavior and circulating catecholamines. *Brain Research,* 1971, *31,* 241–262.

Frankenhaeuser, M. Experimental approaches to the study of catecholamines and emotion. In L. Levi (Ed.), *Emotions: Their parameters and measurement.* New York: Raven Press, 1975.

Frankenhaeuser, M., & Rissler, A. Effects of punishment on catecholamine release and efficiency of performance. *Psychopharmacologia,* 1970, *17,* 378–390.

French, J. W., Ekstrom, R. B., & Price, L. A. *Manual for kit of reference tests for cognitive factors.* Princeton, New Jersey: Educational Testing Service, 1963.

French, J. R. P., Jr., & Caplan, R. Organizational stress and individual strain. In A. Marrow (Ed.), *The failure of success.* New York: AMACOM, 1972.

French, J. R. P., Jr., Rodgers, W., & Cobb, S. Adjustment as person-environment fit. In G. Coelho (Ed.), *Coping and adaptation.* New York: Basic Books, 1974.

French, J. R. P., Jr., Tupper, J., & Mueller, E. F. Work load of university professors. (Cooperative Research Project No. 2171, United States Office of Education.) University of Michigan, Ann Arbor, 1965.

Friedberg, C. K. *Diseases of the heart* (3rd ed.). Philadelphia: Saunders, 1966.

Friedman, E. H., Hellerstein, H. K., Eastwood, G. L., & Jones, S. E. Behavior patterns and serum cholesterol in two groups of normal males. *American Journal of Medical Science,* 1968, *255,* 237–244.

Friedman, M. *Pathogenesis of coronary artery disease.* New York: McGraw-Hill, 1969.

Friedman, M., & Byers, S. O. Effect of environmental influences upon alimentary lipemia of the rat. *American Journal of Physiology,* 1967, *213,* 1359–1364.

Friedman, M., Byers, S. O., & Brown, A. E. Plasma lipid responses of rats and rabbits to an auditory stimulus. *American Journal of Physiology,* 1967, *212,* 1174–1178.

Friedman, M., Byers, S. O., Diamant, J., & Rosenman, R. H. Plasma catecholamine response of coronary-prone subjects (Type A) to a specific challenge. *Metabolism,* 1975, *24,* 205–210.

Friedman, M., & Rosenman, R. H. Association of specific overt behavior pattern with blood and cardiovascular findings. *Journal of the American Medical Association,* 1959, *169,* 1286–1296.

Friedman, M., & Rosenman, R. H. *Type A behavior and your heart.* New York: Knopf, 1974.

Friedman, M., Rosenman, R. H., & Brown, A. E. The continuous heart rate in men exhibiting an overt behavior pattern associated with increased incidence of clinical coronary artery disease. *Circulation,* 1963, *28,* 861–866.

Friedman, M., Rosenman, R. H., & Byers, S. O. Serum lipids and conjunctival circulation after fat ingestion in men exhibiting Type A behavior pattern. *Circulation,* 1964, *29,* 874–886.

Friedman, M., Rosenman, R. H., & Byers, S. O. Response of hyperlipemic subjects to carbohydrates, pancreatic hormones, and prolonged fasting. *Journal of Clinical Endocrinology and Metabolism,* 1968, *28,* 1773–1780.

Friedman, M., Rosenman, R. H., & Carroll, V. Changes in the serum cholesterol and blood-clotting time in men subjected to cyclic variation of occupational stress. *Circulation,* 1958, *17,* 852–861.

Friedman, M., St. George, S., Byers, S. O., & Rosenman, R. H. Excretion of catecholamines, 17-ketosteroids, 17-hydroxycorticoids, and 5-hydroxyindole in men exhibiting a particular behavior pattern (A) associated with high incidence of clinical coronary artery disease. *Journal of Clinical Investigation,* 1960, *39,* 758–764.

Fuller, E. W., Jr., & Eliot, R. S. The role of exercise in the relief of stress. In R. S. Eliot (Ed.), *Stress and the heart.* Mount Kisco, New York: Futura, 1974.

Funkenstein, D. H., King, S. H., & Drolette, M. E. *Mastery of stress.* Cambridge, Massachusetts: Harvard University Press, 1957.

Gatchel, R. J., & Proctor, J. D. Psychological correlates of learned helplessness in man. *Journal of Abnormal Psychology,* 1976, *85,* 27–34.

Glass, D. C., & Singer, J. E. *Urban stress: Experiments on noise and social stressors.* New York: Academic Press, 1972.

Glass, D. C., Snyder, M. L., & Hollis, J. F. Time urgency and the Type A coronary-prone behavior pattern. *Journal of Applied Social Psychology,* 1974, *4,* 125–140.

Gordon, T., & Verter, J. Serum cholesterol, systolic blood pressure, and Framingham relative weight as discriminators of cardiovascular disease. *The Framingham study: An epidemiological investigation of cardiovascular disease.* Section 23. Washington, D.C.: U.S. Government Printing Office, 1969.

Gough, H. G. *The Adjective Check List.* Berkeley, California: University of California Press, 1952.

Gough, H. G. *Manual for the California Psychological Inventory.* Palo Alto, California: Consulting Psychologists' Press, 1957.

Graham, D. T. Psychosomatic medicine. In N. S. Greenfield & R. A. Sternbach (Eds.), *Handbook of psychophysiology.* New York: Holt, Rinehart and Winston, 1972.

Gray, J. A. Sodium amobarbital and effects of frustrative nonreward. *Journal of Comparative and Physiological Psychology,* 1969, *69,* 55–64.

Greene, W. A., Goldstein, S., & Moss, A. J. Psychosocial aspects of sudden death: A preliminary report. *Archives of Internal Medicine,* 1972, *129,* 725–731.

Greene, W. A., Moss, A. J., & Goldstein, S. Delay, denial, and death in coronary heart disease. In R. S. Eliot (Ed.), *Stress and the heart.* Mount Kisco, New York: Futura, 1974.

Greenfield, N. S., & Sternbach, R. A. (Eds.). *Handbook of psychophysiology.* New York: Holt, Rinehart and Winston, 1972.

Greer, J. S., & McGill, H. C., Jr. The evolution of the fatty streak. In A. N. Brest & J. H. Moyer (Eds.), *Atherosclerotic vascular disease.* New York: Appleton-Century-Crofts, 1967.

Groen, J. J., & Drory, S. Influence of psychosocial factors on coronary heart disease: A comparison of autopsy findings with the results of a sociological questionnaire. *Pathologia et Microbiologia,* 1967, *30,* 779–788.

Grundy, S. M., & Griffin, A. C. Effects of periodic mental stress on serum cholesterol levels. *Circulation,* 1959, *19,* 496–498.

Gurin, P., Gurin, G., Lao, R. C., & Beattie, M. IE control in the motivational dynamics of youth. *Journal of Social Issues,* 1969, *25,* 29–53.

Gutmann, M. C., & Benson, H. Interaction of environmental factors and systemic arterial blood pressure: A review. *Medicine,* 1971, *50,* 543–553.

Haan, N. Proposed model of ego functioning: Coping and defense mechanisms in relationship to IQ change. *Psychological Monographs,* 1963, *77* (8, Whole No. 571).

Hackett, T. P., & Cassem, N. H. Factors contributing to delay in responding to the signs and symptoms of acute myocardial infarction. *American Journal of Cardiology,* 1969, *24,* 651–658.

Hagnell, O., & Tunving, K. Mental and physical complaints among alcoholics. *Quarterly Journal of Studies on Alcohol,* 1972, *33,* 77–84.

Hamburg, D. A. Plasma and urinary corticosteroid levels in naturally occurring psychologic stresses. In *Ultrastructure and metabolism of the nervous system: Proceedings of the Association for Research in Nervous and Mental Disease* (Vol. 40). Baltimore: Williams & Wilkins, 1962.

Hathaway, S. R., & McKinley, J. C. *Minnesota Multiphasic Personality Inventory: Manual.* New York: Psychological Corporation, 1951.

Hawkins, N. G., Davies, R., & Holmes, T. H. Evidence of psychosocial factors in the development of pulmonary tuberculosis. *American Review of Tubercular and Pulmonary Diseases,* 1957, *75,* 768–780.

Heckhausen, H. *The anatomy of achievement.* New York: Academic Press, 1967.

Helmreich, R., Stapp, J., & Ervin, C. The Texas Social Behavior Inventory (TSBI): An objective measure of self-esteem or social competence. Unpublished manuscript, The University of Texas at Austin, 1973.

Hill, A. V., & Lupton, H. Muscular exercise, lactic acid, and the supply utilization of oxygen. *Quarterly Journal of Medicine,* 1923, *16,* 135–171.

Hinkle, L. E., Jr., Whitney, L. H., Lehman, E. W., Dunn, J., Benjamin, B., King, R., Piakun, A., & Flehinger, B. Occupation, education, and coronary heart disease: Risk is influenced more by education and background than by occupational experiences, in the Bell System. *Science,* 1968, *161,* 238–246.

Hiroto, D. S. Locus of control and learned helplessness. *Journal of Experimental Psychology,* 1974, *102,* 187–193.

Hiroto, D. S., & Seligman, M. E. P. Generality of learned helplessness in man. *Journal of Personality and Social Psychology,* 1975, *31,* 311–327.

Hirst, A. E., Hadley, G. G., & Gore, I. Effects of chronic alcoholism and cirrhosis on atherosclerosis. *American Journal of Medical Science,* 1965, *249,* 143–149.

Hokanson, J. E., Burgess, M., & Cohen, M. F. Effects of displaced aggression on systolic blood pressure. *Journal of Abnormal and Social Psychology,* 1963, *67,* 214–218.

Hollingshead, A. B. *Two factor index of social position.* Mimeographed booklet, Yale University, 1957.

Hollis, J. F. Expectations of control, the Type A coronary-prone behavior pattern, and reactions to uncontrollable events. Unpublished doctoral dissertation, The University of Texas at Austin, 1975.

Holmes, T. H., & Masuda, M. Life change and illness susceptibility. Unpublished manuscript, The University of Washington at Seattle, 1970.

Holmes, T. H., & Rahe, R. H. The Social Readjustment Rating Scale. *Journal of Psychosomatic Research,* 1967, *11,* 213–218.

House, J. S. Occupational stress as a precursor to coronary disease. In W. D. Gentry & R. B. Williams, Jr. (Eds.), *Psychological aspects of myocardial infarction and coronary care.* Saint Louis: Mosby, 1975.

Insull, W. (Ed.) *Coronary risk handbook.* New York: American Heart Association, 1973.

Jackson, A. S., & Pollack, M. L. Personal communication to A. E. Coleman, January 1975.

Januszewicz, W., & Sznajderman, M. Catecholamines and the cardiovascular system. *Acta Physiologica Polonica,* 1972, *23,* 585–595.

Jenkins, C. D. Psychologic and social precursors of coronary disease. *New England Journal of Medicine,* 1971, *284,* 244–255, 307–317.

Jenkins, C. D. The coronary-prone personality. In W. D. Gentry & R. B. Williams, Jr. (Eds.), *Psychological aspects of myocardial infarction and coronary care.* Saint Louis: Mosby, 1975.

Jenkins, C. D. Recent evidence supporting psychologic and social risk factors for coronary disease. *New England Journal of Medicine,* 1976, *294,* 987–994, 1033–1038.

Jenkins, C. D., Hames, C. G., Zyzanski, S. J., Rosenman, R. H., & Friedman, M. Psychological traits and serum lipids. I. Findings from the California Psychological Inventory. *Psychosomatic Medicine,* 1969, *31,* 115–127.

Jenkins, C. D., Rosenman, R. H., & Friedman, M. Development of an objective psychological test for the determination of the coronary-prone behavior pattern in employed men. *Journal of Chronic Diseases,* 1967, *20,* 371–379.

Jenkins, C. D., Rosenman, R. H., & Friedman, M. Replicability of rating the coronary-prone behavior pattern. *British Journal of Preventive and Social Medicine,* 1968, *22,* 16–22.

Jenkins, C. D., Rosenman, R. H., & Zyzanski, S. J. Cigarette smoking: Its relationship to coronary heart disease and related risk factors in the Western Collaborative Group Study. *Circulation,* 1968, *38,* 1140–1155.

Jenkins, C. D., Rosenman, R. H., & Zyzanski, S. J. The Jenkins Activity Survey for Health Prediction. Boston: Publ. by the authors, 1972.

Jenkins, C. D., Rosenman, R. H., & Zyzanski, S. J. Prediction of clinical coronary heart disease by a test for the coronary-prone behavior pattern. *New England Journal of Medicine,* 1974, *290,* 1271–1275.

Jenkins, C. D., Zyzanski, S. J., & Rosenman, R. H. Progress toward validation of a computer-scored test for the Type A coronary-prone behavior pattern. *Psychosomatic Medicine,* 1971, *33,* 193–202.

Jenkins, C. D., Zyzanski, S. J., & Rosenman, R. H. Biological, psychological, and social characteristics of men with different smoking habits. *Health Service Reports,* 1973, *88,* 834–843.

Jenkins, C. D., Zyzanski, S. J., & Rosenman, R. H. Risk of new myocardial infarction in middle-aged men with manifest coronary heart disease. *Circulation*, 1976, *53*, 342–347.

Kagan, J., Moss, H. A., & Sigel, I. E. Psychological significance of styles of conceptualization. *Monographs of the Society for Research in Child Development*, 1963, *28* (Serial No. 86).

Kagan, J., Rosman, B. L., Day, D., Albert, J., & Phillips, W. Information processing in the child: Significance of analytic reflective attitudes. *Psychological Monographs*, 1964, *78* (1, Whole No. 578).

Kahneman, D. *Attention and effort*. Englewood Cliffs, New Jersey: Prentice-Hall, 1973.

Karlsson, J., Astrand, P. O., & Ekblom, B. Training of the oxygen transport system in man. *Journal of Applied Physiology*, 1967, *22*, 1061–1065.

Kavanagh, T., & Shephard, R. J. The immediate antecedents of myocardial infarction in active men. *Canadian Medical Association Journal*, 1973, *109*, 19–22.

Keith, R. A. Personality and coronary heart disease: A review. *Journal of Chronic Diseases*, 1966, *19*, 1231–1243.

Keith, R. A., Lown, B., & Stare, F. J. Coronary heart disease and behavior patterns. *Psychosomatic Medicine*, 1965, *27*, 424–434.

Kenigsberg, D., Zyzanski, S. J., Jenkins, C. D., Wardwell, W. I., & Licciardello, A. T. The coronary-prone behavior pattern in hospitalized patients with and without coronary heart disease. *Psychosomatic Medicine*, 1974, *36*, 344–351.

Keys, A., Aravanis, C., Blackburn, H., van Buchem, F. S. P., Buzina, R., Djordjevic, B. S., Fidanza, F., Kavonen, M. J., Menotti, A., Pudov, V., & Taylor, H. L. Probability of middle-aged men developing coronary heart disease in 5 years. *Circulation*, 1972, *45*, 815–828.

Keys, A., Taylor, H. L., Blackburn, H., Brozek, J., Anderson, J. T., & Simonson, E. Mortality and coronary heart disease among men studied for 23 years. *Archives of Internal Medicine*, 1971, *128*, 201–214.

Kits van Heijningen, H., & Treurniet, N. Psychodynamic factors in acute myocardial infarction. *International Journal of Psychoanalysis*, 1966, *47*, 370–374.

Krantz, D. S. The coronary-prone behavior pattern, obesity, and reactions to environmental events. Unpublished doctoral dissertation, The University of Texas at Austin, 1975.

Krantz, D. S., Glass, D. C., & Snyder, M. L. Helplessness, stress level, and the coronary-prone behavior pattern. *Journal of Experimental Social Psychology*, 1974, *10*, 284–300.

Kryter, K. D. *The effects of noise on man*. New York: Academic Press, 1970.

Lacey, J. I. Somatic response patterning and stress: Some revisions of activation theory. In M. H. Appley & R. Trumbull (Eds.), *Psychological stress*. New York: Appleton-Century-Crofts, 1967.

Lacey, J. I., Kagan, J., Lacey, B. C., & Moss, H. A. The visceral level: Situational determinants and behavioral correlates of autonomic response patterns. In P. H. Knapp (Ed.), *Expression of the emotions in man*. New York: International Universities Press, 1963.

Langer, E. The psychology of chance. Unpublished manuscript, Yale University, 1973.

Larson, L. A. *Fitness, health, and work capacity: International standards for assessment*. New York: Macmillan, 1974.

Lazarus, R. S. *Psychological stress and the coping process*. New York: McGraw-Hill, 1966.

Lazarus, R. S. A cognitively oriented psychologist looks at biofeedback. *American Psychologist*, 1975, *30*, 553–561.

Levi, L. The urinary output of adrenalin and noradrenalin during pleasant and unpleasant emotional states: A preliminary report. *Psychosomatic Medicine*, 1965, *27*, 80–85.

Liljefors, I., & Rahe, R. H. An identical twin study of psychosocial factors in coronary heart disease in Sweden. *Psychosomatic Medicine*, 1970, *32*, 523–542.

Lown, B., Verrier, R., & Corbalan, R. Psychologic stress and threshold for repetitive ventricular response. *Science*, 1973, *182*, 834–836.

Lykken, D. T. A study of anxiety in the sociopathic personality. *Journal of Abnormal and Social Psychology*, 1957, *55*, 6–10.

Mandler, G., & Sarason, S. A study of anxiety and learning. *Journal of Abnormal and Social Psychology*, 1952, *47*, 166–173.

Mann, G. V. The influence of obesity on health (second of two parts). *New England Journal of Medicine*, 1974, *291*, 226–232.

Mann, G. V., & White, H. S. The influence of stress on plasma cholesterol levels. *Metabolism*, 1953, *2*, 47–58.

Mason, J. W. Organization of psychoendocrine mechanisms: A review and reconsideration of research. In N. S. Greenfield & R. A. Sternbach (Eds.), *Handbook of psychophysiology*. New York: Holt, Rinehart and Winston, 1972.

Mason, J. W., & Brady, J. V. The sensitivity of psychoendocrine systems to social and physical environment. In P. H. Leiderman & D. Shapiro (Eds.), *Psychobiological approaches to social behavior*. Stanford, California: Stanford University Press, 1964.

Matthews, K. A., & Krantz, D. S. Resemblance of twins and their parents in Pattern A behavior. *Psychosomatic Medicine*, 1976, *38*, 140–144.

Maxwell, M. A. *Alcohol, man, and science*. Report of the Hogg Foundation for Mental Health, Austin, Texas, 1966.

McClelland, D. C. *The achieving society*. Princeton, New Jersey: Van Nostrand, 1961.

McGinn, N. F., Harburg, E., Julius, S., & McLeod, J. M. Psychological correlates of blood pressure. *Psychological Bulletin*, 1964, *61*, 209–219.

McGrath, J. E. (Ed.). *Social and psychological factors in stress*. New York: Holt, Rinehart and Winston, 1970.

Metropolitan Life Insurance Company. New weight standards for men and women. *Statistical Bulletin*, 1959, *40*, 1–4.

Miller, N. Behavioral medicine as a new frontier: Opportunities and dangers. In S. M. Weiss (Ed.), *Proceedings of the National Heart and Lung Institute: Working Conference on Health Behavior*. Dept. of Health, Education and Welfare Publication No. (NIH) 76-868, 1975.

Mirels, H. L. Dimensions of internal versus external control. *Journal of Consulting and Clinical Psychology*, 1970, *34*, 226–228.

Mischel, W. *Personality and assessment*. New York: Wiley, 1968.

Mordkoff, A. M., & Parsons, O. A. The coronary personality: A critique. *International Journal of Psychiatry*, 1968, *5*, 413–426.

Mustard, J. F., & Packham, M. A. Platelet function and myocardial infarction. In S. Bondurant (Ed.), *Research on acute myocardial infarction*. New York: American Heart Association, 1969.

Nestel, P. J., Verghese, A., & Lovell, R. R. Catecholamine secretion and sympathetic nervous system reponses to emotion in men with and without angina pectoris. *American Heart Journal*, 1967, *73*, 227–234.

Netter, F. H. *The Ciba collection of medical illustrations: Heart* (Vol. 5). Summit, New Jersey: Ciba Publications Department, 1969.

Nichols, R. C., & Bilbro, W. C. The diagnosis of twin zygosity. *Acta General*, 1966, *26*, 265–275.

Noble, B. J., Metz, K. F., Pandolf, K. B., Bell, C. W., Cafarelli, E., & Simes, W. E. Perceived exertion during walking and running. II. *Medicine and Science in Sports*, 1973, *5*, 116–120.

Olin, H. S., & Hackett, T. P. Denial of pain in acute myocardial infarction. *Journal of the American Medical Association*, 1964, *190*, 977–981.

Otis, A. *Otis Quick-Scoring Mental Ability Test: Form gamma*. New York: Harcourt Brace Jovanovich, 1954.

Paré, W. P., Rothfeld, B., Isom, K. E., & Varady, A. Cholesterol synthesis and metabolism as a function of unpredictable shock stimulation. *Physiology and Behavior*, 1973, *11*, 107–110.

Parke, R. D. (Ed.), *Recent trends in social learning theory*. New York: Academic Press, 1972.

Parkes, C. M., Benjamin, B., & Fitzgerald, R. G. Broken heart: A statistical study of increased mortality among widowers. *British Medical Journal*, 1969, *1*, 740–743.

Paykel, E. S. Life stress and psychiatric disorder: Applications of the clinical approach. In B. S. Dohrenwend & B. P. Dohrenwend (Eds.), *Stressful life events: Their nature and effects.* New York: Wiley, 1974.

Paykel, E. S., Myers, J. K., Dienelt, M. N., Klerman, G. L., Lindenthal, J. J., & Pepper, M. P. Life events and depression: A controlled study. *Archives of General Psychiatry*, 1969, *21*, 753–760.

Peterson, J. E., Keith, R. A., & Wilcox, A. A. Hourly changes in serum choleterol concentration: Effects of the anticipation of stress. *Circulation*, 1962, *25*, 798–803.

Pliner, P. The effects of auditory cues on time-estimation judgments. In S. Schachter & J. Rodin, *Obese humans and rats.* Hillsdale, New Jersey: Lawrence Erlbaum Associates, 1974.

Plomin, R. J. A temperament theory of personality development: Parent-child interactions. Unpublished doctoral dissertation, The University of Texas at Austin, 1974.

Pumroy, D. K. Maryland Parent Attitude Survey: A research instrument with social desirability controlled. *Journal of Psychology*, 1966, *64*, 73–78.

Raab, W., Chaplin, J. P., & Bajusz, E. Myocardial necroses produced in domesticated rats and in wild rats by sensory and emotional stresses. *Proceedings of the Society of Experimental Biology and Medicine*, 1964, *116*, 665–669.

Raab, W., Stark, E., MacMillan, W. H, & Gigee, W. R. Sympathetic origin and antiadrenergic prevention of stress-induced myocardial lesions. *American Journal of Cardiology*, 1961, *8*, 203–211.

Rahe, R. H. Life-change measurement as a predictor of illness. *Proceedings of the Royal Society of Medicine*, 1968, *61*, 44–46.

Rahe, R. H. A start at quantifying stress in life. *Journal of the American Medical Association*, 1975, *232*, 699.   (a)

Rahe, R. H. Liaison psychiatry on a coronary care unit. *Journal of Human Stress*, 1975, *1*, 13–21.   (b)

Rahe, R. H., & Lind, E. Psychosocial factors and sudden cardiac death: A pilot study. *Journal of Psychosomatic Research*, 1971, *15*, 19–24.

Rahe, R. H., O'Neil, T., & Arthur, R. J. Brief group therapy following myocardial infarction: Eighteen-month follow-up of a controlled trial. Unpublished manuscript, National Health Research Center, San Diego, California, January 31, 1975.

Rahe, R. H., & Paasikivi, J. Psychosocial factors and myocardial infarction: II. An outpatient study in Sweden. *Journal of Psychosomatic Research*, 1971, *15*, 33–39.

Rahe, R. H., Romo, M., Bennett, L., & Siltanen, P. Recent life changes, myocardial infarction, and abrupt coronary death: Studies in Helsinki. *Archives of Internal Medicine*, 1974, *133*, 221–228.

Rahe, R. H., Rubin, R. T., & Arthur, R. J. The three investigators study: Serum uric acid, cholesterol, and cortisol variability during stresses of everyday life. *Psychosomatic Medicine*, 1974, *36*, 258–268.

Rahe, R. H., Rubin, R. T., Arthur, R. J., & Clark, B. R. Serum uric acid and cholesterol variability. *Journal of the American Medical Association*, 1968, *206*, 2875–2880.

Rahe, R. H., Rubin, R. T., Gunderson, E. K. E., & Arthur, R. J. Psychologic correlates of serum cholesterol in man: A longitudinal study. *Psychosomatic Medicine*, 1971, *33*, 399–410.

Rahe, R. H., Tuffli, C. F., Jr., Suchor, R. J., & Arthur, R. J. Group therapy in the outpatient management of post-myocardial infarction patients. *Psychiatry in Medicine*, 1973, *4*, 77–88.

Richter, C. P. On the phenomenon of sudden death in animals and man. *Psychosomatic Medicine*, 1957, *19*, 191–198.

Romo, M., Siltanen, P., Theorell, T., & Rahe, R. H. Work behavior, time urgency and life dissatisfactions in subjects with myocardial infarction: A cross-cultural study. *Journal of Psychosomatic Research*, 1974, *18*, 1–8.

Rose, R. M., & Hurst, M. W. Plasma cortisol and growth hormone responses to intravenous catheterization. *Journal of Human Stress*, 1975, *1*, 22–36.

Rosen, B., & D'Andrade, R. The psychosocial origins of achievement motivation. *Sociometry*, 1959, *22*, 185–218.

Rosenman, R. H. Type A behavior pattern—pro and con. Unpublished manuscript, Harold Brunn Institute, Mount Zion Hospital and Medical Center, San Francisco, California, 1975.

Rosenman, R. H., Brand, R. J., Jenkins, C. D., Friedman, M., Straus, R., & Wurm, M. Coronary heart disease in the Western Collaborative Group Study: Final follow-up experience of 8½ years. *Journal of the American Medical Association*, 1975, *233*, 872–877.

Rosenman, R. H., & Friedman, M. Association of specific behavior pattern in women with blood and cardiovascular findings. *Journal of the American Medical Association*, 1961, *24*, 1173–1184.

Rosenman, R. H., & Friedman, M. Observations on the pathogenesis of coronary heart disease. *Nutrition News*, 1971, *34*, 9–14.

Rosenman, R. H., & Friedman, M. Neurogenic factors in pathogenesis of coronary heart disease. *Medical Clinics of North America*, 1974, *58*, 269–279.

Rosenman, R. H., Friedman, M., Straus, R., Wurm, M., Jenkins, C. D., & Messinger, H. B. Coronary heart disease in the Western Collaborative Group Study: A follow-up experience of two years. *Journal of the American Medical Association*, 1966, *195*, 130–136.

Rosenman, R. H., Friedman, M., Straus, R., Jenkins, C. D., Zyzanski, S. J., & Wurm, M. Coronary heart disease in the Western Collaborative Group Study: A follow-up experience of 4½ years. *Journal of Chronic Diseases*, 1970, *23*, 173–190.

Rosenman, R. H., Friedman, M., Straus, R., Wurm, M., Kositchek, R., Hahn, W., & Werthessen, N. T. A predictive study of coronary heart disease. *Journal of the American Medical Association*, 1964, *189*, 103–110.

Rosenman, R. H., Rahe, R. H., Borhani, N. O., & Feinlieb, M. Heritability of personality and behavior pattern. *Proceedings of the First International Congress on Twins, Rome, Italy*, November, 1974.

Roth, S., & Kubal, L. Effects of noncontingent reinforcement on tasks of differing importance: Facilitation and learned helplessness. *Journal of Personality and Social Psychology*, 1975, *32*, 680–691.

Rotter, J. B. Generalized expectancies for internal versus external control of reinforcement. *Psychological Monographs*, 1966, *80* (Whole No. 609).

Rubin, R. T., Rahe, R. H., Arthur, R. J., & Clark, B. R. Adrenal cortical activity changes during underwater demolition team training. *Psychosomatic Medicine*, 1969, *31*, 553–564.

Rubin, R. T., Rahe, R. H., Clark, B. R., & Arthur, R. J. Serum uric acid, cholesterol, and cortisol levels: Interrelationship in normal men under stress. *Archives of Internal Medicine*, 1970, *125*, 815–819.

Russek, H. I. Stress, tobacco, and coronary disease in North American professional groups. *Journal of the American Medical Association*, 1965, *192*, 189–194.

Sales, S. M. Organizational roles as a risk factor in coronary heart disease. *Administrative Science Quarterly*, 1969, *14*, 325–337.

Sales, S. M., & House, J. S. Job dissatisfaction as a possible risk factor in coronary heart disease. *Journal of Chronic Diseases*, 1971, *23*, 861–873.

Saltin, B. Aerobic work capacity and circulation at exercise in man. *Acta Physiologica Scandanavia*, 1964, *62*, (Supplement No. 230).

Schachter, S., & Rodin, J. *Obese humans and rats*. Hillsdale, New Jersey: Lawrence Erlbaum Associates, 1974.

Schachter, S., & Singer, J. E. Cognitive, social, and physiological determinants of emotional state. *Psychological Review*, 1962, *69*, 379–399.

Schmale, A. H. Giving up as a final common pathway to changes in health. *Advances in Psychosomatic Medicine,* 1972, *8,* 18–38.

Seligman, M. E. P. *Helplessness: On depression, development, and death.* San Francisco: Freeman, 1975.

Seligman, M. E. P., & Maier, S. F. Failure to escape traumatic shock. *SJournal of Experimental Psychology,* 1967, *74,* 1–9.

Seligman, M. E. P., Maier, S. F., & Solomon, R. L. Unpredictable and uncontrollable aversive events. In F. R. Brush (Ed.), *Aversive conditioning and learning.* New York: Academic Press, 1971.

Selye, H. *The stress of life.* New York: McGraw-Hill, 1956.

Shapiro, D., Schwartz, G. E., & Benson, H. *Biofeedback: A behavioral approach to cardiovascular self-control.* In R. S. Eliot (Ed.), *Stress and the heart.* Mount Kisco, New York: Futura, 1974.

Shekelle, R. B. Educational status and risk of coronary heart disease. *Science,* 1969, *163,* 97–98.

Shekelle, R. B., Schoenberger, J. A., & Stamler, J. Correlates of the JAS Type A behavior pattern score. *Journal of Chronic Diseases,* 1976, *29,* 381–394.

Sigg, E. B. The pharmacological approaches to cardiac stress. In R. S. Eliot (Ed.), *Stress and the heart.* Mount Kisco, New York: Futura, 1974.

Silverman, A. J., & Cohen, S. I. Affect and vascular correlates of catecholamines. *Psychiatric Research Reports of the American Psychiatric Association,* 1960, *12,* 16–30.

Simpson, M. T., Olewine, D. A., Jenkins, C. D., Ramsey, F. H., Zyzanski, S. J., Thomas, G., & Hames, C. G. Exercise-induced catecholamines and platelet aggregation in the coronary-prone behavior pattern. *Psychosomatic Medicine,* 1974, *36,* 476–487.

Singh, D. Effect of level of manifest anxiety and type of pretraining on timing behavior. *American Journal of Psychology,* 1971, *84,* 134–139.

Singh, D. Role of response habits and cognitive factors in determination of behavior of obese humans. *Journal of Personality and Social Psychology,* 1973, *27,* 220–238.

Sloane, R. B., Davidson, P., Holland, L., & Payne, R. W. Aggression and effects of upbringing in normal students. *Archives of General Psychiatry,* 1962, *7,* 374.

Sloane, R. B., Habib, A., Eveson, M. B., & Payne, R. W. Some behavioral and other correlates of cholesterol metabolism. *Journal of Psychosomatic Research,* 1961, *5,* 183–190

Smith, C. P. The origin and expression of achievement-related motives in children. In C. P. Smith (Ed.), *Achievement-related motives in children.* New York: Russell Sage Foundation, 1969.

Smith, T. Factors involving sociocultural incongruity and change: A review of empirical findings. *Milbank Memorial Fund Quarterly,* 1967, *45,* 23–39.

Steinberg, D. Catecholamine stimulation of fat mobilization and its metabolic consequences. *Pharmacological Review,* 1966, *18,* 217–235.

Sternbach, R. A. *Principles of psychophysiology.* New York: Academic Press, 1966.

Stricker, L. J. Edwards Personal Preference Schedule. In O. K. Buros (Ed.), *The sixth mental measurements yearbook.* Highland Park, New Jersey: Gryphon Press, 1970.

Suinn, R. M. Behavior therapy for cardiac patients: Letter to the Editor. *Behavior Therapy,* 1974, *5,* 569–571.   (a)

Suinn, R. M. Training to relax lowers serum cholesterol levels. *Medical News of the Journal of the Jmerican Medical Association,* 1974, *230,* 19.   (b)

Suinn, R. M. The cardiac stress management program for Type A patients. *Cardiac Rehabilitation,* 1975, *5,* 13–15.

Suinn, R. M., Brock, L., and Edie, C. Behavior therapy for Type A patients. *American Journal of Cardiology,* 1975, *36,* 269–270.

Syme, S. L. Psychological factors and coronary heart disease. *International Journal of Psychiatry,* 1968, *5,* 429–433.

Taylor, J. A. A personality scale of manifest anxiety. *Journal of Abnormal and Social Psychology,* 1953, *48,* 285–290.

Theorell, T. Life events before and after the onset of a premature myocardial infarction. In B. S. Dohrenwend & B. P. Dohrenwend (Eds.), *Stressful life events: Their nature and effects.* New York: Wiley, 1974.

Theorell, T., Lind, E., & Floderus, B. Life events and prospective near-future serious illness with special reference to myocardial infarction: Studies on middle-aged construction building workers. Lecture at the Psychosomatic Symposium held in Hong Kong, March 1975.

Theorell, T, & Rahe, R. H. Psychosocial factors and myocardial infarction. I. An in-patient study in Sweden. *Journal of Psychosomatic Research.* 1971, *15,* 25–31.

Theorell, T., & Rahe, R. H. Behavior and life satisfaction characteristics of Swedish subjects with myocardial infarction. *Journal of Chronic Diseases,* 1972, *25,* 139–147.

Theorell, T., & Rahe, R. H. Life change events, ballistocardiography, and coronary death. *Journal of Human Stress,* 1975, *1,* 18–24.

Thomas, C. B., & Murphy, E. A. Further studies on cholesterol levels in the Johns Hopkins medical students: The effect of stress at examination. *Journal of Chronic Diseases,* 1958, *8,* 661–670.

Thornton, J. W., & Jacobs, P. D. Learned helplessness in human subjects. *Journal of Experimental Psychology,* 1971, *87,* 367–372.

Thornton, J. W., & Jacobs, P. D. The facilitating effects of prior inescapable/unavoidable stress on intellectual performance. *Psychonomic Science,* 1972, *26,* 185–187.

Thornton, J. W., & Powell, G. D. Immunization and alleviation of learned helplessness in man. Unpublished manuscript, Angelo State University (Texas), 1971.

Thurstone, L. L. *A factorial study of perception.* Chicago: University of Chicago Press, 1944.

Thurstone, L. L. *The Thurstone Temperament Schedule: Examiners manual.* Chicago: Science Research Associates, 1949.

Tresselt, M. E., & Mayzner, M. S. Normative solution times for a sample of 134 solution words and 378 associated anagrams. *Psychonomic Monograph Supplements,* 1966, *1,* 293–298.

Turner, L., & Solomon, R. L. Human traumatic avoidance learning: Theory and experiments on the operant-respondent distinction and failures to learn. *Psychological Monographs,* 1962, *76* (40, Whole No. 559).

Wallach, M. A., Kogan, N., & Bem, D. J. Group influence on individual risk-taking. *Journal of Abnormal and Social Psychology,* 1962, *65,* 75–86.

Weiner, B. *Theories of motivation.* Chicago: Rand McNally, 1972.

Weiss, J. M. Somatic effects of predictable and unpredictable shock. *Psychosomatic Medicine,* 1970, *32,* 397–408.

Weiss, J. M., Glazer, H. I., & Pohorecky, L. A. Coping behavior and neurochemical changes: An alternative explanation for the original "learned helplessness" experiments. In G. Serban (Ed.), Psychopathology of human adaptation. New York: Plenum Press, 1977, in press.

Weiss, J. M., Stone, E. A., & Harrell, N. Coping behavior and brain norepinephrine level in rats. *Journal of Comparative and Physiological Psychology,* 1970, *72,* 153–160.

Wertlake, P. T., Wilcox, A. A., Haley, M. I., & Peterson, J. E. Relationship of mental and emotional stress to serum cholesterol levels. *Proceedings of the Society for Experimental Biology and Medicine,* 1958, *97,* 163–165.

Williams, R. B., Jr. Physiological mechanisms underlying the association between psychosocial factors and coronary disease. In W. D. Gentry & R. B. Williams, Jr. (Eds.), *Psychological aspects of myocardial infarction and coronary care.* St. Louis: Mosby, 1975.

Wilson, E. O. *Sociobiology.* Cambridge, Massachusetts: Harvard University Press, 1975.

Winterbottom, M. R. The relation of need for achievement to learning experiences in independence and mastery. In J. W. Atkinson (Ed.), *Motives in fantasy, action and society.* Princeton, New Jersey: Van Nostrand, 1958.

Wolf, S. Psychosocial forces in myocardial infarction and sudden death. In S. Bondurant (Ed.), *Research on acute myocardial infarction.* New York: American Heart Association, 1969.

Wolf, S., McCabe, W. R., Yamamoto, J., Adsett, C. A., & Schottstaedt, W. W. Changes in serum lipids in relation to emotional stress during rigid control of diet and exercise. *Circulation,* 1962, *26,* 379–387.

Woodrow, H. Time perception. In S. S. Stevens (Ed.), *Handbook of experimental psychology.* New York: Wiley, 1951.

World Health Organization. *Epidemiological and vital statistics report.* Geneva: World Health Organization, 1960. P. 147.

Wortman, C. B., & Brehm, J. W. Responses to uncontrollable outcomes: An integration of reactance theory and the learned helplessness model. In L. Berkowitz (Ed.), *Advances in experimental social psychology* (Vol. 8). New York: Academic Press, 1975.

Zwerling, I., & Rosenbaum, M. Alcoholic addiction and personality (nonpsychotic conditions). In S. Arieti (Ed.), *American handbook of psychiatry* (Vol. 1). New York: Basic Books, 1959.

Zyzanski, S. J., & Jenkins, C. D. Basic dimensions within the coronary-prone behavior pattern. *Journal of Chronic Diseases,* 1970, *22,* 781–795.

Zyzanski, S. J., Jenkins, C. D., Ryan, T. J., Flessas, A., and Everist, M. Psychological correlates of coronary angiographic findings. *Archives of Internal Medicine,* 1976, *136,* 1234–1237.

Author Index

Numbers in *italics* refer to the pages on which the complete references are listed.

Subject Index